The Media & Business

The Media

& Business

Edited and with an introduction by
Howard Simons and
Joseph A. Califano, Jr.

 Vintage Books | A Division of Random House | New York

A VINTAGE ORIGINAL
FIRST EDITION, February 1979

Copyright © 1979 by Howard Simons and Joseph A. Califano, Jr.

Library of Congress Cataloging in Publication Data
Main entry under title:

The Media and business.

Proceedings of an October 1977 weekend seminar of leaders from the media and business,
sponsored by the Ford Foundation.
1. Journalism, Commercial—United States—Congresses. I. Simons, Howard. II. Califano,
Joseph A., 1931-   III. Ford Foundation.
PN4888.C59M4   070.4'49'33   78-55714
ISBN 0-394-72741-X

Manufactured in the United States of America

Contents

Acknowledgments

We are indebted to the sponsors of the Princeton Conference: the *Chicago Tribune*, the *New York Times*, the *Washington Post*, the *Wall Street Journal*, the *Boston Globe*, the *Los Angeles Times*, and the Ford Foundation for the opportunity to edit this extraordinary learning experience. A very special measure of appreciation goes to a brilliant, energetic, and witty young lawyer friend of ours—John B. Kuhns. We also thank Richard M. Clurman, Stuart F. Sucherman, and Margaret Drain. Finally, we owe a special debt to the unflagging good-natured help of Donna Crouch.

We alone bear responsibility for the contents of the introductory essays and for editing the conference transcripts.

Introduction:

The Businessman and the Journalist

The press likes to talk about its adversary relationship with government these days. But the press says very little about its relationship with other societal institutions, particularly American business.

In contrast to media silence, the business community is becoming more vocal in its attacks on the press. Of late it feels particularly embattled and embittered. What was once a relatively quiet adversary relationship is fast becoming an openly antagonistic relationship between two powerful and self-righteous institutions.

To the businessman, too often the antagonism boils down to this—business builds up; the media tears down. To the media, too often the antagonism boils down to this—business always hides its wrongdoing; only the media penetrates this stone wall.

Part of the problem can be found in the events of the past few years. Vietnam and Watergate, the CIA and the FBI have contributed to an erosion of the once-blind devotion to institutions known best. Particularly among the young, established institutions are suspect. Business has not been and cannot be immune.

Part of the problem, too, can be found in the excesses of the 1960's and the shortages of the 1970's—and things promise to get worse before they get better.

Illegal campaign contributions, social accountability, health and safety, asbestos, thalidomide, the environment, the energy crisis, investment in apartheid—this is the stuff that fosters suspicion and discontent and investigative reporting.

Did the media cause it all? Not really, say the businessmen, but they have contributed mightily. The businessmen's complaints are not unlike those of government officials and politicians: the media is too powerful; they always get it wrong; you cannot get a fair shake; they don't write about all the good things we do but only the bad; sensationalism sells newspapers; they don't understand what they are reporting; they oversimplify.

From the media perspective, business creates part of the problem. Businessmen don't talk; they stonewall the media. Businessmen seem to live a fairly sheltered life within the corporate cocoon and shy away from the sunlight of the public arena. Not used to the same give-and-take as that of the government official or politician, the businessman becomes defensive and critical and antagonistic.

The businessman retorts that the media, after all, are businesses, too—with awesome power and impact on society, businesses that should be subjected to the same scrutiny, challenge, and accountability that the media demand of government and are now beginning to demand of other business.

But the press is afforded special protection under the First Amendment to the U.S. Constitution—and journalists claim that the free press clause gives the media special rights and privileges not afforded other business enterprises.

These business/press confrontations as often as not mirror larger conflicts in our society. Many of these conflicts actually do not involve legal rights at all, but only the human agony of ethical, moral, and personal dilemmas in situations where the law gives precious little guidance.

The Antagonistic Relationship

Illustrations of the negative business attitude toward the press are ever-present these days. For example, in the April 1978 issue of the *Atlantic*, Louis Banks, a former managing editor of *Fortune* magazine, wrote a stinging article entitled "Memo to the Press: They Hate You Out There." Bank's view is that there are three distinct levels of antagonism between business and the media:

> The first involves everyday operational relationships, i.e., the specific reactions to specific encounters in which the business executive or his company has been involved. The second is attitudinal: a businessman's conviction that the great power of the media is used selectively to sour the body politic on corporate product, profit, or practice. The third is societal: a gut feeling that, behind a façade of constitutional righteousness, First Amendment guarantees are being misused at the expense of other institutional rights no less basic, with a net loss to the American system.

Alfred L. Malabre, Jr., made a similar statement in the April 21, 1978, issue of the *Wall Street Journal*. Malabre, in a review of Tom Wicker's book *On Press*, suggested that Dean Rusk's TET diatribe about press coverage of the Vietnam war "might as well have been spoken by an oil-industry executive upset over press coverage of the oil business or a chamber of commerce official upset over press concentration on crime in a community."

Part of the antagonism comes from a growing awareness not just among journalists but the public at large of aspects of business which until a few decades ago were not questioned very often or very loudly. To be sure, there have been periodic and historic investigations—e.g., Ida Tarbell and Upton Sinclair. But it is only recently that consumerism and environmental concerns and business accountability have received considerable and sustained attention. Heretofore, business pretty much had its way. Some newpapers were owned by business—Anaconda owned papers in Montana, the Florida *Times-Union* in Jacksonville is owned by a railroad, and only recently has DuPont sold the Wilmington newspapers. More telling, most newspapers used to take business handouts and run with them. Some still do.

Arthur Taylor, former president of CBS, Inc., explains the new antagonism between business and the press this way: "At the same time, public interest—and therefore press interest—in business as an institution has greatly increased. Consumerism, greater stockholder activism, environmentalists, and proponents of equal employment opportunities have helped throw the public spotlight on the factory and on the board room. On top of this, recession, inflation, and the energy crisis have further increased public interest. When people are out of work or worried about their jobs, when they cannot afford to buy a house or a car, or obtain heating oil or gasoline, they quite rightly want to know what is causing these difficulties. In a free enterprise system, business is bound to get a good deal of the blame."

Of course, business often blames the press for its image. And like other segments of American society, it wonders why bad news drives out good, why business gets no credit for all its good works but seems to receive publicity when something goes wrong.

The Litany of Complaints

The business community expects the press to treat it differently from government. Businessmen argue that while government is "public," business is "private"; the power of government derives from the consent of the governed, but the power of business derives from its relationship to stockholders, customers, and corporate bylaws. In this view the public has the right to know how its government is handling the public's business, but the concerns of "private" business are the concerns of management and stockholders. Indeed, a private corporation has few affirmative legal obligations to the general public—other than to refrain from injuring the public by neglect or design or deceit. And it is the government's job—not the media's—to enforce those few obligations.

Business criticism of the press is hardly limited to this broad philosophical objection, however. Repeatedly these days, businessmen are attacking the media as inaccurate, unfair, negative, and biased, and are claiming that journalists never apply the same standards to their own actions as they do to those of others.

INACCURACY, CARELESSNESS, NEGATIVISM, AND BIAS

"Operationally," says Louis Banks, "the business bill of particulars tends to be a litany. Careless news stories present business executives as saying things they never said or corporations as doing things they never intended to do. In the reporting of figures, apples are compared to oranges, and decimal points slide back and forth. In the corporate view, sensationalism ignores the 99 percent of constructive progress and gives headline attention to the bizarre, odd, inconsequential, or exceptional. Chronic negativism fortifies this tendency, so that the 'good news' or the positive TV footage does not see light of day in the mass media, while the accident, or the competitor's slur, is surefire copy—and usually wrong in detail. Ignorant reporting tangles business complexities into erroneous conclusions or ducks the complexities in favor of power struggles and personality clashes, real or imagined."

James L. Ferguson, chairman and chief executive of General Foods Corporation, confirms Mr. Banks's views: "There have been cases of out-and-out sloppiness, where the newsman appeared not to know or not to care what he was talking about. There have been instances of extreme overkill. Questions are raised about the safety of a product in such a way as to alarm the public. Then it turns out that there was little or no legitimate basis for the fears."

Mr. Ferguson also accuses the press of anti-business bias: "There have been examples of what looked to us to be flagrant bias: outright slanting of the news. There have been others not so much of bias as such as of underlying hostility toward the business community and all its works."

Mr. Ferguson is far from alone, as evidenced by the statements of a large number of businessmen attending the conference. For example, one industrialist in attendence, when asked to describe the role of the press in environmental concerns, said flatly: "I think the press is biased in favor of the public interest groups."

THE PRESS HURTS AMERICA

Walter B. Wriston, chairman of Citibank, doesn't limit his criticism of the press to the injury it causes business. Rather, in Mr. Wriston's view, all of American society suffers from what he sees as an irresponsible press:

"Yet the accent today is not on the evidence of progress in a multitude of fields; the heaviest emphasis is upon failure. The media, supported by some academic 'liberals,' would have us believe that things are not just going badly, they are growing progressively and rapidly worse. The dominant theme is the new American way of failure. No one wins; we always lose. Jack Armstrong and Tom Swift are dead. If an individual says anything important, it is either ignored or nitpicked to death by commentators. Logical argument has given way to sniping. We no longer have great debates. The accusatory has replaced the explanatory. Let one scientist resign and say that nuclear power is a lethal accident waiting to happen, and he is awarded the front page with pictures. He has unlimited interviews on television. The massive achievement of hundreds and hundreds of scientists and the comfort of millions of citizens who enjoy the products of nuclear power go for nothing. We daily see illustrated a point made by the jurist Oliver Wendell Holmes: 'When the ignorant are taught to doubt, they do not know what they safely may believe.' The media should beware of sowing the dragon's teeth of confusion."

SPECIAL CRITICISM FOR TELEVISION

Essentially, television is a headline medium. Headlines get newspapers into trouble. The reason is straightforward. An editor must squeeze a complicated story, complete with caveats and nuances, into several dozen letters. The long telling is lost in the shorthand.

To get some idea of just how compressed television is, take one statistic—an average hour-long television news show is comprised of 30 items, and the script is equal to 4,000 words. In contrast, a 72-page daily newspaper has an average of 250 items and 150,000 words.

Journalists as well as businessmen have made this point. Walter Cronkite, for example, characterized television's problem in covering complex issues as "the inadvertent and perhaps inevitable distortion that results through the hypercompression we are all forced to exert to fit one hundred pounds of news into the one-pound sack we are given to fill each night."

Herbert Schmertz, a vice-president of Mobil Oil Corporation and a forthright critic of the press and television, suggests that the structural defects of television result not in bias but in weak and inadequate reporting. "The stories that don't make television news," Schmertz has said, "are those that are too complicated to adapt easily to network reporting formulas, or are not controversial enough to draw national interest, lack the requisite drama and activity for exciting film footage, or are produced by non-network, free-lance producers.

"Most business stories, save those involving national strikes, layoffs, shortages, or rising prices, fail to meet network entertainment requirements. The oil industry story is a perfect case history."

ACCESS—THE BUSINESSMAN'S ATTEMPT TO PRESENT HIS SIDE

Mobil has been waging a continuing battle against the television networks to engage in what Schmertz calls "advocacy advertising." It is in effect an attempt by Mobil to tell its side of a controversial issue, be it energy or environment. The struggle is over *access*. Mobil makes no bones about its displeasure with the views expressed on an many editorial page. So, to counterpunch, Mobil began to develop a series of advertisements and bought space in newspapers—usually opposite the editorial page—to display its point of view.

Mobil's success in getting the television networks to take similar commercials has been far less satisfying. Essentially, the networks take the view that the public interest will be best served, especially on controversial issues, by the network news departments. This position was put forth in 1973 in a letter to Schmertz from CBS which said that "it is the general policy of CBS to sell time only for the promotion of goods and services and not for the presentation of points of view on controversial issues of public importance. CBS has adopted this policy because it believes that the public will best be served if important public issues are presented in formats generally determined by broadcast journalists. Thus, time is not sold for presentation of an advertiser's position or public attacks on the advertiser of the product . . ."

Mobil even offered to pay for equal air time under the fairness doctine so that oil industry critics could answer Mobil's idea commercials, as they call them. It didn't work. "All we want is a fair chance to be heard," says

Mobilman Schmertz. "The media have a right to criticize and investigate, but we also have a right to *our* day in the court of public opinion to answer our accusers and present our position."

Not everyone in the business community embraces, endorses, or even likes Mobil's cantankerous carping at the media. Nevertheless, Schmertz has raised some serious questions regarding access to the media.

PRESS HYPOCRISY—THE DOUBLE STANDARD

Businessmen are especially angered by what they think is a double standard utilized by the press. For example: If Boeing or Lockheed pays bribes to foreigners for contractual favors, that's viewed as a "no-no." If the press pays for a story, that's a "yes-yes."

Inducing someone to commit a crime is a crime for most persons. But the press seems to think it is all right to induce a grand juror, for example, to break the law, or to induce someone to steal a document and provide it with a copy.

The average journalist says that he or she will go to jail rather than reveal the source for a story if that source has asked for confidentiality. But the press cannot wait to publish the secrets of government and business.

This perceived hypocrisy was described by one businessman at the conference in the following manner: "What I got out of this, and what I think disturbs me most, is the double standard between the press and business on matters of responsibility. I was, frankly, surprised to hear a television executive say that he wouldn't wait a day or two to go to press, or go on the air, with the story about an [CIA] agent, even though it might cost him his life, for fear of competition. Whereas I don't think the press would stand for it if a drug company rushed its product out quickly, for fear of competition.

"I heard it said that the press will protect confidentiality at almost all cost, whereas if a business tries to, it will be considered a cover-up.

"I heard it said that the press will one way or another buy information, while business will be castigated for questionable or sensitive payments.

"And finally, I heard, today, that the press reserves its right to observe orders of the courts, even when none of us would tolerate the fact that the President of the United States raised that reservation. No businessman could say, 'I will reserve the right to observe an order of the Court.'

"I think, in looking at business, perhaps the press could look at it from its own perspective of its engaging in competitive practices and perhaps the coverage might be a little more balanced."

It brought the house down with applause.

The Press Defends Itself

There is something very real about the businessman's plaint that the media isn't doing its job properly. It is only now, for example, that the media is beefing up its economics and business staffs; only now that business seminars and fellowships for reporters are being established and sought after. Credit/blame the energy crisis and the dollar crisis and the fact that the media—like the State Department and the corporate executive—has a crisis mentality. It's happened several times before, most dramatically in the post-Sputnik days when science writing became not only the fashionable thing to do but a must.

News stories are often incomplete. Sometimes they are inaccurate. Reporters and editors can be captives of pseudo-events staged for their benefit. Some of these problems attend the human condition: People who know do not speak, at least not soon enough; people who think they know tell only part of the story; some lie, others obfuscate, all of us try to protect our own interest. Other problems stem from institutional limitations of newspapering: the daily component of daily journalism; the pressure of space limitations in increasingly expensive newsprint; the different metabolisms, skills, sources, and perceptions of individual editors and reporters.

Particularly daily journalism, but weekly journalism and television specials as well, are at best a quick glance at history on the run. Still, without what the press does—however incomplete or inaccurate or irritating or seemingly destructive—we could very well have a different form of government and see the end to free enterprise.

ON OBJECTIVITY

There can be no such thing as an objective press. This is so because there is no way a editor or a publisher can squeeze the inculcations of a lifetime from a reporter or an editor. And these inculcations—parentage, regionalism, education, friends, religion, experiences ad infinitum—subliminally shape every story and subliminally suggest what a reporter leaves in or omits from a given story.

But unlike the businessman, a reporter is directly open to criticism and correction. Take the byline, for example. When one buys a pair of pants or a shirt, sometimes there is the little paper notation in the pocket that says "Inspected by No. 7." Most of us have never met No. 7. By contrast, in the media either the reporter is there to be seen on television or he or she has a byline on the page of the newspaper. And the byline sits on the reporter's shoulder while he or she is writing the story so that the reader can call that person the next day if something is wrong.

Although the press cannot be objective, it strives to be fair. The best journalists feel singularly dedicated to maintaining credibility. They regard credibility as the most precious commodity of journalism. They will go to tremendous lengths to check out a tip on a story. Most will not publish until completely satisfied that they have all the information available—at least within the deadline restrictions and institutional limitations of newspapering.

Among good reporters the rule is to call the "other guy." Put another way, if someone attacks an individual, the attack should not be printed without providing that individual with an opportunity to answer. Blind criticism from confidential sources who refuse to identify themselves should be allowed only in extremis, although such a rule can be difficult for editors to police.

All this does not mean fairness in any sense of reporting, inch for inch, all sides to the same story. It does mean fairness in hearing out the other side and making an independent judgment.

But business frequently doesn't let the press hear its side. Arthur Taylor put it this way: "Much of the difficulty comes from the fact that many people in business, particularly senior executives, have worked their way up inside the corporate structure and within the business community, shielded to a great extent from public scrutiny and criticism. Unlike politicians or public advocates, their professional skills usually tend to be directed inward, toward their companies, rather than outward toward the public. A middle-level corporation executive generally will not have to undergo the same rough-and-tumble give-and-take in the public arena from people who do not understand how business works that his or her counterpart in politics might have to. And when he or she gets to the top and becomes a captain of industry, the isolation will be even further enforced by a protective staff."

The huge international grain companies exemplify the problem of secrecy. These companies were thrust into the public spotlight first in the 1972 Soviet-American grain transactions. This was a year before the big oil companies had to take a public bow during the Arab embargo. But the grain firms proved to be more stubbornly impenetrable, and considerably less forthcoming, when their own interests suddenly conflicted with the perceived interests of the public and the government. These companies resist disclosing more than the most superficial details about their global operations. The policy of the companies was, and still is: volunteer nothing. All of the "Big Five" (Cargill, Continental, Louis Dreyfus, Bunge, and Andre) are closely held, privately owned family companies. Most of the stock is controlled by seven or eight families who prefer anonymity. As private companies, these giant firms which control the lion's share of the world food trade are not even required to disclose their financial statements to the Securities and Exchange Commission, as the oil companies are. Consequently, they seriously handicap the media in its quest to provide the public with information about business having a substantial impact on world affairs.

ON THE PRESS HURTING AMERICA

It's fashionable today to carp that the press prints only bad news and that somehow if it buried such news or ignored it completely, the country would be better off. But this kind of kill-the-messenger notion is not a sound criticism. For example, it would be difficult to argue that the nation's economic problem would be directly improved if the media remained silent or were silenced. Indeed, many members of the press feel they have been terribly remiss over the past few decades in not vigorously pursuing some of the same stories that are now causing so much business criticism. The media was late and inadequate on pollution (quality of life). The media was late and inadequate on equal employment opportunities. The media was late and inadequate on job safety. The media was late and inadequate on car safety. Everyone can add to this list.

ON THE DOUBLE STANDARD—IS THE PRESS DIFFERENT?

The press is the first to concede that its own standards are different from those which it applies to others. Take the confidential source issue, for example. The often unspoken but nonetheless sacred pledge of every journalist is this: "I will go to jail before revealing the identity of anyone who tells me something confidentially." This moral code is in the heart, mind, and blood of every good journalist. Indeed, the very fact that people have this impression of journalists—that they will go to jail to protect their sources—has brought a wealth of news tips to newpapers and television stations across this nation and has profoundly affected the course of story telling and news reporting.

Unless their need to protect confidential sources is given the sacrosanct status accorded the rights of priests to withhold what penitents tell them in the confessional, of doctors to honor their patient privileges, of lawyers to honor their client privileges, reporters and editors are convinced that the free flow of information to them will slowly diminish and eventually newspapers will be printing public relations handouts and press releases. As far as the journalist is concerned, without this protection lives and livelihoods of news sources would be jeopardized. Put bluntly, only the very dumb or the eternally secure would come forward to offer material to the press that by its nature will upset those in power or those who have power over them.

At the same time, the press has little respect for secrecy in business. But the press has a good answer for this apparent inconsistency. One distinguished First Amendment lawyer at the conference explained it this way: "There is absolutely no doubt that the press takes positions for itself which it would condemn in others, and that the courts, indeed, have gone far toward recognizing those positions for the press, as they would for no one else.

"Justice Stewart gave a speech a few years ago at Yale Law School, in which he ran through a whole list of things; confidential sources are one example. He said, in effect, 'Look, if it were anyone but the press, we wouldn't even listen to them. It's a ridiculous thing for anyone else but the press to say that they should not be obliged to divulge information otherwise relevant because it was obtained on confidentiality.'

"Justice Stewart's position was that the press was specifically set forth in the Constitution as being not the same as any other entity in American life.

"Let's pass the history part . . . the kinds of questions we have to consider are, in effect, how free a press do we want to have?

"We have to understand—and all the businessmen know this from personal experience—that the freer the press is, the freer it is to be offensive and reckless and to say things which are often untrue.

"Now, either we get enough societal benefits out of that or we don't. In asking the question of what the framers meant and what the courts have said, each of us has to make our own kind of decision as to whether the price, and it is a real price that we pay for that, is a price we choose to pay.

"I would hope that a number of businessmen here would think it is a price worth paying. It is a responsible position, I must say, to say it is not. Many democratic countries don't choose to pay that price, but I think this is the way to view the issue."

There was no applause.

Another participant—an editor—defended the press this way: "The press . . . is the only private institution in this country that has a constitutional privilege. It's the only one.

"The First Amendment says that the Congress shall not enact any law that will abridge the freedom of the press and the freedom of speech. Now, that franchise, it seems to me, puts the press in a very special category. As I read the origins of our Constitution . . . the purpose of that was to create some kind of a balancing force that would exercise some kind of restraint upon government. The founders of our government were very concerned about tyranny. They were revolutionaries. And for that purpose, the First Amendment created a balancing force which would have some restraint on government.

"That creates a very special relationship between the press and the government. It's a relationship which business does not share. I think it is perfectly proper for a businessman to share information with the government. I can't see any real problem there at all. But when the press begins to share information with the government, it begins to lose its credibility. . . ."

Chief Justice Warren E. Burger has a somewhat different view on the First Amendment protection accorded the media. Burger believes that big media is no different from any other big business and has no special constitutional protection. In a recent concurrence to an opinion on political free speech, the Chief Justice told media conglomerates that they might not be privileged institutions after all. But Burger's view doesn't undermine the First Amendment positions taken by journalists—it merely recognizes that all persons have equal rights to engage in freedom of expression. Whether anyone else on the bench agrees with Burger is unknown, though none of the other justices chose to endorse Burger's view.

Parenthetically, Burger takes the view we have always taken—the First Amendment is for everyone, from the lone Tom Paine with the mimeograph machine to the *Los Angeles Times* and its million plus Sunday papers.

Some Observations

The business community, in its quest for privacy, likes thinking that the laws, coverage, attitudes, and ethics that govern relationships between the media and the government have no applicability to media-business relationships. This is simply not the case. However valid the distinctions between business and government may have been in a simpler era, they have become blurred in our complex world.

Today business is remarkably similar to government in its power, its pervasiveness, and its impact on individual life. A relatively small group of corporations critically influence the life of every American by their routine decisions:

- What drugs shall be developed, and how shall they be marketed?
- What chemicals shall be discharged into the environment and with what effects—perhaps on unborn generations?
- What new medical technologies will be available to the American people?
- What will be offered for our children to see on television?
- What kind of food shall we eat?
- What kind of housing will we finance—and hence build—and where?

Arguments about whether large corporations *control* all these critical decisions, or merely respond to market demands, obscure the central fact—big business does exercise great power, power rivaling that of big government. And the American public increasingly demands that business, like government, be held accountable.

One other aspect of the business-government relationship has changed in the last few years. There are more and more partnerships between business and government, as often as not at business request—to build supersonic transports, to finance maritime fleets, to create an entire space industry, or to maintain a defense industry.

As a result of these changes, government regulation of business abounds. This extraordinary profusion, during the past few years, of government regulations has the most profound implications for the relationship between the media and business. Increasingly, media coverage of government is aso coverage of business, the line between "private" and "public" sectors has eroded—especially with respect to the largest and most highly regulated corporations. The real world of government and business is a world in which a Lockheed can become a ward of the U.S. Treasury; a world in which DuPont is subject not only to the usual market pressures but to legal obligations imposed by a dozen federal agencies; a world in which a corporation like AT&T, for each *hour* it spends in stockholder relations, probably spends a *year* on government regulations.

In such a world, the press rightfully asks, why should the chairman of AT&T be any less the subject of press attention than a member of the Federal Communications Commission?

In such a world, the press rightfully asks, why should the affairs of Northrop Corporation be any less the subject of press scrutiny than the affairs of the Air Force Procurement Office?

In such a world, is it more important for the media to pursue its First Amendment rights to inform the public about Pat Harris and Cecil Andrus than about Katharine Graham and Punch Sulzberger?

Our own sense is that the media has hardly begun to fulfill its responsibility to cover business for the general public in this country. But if they are to play that role effectively, the media will have to elevate their standards of independence, vigor, and competence where business reporting is concerned.

There is a large, influential, and generally sympathetic business press: journals from *Fortune* to *Barron's* to the *Harvard Business Review* to the *Wall Street Journal* and the financial pages of major newspapers—all written largely for a business audience.

In most newspapers, business coverage is a melange of stock market quotations and wire service stories on economic indicators and crop predictions. For most of the media, the precious opportunity to inform the general public about our financial system, the major issues confronting business, or the impact of government regulation on business is a missed opportunity.

The print media cover business sketchily—and the electronic media hardly at all—except when business is implicated (and we use the word advisedly) in a national news story. And so the general public's diet of business news consists largely of stories about corruption or unsafe products or corporate bribery and about good lawsuits against bad corporations.

The other news of business—its structural problems, its achievements, its basic processes, even when spectacular—rarely appears on the journalistic menu.

Whatever the reasons for this—be it media inattention, corporate habits of secrecy, or a combination of the two—it hurts. It hurts the public and, we suggest, it hurts business.

For the underreporting of business in America deprives the business community of two resources it desperately needs—though it may *want* only one of them. *First*, a well-informed, competent channel of communication to the public, and *second*, an attentive, persistent, and perhaps even constructive critic. Both of these are, of course, daily facts of life for government.

Without these, the business community lives with a public that is ignorant of the way business works, suspicious of its motives, unsympathetic to its problems—and easy prey to ill-conceived schemes for government intervention into business affairs.

The Bert Lance affair raised many questions about the role of the press—most of them unjustified.

What did concern us about that coverage was this:

The media knew so little about banking practices and procedures that it failed for months, beginning with the confirmation hearings, to recognize suspicious leads—and when the media did begin its searing coverage in August and September, 1977, that coverage reflected and created a great deal of confusion because so many reporters and editors did not know what constituted ethical, appropriate, and customary banking procedures and practices.

The press and the government blundered to the inevitable resolution and resignation. But the good banks will spend years explaining how they do business—with little hope of coverage outside the narrowly read business pages.

If we are to avoid such events in the future, and if business is to earn and keep the confidence of the public, it must—like government—assume the risks of increased exposure and accessibility. It must argue its position vigorously and confidently, and not shrink from controversy. And—like government—it cannot accomplish these things without the media.

For their part, the media must marshal more resources for covering business in a sustained, evenhanded way. This will require that reporters and editors educate themselves about economics, international competition, the mechanics of business organization and the styles of business decision-making. It may even mean that media people will have to divest themselves of some cherished preconceptions about business—and that the media will have to examine claims made by the critics of business at least as skeptically as they examine the claims of business!

The media could perhaps begin by asking: To whom, if anyone, are the *media* accountable?

The media, after all, are businesses too—with awesome power and impact on society, businesses which should be subjected to the same scrutiny, challenge, and accountability that the media now demand of government; that they are only beginning to direct at other businesses—and almost never demand of themselves and of one another.

Even if these marvelous transformations occur, of course, the media and business will probably still confront each other as adversaries, each pursuing what it regards as its prerogatives and responsibilities, and each regarding the other with some suspicion. For these confrontations, as often as not, mirror larger conflicts in our society, conflicts that are only obscured by the compelling claims advanced by each of the contenders: the right of privacy versus the public's right to know; the right to publish versus national security; the rights of stockholders versus the rights of the community, private profit versus public responsibility.

- What, for example, are the obligations of a corporate employee who believes that his or her employer is engaged in improper conduct but who fears that disclosure to the government or a journalist may harm innocent people?

● At what point—if ever—does business's failure to follow the law, or government's refusal to enforce it, justify the media in stealing documents or purchasing news-gathering interviews?

● At what point is a company on notice that its products may be dangerous? And, once it is on notice, what are its obligations to the media, the public and the government?

The list of moral conundrums that figure in conflicts between the media and business is endless. The laws of libel, freedom of information, trade secrets, national security, privacy, stockholders' rights, and the First Amendment do not begin to answer many of them.

On these issues, as on so many others, where one stands will often depend on where one sits. We are dealing with institutional biases that tempt us to see much of the world in one-dimensional terms—to see "rights" where there are really conflicting vested interests, to see the "public interest" where there are really competing visions of private and public good; to attribute unworthy motives to one's adversary, and unblemished virtue to oneself.

The business community has a right to press for media to be competent, fair, and accurate—and to point out when such is not the case. But business must recognize that the First Amendment does not guarantee a competent, fair, and accurate press. The guarantee is for a *free* press—which oftens means a cantankerous, suspicious, and inaccurate press.

Business must remember that a truly fine newspaper is not a public relations operation or a business blotter or a booster for the community in which it is published. It is not a mouthpiece for official statements and pronouncements. Nor at the same time is it an activist cause-oriented instrument in the hands of an elite group of the leaders or individuals who think they have the sole perception of what society is or should be. A newspaper certainly is not the last word on the news. Nor is it even a comprehensive, utterly fair, totally accurate, always excellent, completely objective chronicle of its times. And it does not have to be correct all of the time. Nor could it be, putting out a totally new product every day of the year.

A truly excellent newspaper is a collection of bright, eager, and hardworking human beings reporting what they see as best they can, trying to determine what is new and profound, significant or funny, sad or telling, different or important. More often than not, what is printed has more to do

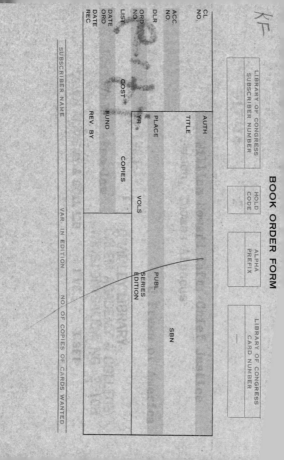

with what is wrong than with what is right; more to do with keeping people honest than with honest people; more to do with eliminating dark places than reflecting sunlight; but always, mostly to do with seeking truth.

The public is best served, and the truth is most likely to emerge, through a certain amount of lively disagreement. In our society, powerful institutions *should* be challenged vigorously by other powerful institutions; every institution should have to justify its public positions, its claims of power, its special vision of the public interest.

—Joseph A. Califano, Jr.
Howard Simons

Preface

On a crisp 1977 fall weekend near Princeton, New Jersey, dozens of eminent journalists and dozens of prestigious business leaders gathered together to lock biases and to exchange fundamental beliefs and fundamental differences. The occasion was the first seminar on the media and business sponsored by the Ford Foundation and six distinguished American newspapers: the *Chicago Tribune*, the *New York Times*, the *Washington Post*, the *Wall Street Journal*, the *Boston Globe*, and the *Los Angeles Times*.

This particular seminar was modeled after the older and highly successful law and media seminars which the Ford Foundation and various newspapers have cosponsored throughout the United States, in England and India.

As Fred W. Friendly, Ford Foundation host and godfather to all the seminars, wrote to the participants of this first business and media meeting:

> We propose to use the interrogatory, hypothetical case method that has served us so well in many past meetings on the subject of the media and the law. This time we will use that format to examine the important ambiguities of the business and media relationship, which is certainly tangled and often hostile. Our objective is not to try to reach any conclusions but to bring the participants and observers into learning proximity to each other, stimulated by this special method of discussion. At each of the three sessions, at which a hypothetical case will be "tried," there will be approximately forty participants around a horseshoe table, a mixture of representatives from business and the media, along with some government regulators and a sprinkling of lawyers and perhaps a judge. At each session also there will be an equal number of observers who may participate if they are so moved.

For a day and a half, editors, publishers, and reporters would square off with business moguls and bankers and industrialists in a Socratic ring where three law professors would bait and sting and goad and push and pull the participants into exploring the roots of antagonism between these two powerful and important American institutions.

During a fourth session there was no hypothetical case. Rather, the dean of the Harvard Business School asked participants all to speak their minds and their emotions, and they did.

Generally speaking, the feeling during the seminar was that, when all is said and explained, business feels it builds up and the media tears down, and moreover, the media gets it wrong and doesn't know what it is talking about, whereas the media feels that business lies and obfuscates and stonewalls and does a hundred things you and we would never dream of.

To be sure, minds and mind sets were not necessarily changed as a result of this brief learning clash. That was not its purpose. Its purpose, rather, was to make journalists and business people more aware of the reasons for each other's conduct and behavior and to provide a sense of the institutional limitations facing each of these institutions.

The level of discussion and argumentation during the sessions—as is evident in the transcripts that follow—was intelligent, sophisticated, articulate, and emotional, as well as barbed and sarcastic and even, at times, humorous.

Consequently, the personal experience was telling.

Afterwards, for example, one of the news participants put it this way: "Between the table and the corridor talk, and the occasional insightful moments in the formal sessions, my consciousness was raised a bit (not enough, however, to erode that red-blooded adversary relationship we all cherish). I hope it worked the same way with the businessmen."

On the other hand, a business representative put it this way: "It was not my idea to go and complain to the press about bad treatment or unfair stories. I went to understand how they look at business in general and how they approach not only business stories, but stories crucial to other segments of our American society."

And, finally, this note from an observer who is neither journalist nor businessperson: "What you've done is to focus on an area of harmful friction in American public life—more important in this country, perhaps, than in any other because of the great power of both American businessmen and American journalists. . . . It's important because differences and issues of this sort can rarely be resolved by ballot, they cannot be resolved in courts, legislatures or by the executive, and yet they continue to bedevil our society."

Some procedural notes are in order. A list or participants and observers who were at the Princeton seminar are to be found below. The hypothetical case precedes each of the discussion transcripts. In the text of the
dialogue of each transcript, participants are identified only as "judge,"
"banker," "editor," "pharmaceutical manufacturer," "lawyer," and so
forth. This is so because prior to the seminar all participants and observers
agreed that the views expressed would not be attributed to specific individuals.

The transcripts of the dialogues are substantially accurate reflections
of what was said and argued and expounded at the seminar. There has
been some editing to make points clearer, to explain references, to disguise
the identities of speakers, and to eliminate repetition.

Only the professors conducting each of the sessions are named on the
transcript pages. They are expert in the use of the Socratic method as a
discussion and teaching device. Therefore, their comments and their questions and their observations do not necessarily reflect their personal views.
Their job was to force the participants to confront the issues, and this they
did.

Participants

A. ROBERT ABBOUD
Chairman of the Board
The First National Bank of Chicago

FLOYD ABRAMS
Attorney
Cahill, Gordon & Reindel

RICHARD R. ALBRECHT
Vice President/Secretary
The Boeing Company

THOMAS G. AYERS
Chairman and President
Commonwealth Edison Co.

ROBERT L. BARTLEY
Editorial Page Editor
Wall Street Journal

GERHARD BLEICKEN
Chairman and Chief Executive Officer
John Hancock Mutual Life Insurance
Co.

BENJAMIN C. BRADLEE
Executive Editor
Washington Post

THORTON F. BRADSHAW
President
Altantic Richfield Company

WARREN E. BUFFETT
Publisher
Buffalo Evening News
Omaha Sun Newspapers

MCGEORGE BUNDY
President
The Ford Foundation

BYRON E. CALAME
Pittsburgh Bureau Chief
Wall Street Journal

JOSEPH A. CALIFANO, JR.
Secretary, U.S. Department of
Health, Education and Welfare

ROBERT B. CLARK
President
Hoffmann-LaRoche, Inc.

RICHARD M. CLURMAN
Richard M. Clurman & Associates

WILLIAM E. COLBY
Colby, Miller & Hanes
(Former Director, CIA)

STANTON R. COOK
Chairman and Publisher
Chicago Tribune

RICHARD P. COOLEY
President
Wells Fargo Bank

ANN CRITTENDEN
Financial Reporter
New York Times

DAVID M. DAVIS
Officer-in-Charge
Office of Communications
The Ford Foundation

The Media & Business

Case Study
1: Rothwell Labs

Professor Nesson

The Case:

Prothorin, a drug initially developed as a treatment for pneumonia, was discovered to concentrate in the urine and to be effective in counteracting some persistent forms of urinary infection. The drug received FDA approval for general distribution in 1972, having passed through the various stages of testing.

It has since become the primary drug of choice in the treatment of urinary infections. In the highly competitive market for urinary drugs, Prothorin has claimed a larger market share each year since its approval, and now accounts for 30 percent of the sales of Rothwell Laboratories. Largely on the strength of Prothorin's success, the stock of Rothwell Labs, which is a multimillion-dollar publicly held corporation, is riding high.

Since 1972 several cases of sudden total alopecia (baldness) have been reported in the medical literature. No specific cause has been determined, but prior treatment of the subjects with Prothorin has been noted as one of the possibly suggestive data.

Herb Reporter writes about science and medicine for the *Metropolis Star*. While attending the annual meeting of the Society of Hematologists he hears Dr. Murray Fine deliver a paper describing an advance in spectrographic assay techniques. According to Dr. Fine, his new technique permits the detection of the presence of smaller quantities of chemicals in the blood and body tissues than could be detected with previous technology. An example Dr. Fine describes is his detection of minute traces of Prothorin in the hair follicles of patients who had been treated with it.

Herb questions Dr. Fine at the end of his presentation. Fine states that he has submitted his paper for publication to the *Southern States Journal of Medicine*. Asked whether his findings indicate that Prothorin causes baldness, Fine replies that his data are certainly suggestive.

Herb calls Mr. Mark Avid, medical advisor to the Health Environment Law Project (HELP), a national advisory group vocally critical of the drug industry and the FDA. Informed of Dr. Fine's results, Avid asserts that, once again, the FDA has failed to protect the public interest. "Millions of people have taken and are taking this drug. It now appears to have a serious unforeseen side effect. The FDA simply fails to protect the public against drugs that have long-term cumulative toxic consequences."

Herb calls Rothwell Labs and asks to speak to its chief executive, Robert Rothwell.

Some Questions

1. How should Rothwell handle the call?

2. Suppose Rothwell's vice-president for public relations calls Reporter and asks for a guarantee of total confidentiality and nonattribution to the company, and informs Reporter that Dr. Fine holds a short position in Rothwell Lab stock. How should Reporter handle this information?

3. Suppose that the FDA obtains a copy of Dr. Fine's paper. How should the agency proceed?

4. Suppose that instead of finding traces of Prothorin in hair follicles, thus suggesting a link between Prothorin and baldness, Dr. Fine found traces of Prothorin in bone marrow, suggesting some link between Prothorin and bone cancer. Would this lead Reporter, the *Metropolis Star*, Avid, Rothwell, or the FDA to respond differently?

The Seminar:

PROFESSOR CHARLES NESSON, HARVARD LAW SCHOOL: Well, good morning to you all. (*To a pharmaceutical manufacturer*) Good morning. What do you think this story is going to look like when it hits the paper?

FIRST PHARMACEUTICAL MANUFACTURER: Well, I really haven't decided yet.

PROFESSOR NESSON: What do you think?

FIRST PHARMACEUTICAL MANUFACTURER: I have my suspicions that it might not come out as well as some of us might expect.

PROFESSOR NESSON: Write it for us.

FIRST PHARMACEUTICAL MANUFACTURER: Right now?

PROFESSOR NESSON: Yes. What's the headline?

FIRST PHARMACEUTICAL MANUFACTURER: How much time will you give us? That's one of the problems I see in this. In fact, I suspect that maybe the headline will be written by someone who hasn't written the body of the article.

PROFESSOR NESSON: You write it.

FIRST PHARMACEUTICAL MANUFACTURER: The headline?

PROFESSOR NESSON: Yes. What's it going to be?

FIRST PHARMACEUTICAL MANUFACTURER: Well, as a matter of fact, I'm not certain that at the present time there ought to be a headline at all.

PROFESSOR NESSON: I know you're not certain, but what do you expect?

FIRST PHARMACEUTICAL MANUFACTURER: What do I expect?

PROFESSOR NESSON: Yes.

FIRST PHARMACEUTICAL MANUFACTURER: I expect a headline that says something like "Prothorin"—is that the way you want us to pronounce it?

PROFESSOR NESSON: Fine with me, it's your drug. (*Laughter*)

FIRST PHARMACEUTICAL MANUFACTURER: I don't think that was so fair.

(*Laughter*) I suspect it might read something like this: "Prothorin Implicated in Important Disease." (*Laughter*)

PROFESSOR NESSON: (*Turns to second pharmaceutical manufacturer*) Do you think that's right?

SECOND PHARMACEUTICAL MANUFACTURER: I don't think that's how the headline will read.

PROFESSOR NESSON: What's your expectation?

SECOND PHARMACEUTICAL MANUFACTURER: "Wonder Drug Causes Baldness." (*Laughter*)

PROFESSOR NESSON: What's the lead line in the story?

SECOND PHARMACEUTICAL MANUFACTURER: I can't tell the reporter what the lead line should be.

PROFESSOR NESSON: You've had a lot of experience reading these things.

SECOND PHARMACEUTICAL MANUFACTURER: Reading them, not writing them. "New research implicates Prothorin, well-known wonder drug, as possible cause of serious baldness, and perhaps other side effects." (*Laughter*)

PROFESSOR NESSON: (*Addresses the third pharmaceutical manufacturer*) Do you have expectations as to what this story is going to be?

THIRD PHARMACEUTICAL MANUFACTURER: Yes. I don't think the story will look like that at all, actually. The science writer, who is a good writer, won't in fact write the story. But on the financial page, there will be a story: "Investors and Brokers Tearing Their Hair over Side Effects of the Drug." (*Laughter; applause*)

PROFESSOR NESSON: (*Turns to first science reporter*) Is there a story in this?

FIRST SCIENCE REPORTER: I'm not sure.

PROFESSOR NESSON: Why aren't you sure?

FIRST SCIENCE REPORTER: Well, for several reasons. For one thing, we are told that somebody or other has submitted a paper for publication in the *Southern States Journal of Medicine*. Submitting a paper is one thing.

First of all, I want to know about this journal. Is it a reference journal? Is it a throwaway? What is it? Second, I'd like to know whether the paper was accepted.

PROFESSOR NESSON: Suppose it hasn't been accepted yet.

FIRST SCIENCE REPORTER: Well, I'd like to know who gave the paper.

PROFESSOR NESSON: Fine, Dr. Murray Fine.

FIRST SCIENCE REPORTER: Yes, I know that, but we need to know more about Fine.

PROFESSOR NESSON: A young researcher at the University of Alabama.

FIRST SCIENCE REPORTER: I'd like to find out where he got his training.

PROFESSOR NESSON: He trained at the Yale Medical School.

FIRST SCIENCE REPORTER: The only other thing is, the case is set up in such a way—and I won't dwell on the details—that it doesn't make an awful lot of scientific sense. There may be a story here, all right, but I'm not sure this one is it.

PROFESSOR NESSON: What do you want to ask?

FIRST SCIENCE REPORTER: Well, I want to ask, for example, if it is really true that this was a drug initially developed as a treatment for pneumonia, and nobody realized for months that it was also effective against urinary infections. I would have expected that if it was active against certain bacteria in one body site, it would have been active in others. I'd like to know whether people have been looking at side effects for a long time, or whether anybody has been looking at this, or whether it's been something the company has been trying to ignore.

PROFESSOR NESSON: There's no question, if I hear you right so far, that your interest in this story is in the possible side effect of this drug, rather than in this new method of spectro-whatever-it-is that this doctor has come up with.

FIRST SCIENCE REPORTER: Well, that is very possibly another story, but I'm not really sure that it's—

PROFESSOR NESSON: Why do the side effects of the drug interest you more than the other thing?

FIRST SCIENCE REPORTER: It doesn't necessarily interest me. You started out asking the first pharmaceutical manufacturer what the headline was going to be about his drug, and that's what you're primarily interested in, I gather.

PROFESSOR NESSON: You're not interested in that?

FIRST SCIENCE REPORTER: New assay techniques are a dime a dozen. They come along all the time.

PROFESSOR NESSON: All the time? All the time?

FIRST SCIENCE REPORTER: Yes.

PROFESSOR NESSON: And side effects for drugs, they are not a dime a dozen?

FIRST SCIENCE REPORTER: Well, they more directly impact on the reader immediately.

PROFESSOR NESSON: And that's your concern?

FIRST SCIENCE REPORTER: I'm not even sure there's a story here. I'm going to go and look at them. And I'm sticking to that. (*Laughter*)

PROFESSOR NESSON: (*Turns now to the second science reporter*) Do you think there's a story here?

SECOND SCIENCE REPORTER: I think there's a story here and I don't think it has anything to do with side effects. I don't think that it has anything to do with the new spectographic assay method. As I read down through this thing, and get into some questions, I find that the vice-president for public relations can call me up and try to swear me to secrecy, and then tell me something about the person who delivered this paper at the Society of Hematologists. But you see, the third paragraph [of Case Study 1] reads: "but prior treatment of the subjects with Prothorin has been noted as one of the possibly suggestive data." We've already got a story that Prothorin is implicated in important disease. We've already had the story "Wonder Drug Causes Baldness." And what's new?

What I want to know is why this guy is calling me out of the clear blue sky and saying, "If you promise not to tell anybody who told you, I will tell you something about this insignificant doctor down in Alabama who has written a third-rate paper for a fifth-rate journal." I would want to know why he is overreacting as much as he is.

PROFESSOR NESSON: We can get to that. There's been some indication in the literature that there have been some effects noted, but not connected with the drug. The interest of this story is that for the first time there is somebody that seems to link, in some way that looks causal, the drug with the side effect. It's the first time anybody's got a basis for saying this wonder drug causes that side effect.

SECOND SCIENCE REPORTER: I don't think he's got a basis for saying that any more than—

PROFESSOR NESSON: So you don't think it's a story.

SECOND SCIENCE REPORTER: I don't think *that* is a story. I think the overreacting of the drug company's flack is the story. That's the one I want to get into.

PROFESSOR NESSON: Do you note some overreaction from the drug companies already? That is, what they expect the story is going to be.

SECOND SCIENCE REPORTER: I sensed a little paranoia here about "Wonder Drug Causes Baldness" and that kind of thing, and what would happen on the financial pages, but—

PROFESSOR NESSON: Paranoia, that would never happen.

SECOND SCIENCE REPORTER: No.

PROFESSOR NESSON: (*To the first science reporter*) That would never happen. This is just unjustified paranoia that we hear around the table.

FIRST SCIENCE REPORTER: Well, frankly, I don't think it would happen very often. But let me just say one thing about your playing on side effects.

There is no such thing in this world as a drug without side effects. There is no such thing as a free lunch. Every science writer knows this, and no science writer is going to get very excited until and unless there is very well-documented evidence.

SECOND SCIENCE REPORTER: That's why I talked about the overreaction.

PROFESSOR NESSON: No such thing as a free lunch? No such thing as a drug without a side effect?

FIRST SCIENCE REPORTER: That does not have a side effect on someone.

PROFESSOR NESSON: You know that to be true?

FIRST SCIENCE REPORTER: It's kind of Science Writing 101.

PROFESSOR NESSON: Do your readers know that to be true?

FIRST SCIENCE REPORTER: We try to tell them all the time.

SECOND SCIENCE REPORTER: By telling them about all the side effects that drugs have. (*Laughter*) "Wonder Drug Has Side Effects." Of course you know that, but we're going to tell you *all* wonder drugs have side effects. That's the way we write these stories.

FIRST SCIENCE REPORTER: We try to write that about any drug because it's a very important thing for people to know. My job is to inform our readers so they can perhaps make a more intelligent decision.

PROFESSOR NESSON: (*Turns to the first editor*) Can you describe for us when it's newsworthy that you learn something about a drug's side effect?

FIRST EDITOR: Well, when it has a very serious effect on patients, who of course have a right to know something that's going to affect their health in a vital way. Here, you're beginning to get on the trail of a possibly serious effect for a drug that's being very widely used, for a lot of reasons other than those for which it is the drug of first choice. Therefore, it's important to know whether or not there are going to be serious side effects.

Now, in the literature, you're beginning to pick up some clues that this drug may in fact cause baldness. You have a fellow who is adding another little bit of evidence to that, but you have to check him out eight ways from Sunday. As of now, as this story is presented here, it may or may not even make the paper. If it made the paper at all, it would be in a very minor, small, and extremely cautious presentation.

PROFESSOR NESSON: (*Notices the first business reporter*) You shake your head.

FIRST BUSINESS REPORTER: It's going to make the paper.

PROFESSOR NESSON: It's going to make the paper?

FIRST BUSINESS REPORTER: As soon as this word gets out, the stock of this company is going to take a terrible beating. That's not because someone wrote the story. It's because this journal will get around and a few investors will hear about it. Wall Street will learn, and they'll all say: "Hey, here's a good short sale." Or if they don't say that, they will at least start selling the stock because they fear that the news is going to get out; that some reporter will write about it, and the result will be that the stock is going to go down and they're going to lose money.

PROFESSOR NESSON: What's the story going to be?

FIRST BUSINESS REPORTER: The story is going to be reaction to the loss in value of the stock. The stock is down five points, and you write about it. Here's a great drug company with a drug that is the primary drug of choice in urinary infections, and an obscure journal has suggested that there is a cause-and-effect relationship between the use of this drug and baldness. As a result, investors sold the shares heavily in the market, thinking that perhaps the stock was overvalued, as most drug companies appear to be. (*Laughter*) So this stock is going to start tumbling, and that's why you've got a story, regardless of whether or not any of the rest of this means anything.

PROFESSOR NESSON: (*Returns to the first science reporter*) You're checking this story out. You check with Dr. Fine. You find out he's a reputable fellow—at least he looks that way. He's well-regarded at his institution. The *Southern States Journal* hasn't absolutely decided it is going to take this article, but it is certainly a reputable journal. Do you check with anyone beyond Dr. Fine and that journal?

FIRST SCIENCE REPORTER: One of the things I think most science writers do is get out what's called the PDR—the *Physician's Desk Reference*—and a basic text by Goodman and Gilman [*The Pharmacological Basis of Therapeutics*].

PROFESSOR NESSON: You're going to look to see what side effects have already been described

FIRST SCIENCE REPORTER: Well, I'm going to look to see perhaps to what drug this is related, and look at the previous experience with that.

PROFESSOR NESSON: Are you going to get in touch with Rothwell Labs, in any way?

FIRST SCIENCE REPORTER: Sure. *If* I'm going to do the story. I again repeat, I'm not a bit sure I'm going to do the story—one thing I think needs to be said is that science writers have more than enough to do, and you have to decide what you're going to write and what's worth pursuing. Yes, of course I'm going to call Rothwell Labs for a comment. I might call people I know in pharmacology departments of medical schools. I might call the FDA [Food and Drug Administration]. I might call some health research groups.

SECOND EDITOR: What you're trying to deal with here is whether in fact this is a newsworthy story. I'd like to just step back and suggest that there are three basic criteria for evaluating information that editors and reporters subconsciously or consciously use at any time that information comes at them.

The first is whether the information is new. We get information coming at us every day. Some of it is new and some of it isn't. When

Billy Carter announces that he's coming to Boston to open a pizza parlor, as he did last week, this is—

PROFESSOR NESSON: That's news.

SECOND EDITOR: It's new, it's news, and we run it. If he comes ten times, which he may very well do, given Billy Carter, the tenth time probably isn't news. It's not new. So is it new?

The second question we ask ourselves is, is it important? Is it relevant in any way? If Jerry Lewis comes to Boston and opens a pizza parlor, it's not particularly surprising or interesting.

PROFESSOR NESSON: But if Billy Carter does, that's important?

SECOND EDITOR: If Billy Carter does, there's a certain bizarreness about that situation that justifies a news story. So is it new? Is it relevant?

The third question that we ask ourselves is, is it accurate? Is it true? And I would suggest that if we got a telephone call to the effect that Jimmy Carter was to come to Boston to open a pizza parlor, certainly this would be a major story—and he may very well do that, given some of his other decisions.

PROFESSOR NESSON: Let me take this one.

SECOND EDITOR: Let me just follow this one minute. If we discover that, in fact, he's not coming to Boston—it's a hoax—then of course it's not a story. Now, applying this to the case at hand, we have information that has been in obscure literature, apparently, but this is the first time that we have an official—semi-official—indication that this drug causes a serious side effect.

PROFESSOR NESSON: It's new.

SECOND EDITOR (*Who is bald*): It's new information. And this side effect, I would consider to be very serious. (*Laughter*)

PROFESSOR NESSON: Right.

SECOND EDITOR: So it passes, in my judgment, two criteria. It's both new and very relevant.

The third question that we ask ourselves is, is it accurate? It seems to me that this is where this story, as most others, bogs down. Is this information in fact legitimate, valid, scientifically provable, or at least sufficiently enough—

PROFESSOR NESSON: How are you going to find that out? You're an editor, right? You didn't go to medical school. You haven't got a science degree. How do you assure yourself, sitting at the editor's table, that you've got a story that's accurate?

SECOND EDITOR: Well, in this case, a medical story, a research story is going to be the hardest story that you could find to pin down the truth of the situation absolutely, irrevocably. But it seems to me that you certainly begin by questioning and assuring yourself of the medical capability of the man who is making this charge.

PROFESSOR NESSON: Okay, that we can do. The first science reporter has done that for you.

SECOND EDITOR: But have we done it?

PROFESSOR NESSON: Yes.

SECOND EDITOR: How have we done it?

PROFESSOR NESSON: We've checked and found out that he went to Yale Medical School.

SECOND EDITOR: Is that sufficient? A lot of people go to—

PROFESSOR NESSON: The University of Alabama. He's well respected, he's coming along on the tenure track. (*Laughter*)

SECOND EDITOR: I would find that quite reassuring. If this man was well respected, by both his former medical professors and his peer group, I think that is something you can't just pass off. You've got to check this out. You've got to ask some people. You've got to make telephone calls. Is this man considered a serious researcher in his field, or is he considered somewhat loose in his research techniques?

PROFESSOR NESSON: Would you consider using any of your newspaper's resources to hire someone who had expertise to check out this story?

SECOND EDITOR: I would if I wanted to give that amount of time to it. In this case, we have, in fact, a paper that has been delivered. Now, my impression is that that paper did not specifically connect this drug to the baldness. That piece of information was elicited by the reporter after the session.

PROFESSOR NESSON: Suppose you called a physician. You say, "Doctor, would you read this paper for us?" He reads it. "What do you think of it?" He says, "Well, it's certainly very interesting. [*Laughter*] But it would take me a lot more time and effort to really check into it, to see if I thought that this was valid. My rates are—"

Are you ready to go for that?

SECOND EDITOR: If you're asking whether I'm willing to pay somebody to get some information—

PROFESSOR NESSON: Yes.

SECOND EDITOR: I'm willing to get information any way I can; if I have to do it that way, perhaps I will. I hope I could get some other doctor who would read it and study it—

PROFESSOR NESSON: Do it for free?

SECOND EDITOR: Do it for free. (*Laughter*) I would also suggest that the FDA is an organization that perhaps would have some immediate insight into this whole area. I think I'd be inclined to call them first. I certainly wouldn't call Mr. Avid first.

PROFESSOR NESSON: (*Says to the second editor*) What do you ask the man from FDA?

SECOND EDITOR: Well, I ask him, first of all, whether he has had any prior reason to connect Prothorin with this very serious disease mentioned.

PROFESSOR NESSON: (*Turns to the first health official*) What kind of an answer is he going to get?

FIRST HEALTH OFFICIAL: He's going to get me telling him that we'd like to take a look at the paper ourselves.

PROFESSOR NESSON: You'd like to take a look at it. How long is it going to take you to look at it? (*Laughter*)

FIRST HEALTH OFFICIAL: Do you want it in epochs or eons? (*Laughter*)

PROFESSOR NESSON: (*To the second editor*) Where are you now?

SECOND EDITOR: My deadline is getting closer and closer and I'm getting nervous. If nothing else, I certainly have the fact that the paper was presented, and whatever—

PROFESSOR NESSON: I see. The way you write the story is, let's not put the paper behind this damned thing. Let's lead it with "Paper presented, which says . . ." and then it's out, fine, the hell with it.

SECOND EDITOR: Well, not the hell with it. If I haven't convinced myself that there's any reasonable truth to this very serious medical implication, then I don't think I can go at deadline that afternoon with anything in addition to the fact that the paper was presented and what was said in an official legal meeting.

PROFESSOR NESSON: And what's the headline on that story going to be?

SECOND EDITOR: Well, I don't know what the paper itself said, but the news story will say whatever the man said. Hopefully, no more and no less.

PROFESSOR NESSON: (*Turns to the third editor*) How does a newspaper deal with this problem? This problem being the difficulty of trying to authenticate a story in an area where you don't have expertise.

THIRD EDITOR: Obviously, you go to the sources of expertise. In this case, I think everybody's right, that so far there's no story at all. Perhaps there is a coincidental relationship between this new analysis method and what he discovered. I would think that you'd begin by asking this fellow a few other questions. For example, did he find Prothorin in the hair follicles on nonbalding people, and other questions along that line, to find out whether, indeed, you could narrow this down to any kind of possible causal relationship. I certainly would pursue the FDA about as hard as I could, and say, "Look, don't you think that people are going bald at a great rate because of using a drug called Prothorin? You owe it to the public to get this out in less than epochal time frames."

PROFESSOR NESSON: (*Asks first health official*) Do you want to respond to the third editor? This is a much stronger appeal than was that of the second editor.

FIRST HEALTH OFFICIAL: Yes, he is more persistent. I think we would obviously take a very quick look, in any such preliminary report. We'd ask Fine for a copy of his full manuscript. We'd ask him if he was willing to have us comment on it publicly or not. We'd take his judgment on that. Very often, you know, editors of medical and scientific journals won't take a paper the main conclusions of which have already been released. So we would feel, in that case, a strong obligation to Dr. Fine to make sure that his prior publication claim to that material is recognized. That's an ethical issue that isn't often recognized in this area.

PROFESSOR NESSON: That's interesting. Your concern is that he get his paper published.

FIRST HEALTH OFFICIAL: Not the primary concern, but that's a concern.

PROFESSOR NESSON: Enough so that you would defer getting into this question, yourself?

FIRST HEALTH OFFICIAL: If we got an unpublished paper from an individual scientist, and he says, "Look at it but don't comment publicly," we will observe his request not to comment on it publicly and not to release it publicly unless it's—

PROFESSOR NESSON: And not to act on it.

FIRST HEALTH OFFICIAL: No, I didn't say that. We're talking about a conversation with a reporter. We would certainly act on it, and if in taking action in a public policy sense, we *had* to release it, we would have to do that. But in terms of treating this material with respect to the press, we'd observe the strictures that he'd put on it.

PROFESSOR NESSON: (*Turns to the fourth editor*) Here you've got a story, a story about people possibly getting bald, real bad stuff. (*Laughter*) Interesting. Does it seem like a story to you?

FOURTH EDITOR: Sure it is.

PROFESSOR NESSON: Sure it is. Your bias is to go with the story, yes?

FOURTH EDITOR: Not in a way that the first pharmaceutical manufacturer said. You wouldn't say: "Prothorin Causes Baldness."

PROFESSOR NESSON: How would you go with the story?

FOURTH EDITOR: "Prothorin May Cause Baldness."

PROFESSOR NESSON: "Prothorin May Cause Baldness." (*Laughter*)

FOURTH EDITOR: It would depend entirely on the research we did on Dr. Fine.

PROFESSOR NESSON: Would you consider running a picture of somebody who is totally bald? (*Laughter*) Let us suppose (*Addresses first science reporter*) that you've checked this thing through, and you've gotten to the point where you are pretty satisfied that Dr. Fine is reputable, his research is pretty solid, there is definitely, if not a solid causal connection fully established, at least grounds for serious suspicion. And you decide you're ready to go with the story. It's new, it's important, and you have verified it as much as you're capable of verifying it.

At that point, are you ready to contact Rothwell Labs to see what kind of reaction?

FIRST SCIENCE REPORTER: Of course.

PROFESSOR NESSON: Tell me how you do it. Who do you call?

FIRST SCIENCE REPORTER: Well, it depends on which company it is. Ordinarily, if I knew their public information person to be on the level—reasonably bright, reasonably well-informed—I would call that person. I doubt that I would call the president of the company, in the first place. He probably may not be aware of the scientific details.

PROFESSOR NESSON: The presidents of companies, what do they know? (*Laughter*) Call the PR man. There's the man to get the facts from. (*Laughter*)

FIRST SCIENCE REPORTER: Well, the PR man usually knows who in that company worked on that product.

PROFESSOR NESSON: Call the first company official for me. What do you ask him?

FIRST SCIENCE REPORTER: I say there has been a paper given. Are you aware of it. Have you read the paper? The paper contains suggestive evidence that this drug is linked to an increased risk of baldness. What do you have to say about it? And what scientist in your company can I speak to about this?

PROFESSOR NESSON: (*To the first company official*) All right, there you are. You've got a feeler from a reporter. She's obviously on to something. It's your company, your drug. She's about to run a story that will make it look bad. The stock is going to go to hell.

FIRST COMPANY OFFICIAL: Am I on a deadline? Is she on a deadline?

FIRST SCIENCE REPORTER: Yes.

FIRST COMPANY OFFICIAL: I'm sorry to hear that. (*Laughter*) I would say, give me the precise nature of your questions. I will write them down. I will read them back to you, and I will get back to you as quickly as I can, with whatever I find out.

FIRST SCIENCE REPORTER: Well, the reason I say I am on a deadline is that this paper was given at a public meeting. That means the chances that I was the only reporter there are very, very slim, and I think this relates to a point brought up by the first health official. There's a lot of fuss in the scientific community about, we don't want our stories reported. The *New England Journal of Medicine* won't take my paper if a word is breathed of it elsewhere. But the fact is that once the paper is given at a public meeting, this is really impossible—

FIRST COMPANY OFFICIAL: I think the accuracy of my response is more important than your deadline.

FIRST SCIENCE REPORTER: That may be true, but my editor may not think so.

FIRST COMPANY OFFICIAL: I understand, but that's nothing I can control.

FIRST SCIENCE REPORTER: Well, in that case, what I am going to do is to say that for lack of time Company X was unable to comment on this.

PROFESSOR NESSON: (*To the first company official*) There it is, the story down there in column two: Rothwell Labs were asked for information, and they responded: "We're sorry, we're unable to comment."

FIRST COMPANY OFFICIAL: That is not as bad as rushing ahead with a comment that is not fully reasearched and fully accurate. I understand the implications of it, and there's nothing I can do about it when the call comes in on deadline.

PROFESSOR NESSON: Tough luck.

FIRST COMPANY OFFICIAL: On me.

PROFESSOR NESSON: And on your company.

FIRST COMPANY OFFICIAL: Right. But it is worse to try to pull together a comment that is later going to be proven to be inaccurate.

PROFESSOR NESSON: (*To the first science reporter*) Do you think he's right about that?

FIRST SCIENCE REPORTER: Yes, because I'll hold back, if I can, to the next edition, and pick it up.

FIRST COMPANY OFFICIAL: You'll hold back. So now I have a day?

FIRST SCIENCE REPORTER: No, you won't have a day. You'll have between the first edition and the second. (*Laughter*)

PROFESSOR NESSON: (*Turns now to the first TV executive*) Suppose you're going with this on broadcast. You've got a deadline. You've got a little story to stick in the six-thirty news. Do you get in touch with the public relations official? Or do you try and get the head of the company?

FIRST TV EXECUTIVE: You make a supposition I don't accept. I don't think it's a story yet that we would go with on television, at least, on a network program. *Eyewitness News* and a local station probably would go on and comment on the fact that Howard Cosell wears a toupee and would wonder if Prothorin had affected him.

PROFESSOR NESSON: You mean, local news. That's fine with me. I want you going with this story. If you don't think this is big enough and important enough to make the national news—

FIRST TV EXECUTIVE: It isn't.

PROFESSOR NESSON: Not—

FIRST TV EXECUTIVE: No way.

PROFESSOR NESSON: If it was cancer?

FIRST TV EXECUTIVE: Cancer, yes.

PROFESSOR NESSON: Cancer, that would be good. (*Laughter*) All right, take your pick. You're either on the local news with baldness or you're on the national news with cancer. (*Laughter*) Are you going to call our company official here?

FIRST TV EXECUTIVE: I'm going to make absolutely certain before I go that my correspondent (and we do have a science correspondent—the networks now are providing them and they are also providing consultants) has pretty well checked out every aspect we can, from Fine to the company PR man and others, because in fact I have a luxury that newspapers don't have. One of the luxuries I have is a negative, and that is, I don't have very much air time every night. I have to make decisions on elimination. I *have* to leave things out. I would just as soon leave out this item until I am dead certain that I am correct, because I have thirty-five other items that I probably am able to be more secure on than this one. That's the difference.

PROFESSOR NESSON: Take it at this point. You checked out the story, not absolutely established that there is cause and effect, but awful good grounds to think so. Solid source, solid paper, you're ready to go with it. The question I've got for you is, do you go to the company PR person and try to get a comment from him?

FIRST TV EXECUTIVE: Darn right, probably on film.

PROFESSOR NESSON: Do you go to the head of the company and try to get a comment from him?

FIRST TV EXECUTIVE: Darn right, and I won't get it from either one of them.

PROFESSOR NESSON: Why not?

FIRST TV EXECUTIVE: Because they're afraid of us.

PROFESSOR NESSON: (*Turns to the first company official*) Is that true?

FIRST COMPANY OFFICIAL: No.

FIRST TV EXECUTIVE: Well, let's talk about practice rather than theory. I've done stories about the FDA. I spent a career doing documentaries about the FDA. If you'll bear with me, let's get into this just slightly. And we are very used to the stall. We are very used to having to go at six o'clock or six-thirty by saying there has been no comment yet. The difference is also that we don't have a second run on a given night. The difference in television is that you go on the air when you go on the air. Your options are either to go with it or not to go tonight, but go tomorrow night.

PROFESSOR NESSON: Suppose I make you a consultant, a public relations consultant, to this drug company. You know the broadcast business backwards and forwards. They get a call from your equivalent now with the broadcast company. Can you advise them of how to respond to it? Are you with our first company official—"No comment until we get a chance to look at this?"

FIRST TV EXECUTIVE: Correct.

PROFESSOR NESSON: Granted, that means we're never going to get a comment, because you're not going to run the story twice. We've got one shot—that's tonight on the evening news. Maybe we get ten seconds' worth of your air time. Forget it, Company. Is that what you're saying?

FIRST TV EXECUTIVE: No, I don't think I said that. I think I stand with what the first company official said. If we are serious journalists—and I don't care if it's print or electronic—it is our obligation to check out a story before we go on the air with it. If he said to me, "We have no comment," I would report that at this point—if I thought this story was worth putting on the air—there had been no comment. Or perhaps we would even say something like this: "We have asked for a comment from Rothwell Labs, and they have not given it to us yet."

FIRST COMPANY OFFICIAL: I didn't say that. I said I would like your questions and I will write them down so I have them precisely. And I'll read them back to you so that we agree on the questions. I will immediately start to ask the people in the company who I think might have knowledge or lack of knowledge about this, and get back to you as soon as I possibly can. It is not a question of no comment.

FIRST TV EXECUTIVE: We have asked Rothwell, and so far they are studying the matter and we will follow this up tomorrow, if indeed I went with it tonight. And I don't think I'd go with it tonight. I think I'd give them twenty-four hours.

PROFESSOR NESSON: (*Asks the first company official*) Is that all the time it's going to take?

FIRST COMPANY OFFICIAL: I have no idea.

PROFESSOR NESSON: Suppose you've checked into it. You say give it to me in written form. Let me read it back to you. Send them interrogatories. They give you fourteen interrogatories. You check it through, and you come up with a relatively complicated picture. I mean, your company is interested in this. Your company doesn't know that much more than Fine does. In fact, maybe a lot less. There's a lot of good to be said about this drug; it has saved a lot of people from a lot of pain. There's something bad to be said about the possible side effects. What's your answer going to look like?

FIRST COMPANY OFFICIAL: Well, at that point I would call the reporter and ask him if he would be willing to come over and meet with some of our scientific people to go over all aspects of the drug as we know them.

PROFESSOR NESSON: (*Asks the first science reporter*) And you're willing to do that?

FIRST SCIENCE REPORTER: Depending on how big a story it is, yes.

PROFESSOR NESSON: (*Turns to the first company official*) Are you willing to sit down with our TV executive on film?

FIRST COMPANY OFFICIAL: At some point I would be, yes.

PROFESSOR NESSON: Does it bother you? How long are you going to sit down for? ·

FIRST COMPANY OFFICIAL: Well, it depends on what procedures he's going to use. If he's going to come in and film me or anyone else for half an hour or so and then edit it, or have somebody else who wasn't even at the meeting edit it down to ten seconds, I would seriously doubt that I'd do it.

PROFESSOR NESSON: You say, *if* he's going to do that?

FIRST COMPANY OFFICIAL: Yes.

PROFESSOR NESSON: Of *course* he's going to do that.

FIRST COMPANY OFFICIAL: Of course he's going to do it, right. (*Laughter*) Not necessarily. There have been situations where there's been an agreement that there will be a ten- or thirty-second interview, without editing. Rare, but it's happened.

PROFESSOR NESSON: Are you going to let the head of the company talk to him?

FIRST COMPANY OFFICIAL: I may well.

PROFESSOR NESSON: (*Asks the first pharmaceutical manufacturer*) Are you going to let your PR official talk to him?

FIRST PHARMACEUTICAL MANUFACTURER: Yes. He seems to me to be a pretty intelligent fellow. (*Laughter*)

PROFESSOR NESSON: What I'm asking is, is this a PR problem or is it a president's problem?

FIRST PHARMACEUTICAL MANUFACTURER: This is a scientific problem.

PROFESSOR NESSON: That's not your problem.

FIRST PHARMACEUTICAL MANUFACTURER: This is a professional problem.

PROFESSOR NESSON: That's not your problem.

FIRST PHARMACEUTICAL MANUFACTURER: Of course it's my problem.

PROFESSOR NESSON: Why do you let your PR person handle it?

FIRST PHARMACEUTICAL MANUFACTURER: He's just the input. He is going to seek out the information from the vice-president for medical affairs, perhaps from the director of the research institute, to find out what information is really available and what the data behind this are. There are a good many things behind this that have never been explained to any of us. Is it baldness in men alone, or is it baldness in men and women?

PROFESSOR NESSON: Both.

FIRST PHARMACEUTICAL MANUFACTURER: How do you know that?

PROFESSOR NESSON: I made it up—it's hypothetical. (*Laughter*)

FIRST PHARMACEUTICAL MANUFACTURER (*Who is also bald*): Then let me give you my hypothetical answer. (*Laughter*) If it happens in women, it's a lot more serious than if it happens in men. Look at the second editor and at me: baldness isn't exactly a fatal disease. (*Laughter*) We have managed to get along with this. Now what you've got to know is how many people have gotten it, how many times this possible side effect has occurred. Has it been in all sexes? Has Fine found it in other body tissues as well? This is not something that you answer in five minutes. You've got to have the interrogatories. In the last analysis, I might respond to it.

PROFESSOR NESSON: You *might* respond.

FIRST PHARMACEUTICAL MANUFACTURER: I might.

PROFESSOR NESSON: Do you talk to your lawyer about this?

FIRST PHARMACEUTICAL MANUFACTURER: Yes, I do. That's why one is sitting beside me. (*Laughter*)

PROFESSOR NESSON: What do you want to know from your lawyer?

FIRST PHARMACEUTICAL MANUFACTURER: Well, in these days, I think—you know, legal fees are the largest upremeditated expense in my budget. These days you have to talk to an attorney before you make public statements.

PROFESSOR NESSON: Say that again.

FIRST PHARMACEUTICAL MANUFACTURER: That is why I would like to come and be your student. I think I need some of that background, as well. I have a feeling you could teach me.

PROFESSOR NESSON: The largest unpremeditated expense?

FIRST PHARMACEUTICAL MANUFACTURER: Is legal.

PROFESSOR NESSON: Is that different from the largest expense?

FIRST PHARMACEUTICAL MANUFACTURER: I said the largest unpremeditated one. We have a lot of large expenses, but the ones that can never budget accurately are those for the legal profession. And we need them desperately.

PROFESSOR NESSON: What do you want to ask him?

FIRST PHARMACEUTICAL MANUFACTURER: Before I make the statements in which we would reply to the interrogatories, I would like to have him go over them with me.

PROFESSOR NESSON: Why?

FIRST PHARMACEUTICAL MANUFACTURER: Because I want to be absolutely certain that I do not say anything that would be a violation of a federal regulation, in the first instance; that I would not say anything that would do damage to a patient, in the second instance; and that I would not do damage to my company, in the third instance. I don't think I know all the answers, Mr. Nesson. I think I should consult with as many people as is necessary, concerning a subject such as this, in order that all can be protected.

PROFESSOR NESSON: (*Turns to the third editor*) Let me come back to you. There's no question that many people in the drug industry think they're not treated that fairly in the newspapers.

THIRD EDITOR: No secret there.

PROFESSOR NESSON: No secret there, right? Do you have any advice for drug companies, when it comes to how they handle the inquiries from reporters? Do you think that our company official is on the right track or the wrong track? Do you think he's going too fast or too slow?

THIRD EDITOR: No, I think he's behaving exactly as I would expect a responsible public relations representative to behave. And the only advice one could give to the drug companies—and this is very presumptuous of me—is to be as candid as they possibly can, so long as they know they're dealing with a responsible news organization. Say, "Look, we don't know exactly how far this thing has gone. We'll try to find out. We're trying to find out." Present all the pertinent data that would obtain here.

You know, nobody's made the point that if this story comes out, obviously it's a tremendously damaging story to this company, so I doubt that anybody will irresponsibly and in too great a hurry rush forward with it. I should qualify that—I doubt that any *responsible* news organization would do that, which means then that you *would* have to check it out.

Now, if you had discovered that baldness in women is connected with this, too, then the urgency becomes greater. Then you do go to the head of the company and say, "For God's sake, you've got a problem.

We can't keep this quiet forever." And we've got to find out what is true about this, or at least what is most likely to be true about it.

PROFESSOR NESSON: (*Turns to the second pharmaceutical manufacturer*) Let me ask you a question of similar generality. Can you state for me what your theory is about why the drug companies are treated badly in the press. Not just drug companies, industrial companies putting out products that may have toxic side effects.

SECOND PHARMACEUTICAL MANUFACTURER: Well, I'll do that; then I want to come back to one other thing about the case itself that we're talking about.

My theory is not very profound: I think it's generally that what the press views as news tends generally to be, perhaps, hurtful. What we might view as news—namely, the advent of a great new drug—is perhaps of less interest to them. I think it's really their view of what's going to interest their readers, and, unfortunately, bad news tends more often than not to be the thing that gets into the papers.

PROFESSOR NESSON: The readers are scared, and therefore a story that comes out appeals to something that's of interest to them.

SECOND PHARMACEUTICAL MANUFACTURER: I think press people are trying to find out what will be of interest to their readers. And often, an airplane crash has more interest than the fact that eighty million airplanes have landed safely.

PROFESSOR NESSON: (*Asks the first health official*) Is it your judgment that the public in the United States has the understanding that our first science reporter holds—that is, there are side effects to everything, nothing is safe?

FIRST HEALTH OFFICIAL: No, I don't think so.

PROFESSOR NESSON: You think that a lot of the public think drugs are pretty safe.

FIRST HEALTH OFFICIAL: Yes, I think that's at least a fairly widely held view.

PROFESSOR NESSON: In fact, FDA is in the business of saying this drug is safe and effective.

FIRST HEALTH OFFICIAL: No, it's not, actually. I think FDA has always made a fairly determined effort to try to get public understanding that the use of any drug is a risk-benefit decision.

PROFESSOR NESSON: The FDA has always made that effort. What does the statute say?

FIRST HEALTH OFFICIAL: The statute talks about safety and efficacy, and it talks about them in, I think, very long-winded and confusing terms, and

I think that's part of the problem. It's one of the reasons the FDA is trying to get the statute changed.

PROFESSOR NESSON: It wants it changed to say that the FDA is going to approve drugs that are pretty safe.

FIRST HEALTH OFFICIAL: It's going to say that FDA is going to approve drugs for particular indications, on the grounds of the risk-to-benefit ratio that they afford in that indication.

PROFESSOR NESSON: It would like to educate the public that there are risks associated?

FIRST HEALTH OFFICIAL: Oh, absolutely.

PROFESSOR NESSON: Absolutely, absolutely. Why doesn't the FDA insist on putting inserts into the packages the patients get when they take a drug, that says, here are the risks with this drug, patient.

FIRST HEALTH OFFICIAL: It is doing it. And getting sued.

PROFESSOR NESSON: How many drugs is the FDA doing it for?

FIRST HEALTH OFFICIAL: The FDA did it for oral contraceptives. The FDA did it for IUDs. The FDA is doing it for the estrogens, and the FDA had to fight each one of them in the courts.

PROFESSOR NESSON: Funny, three items like that—estrogens, IUDs, contraceptives. Why not for Prothorin? Why not for penicillin?

FIRST HEALTH OFFICIAL: Like any other problem, you take it in pieces—

PROFESSOR NESSON: One at a time. We've got about four million drugs here. A few epochs and eons down the road, we'll finally get to one of these.

FIRST HEALTH OFFICIAL: That's about the way it goes.

PROFESSOR NESSON: (*Asks the second health official*) Do you have any problem with patient inserts?

SECOND HEALTH OFFICIAL: No.

PROFESSOR NESSON: Why not?

SECOND HEALTH OFFICIAL: Do you mean would I have any problems if they were there?

PROFESSOR NESSON: Yes.

SECOND HEALTH OFFICIAL: I think there could be problems, but I personally wouldn't have a problem in seeing them there. I think inserts, like any effort at communication with the patient, could conceivably develop problems for the doctor-patient relationship that don't exist now. But I think—

PROFESSOR NESSON: (*Turns to the first businessman*) When you go to see your doctor, and he prescribes some drug for you, do you ask him about the side effects of the drug?

FIRST BUSINESSMAN: Never.

PROFESSOR NESSON: Did you say never?

FIRST BUSINESSMAN: Never.

PROFESSOR NESSON: It's an article of faith with you.

FIRST BUSINESSMAN: I've got a pain, he's got a cure. (*Laughter*)

PROFESSOR NESSON: And if your hair were to suddenly fall out, you would say, "Oh, well, that's the breaks of the game."

FIRST BUSINESSMAN: No, I'd sue the doctor. (*Laughter*)

PROFESSOR NESSON: (*Asks the fourth pharmaceutical manufacturer*) When you go to the doctor, do you ask any questions about side effects?

FOURTH PHARMACEUTICAL MANUFACTURER (*Who is also bald*) Well, certainly not about alopecia. (*Laughter*) I would. Yes, of course, it's my business.

PROFESSOR NESSON: Why not, right? You're an informed person. You want to make an intelligent judgment.

FOURTH PHARMACEUTICAL MANUFACTURER: But in the last analysis, I will follow the doctor's advice, of course.

PROFESSOR NESSON: Do you take a position in favor of package inserts for patients?

FOURTH PHAMACEUTICAL MANUFACTURER: I have a very mixed position on it. I go back to the time when I was suffering from a cardiac problem. The doctor told me to give him a ring if anything went wrong, and tell him what was happening. So I called him up and said, "What should I be looking for?" He said, "If you think I'm going to tell you that, you're crazy, because you'll have it."

I think it's a very serious question as to whether you give this list of side effects that only the FDA can conjure up to every patient who may be put on a drug. I don't think we've examined the case that carefully.

PROFESSOR NESSON: (*Asks the second health official*) Is he talking to you?

SECOND HEALTH OFFICIAL: Well, I understand what he's saying. I think that's what I meant by the fact that such a practice would cause certain problems to develop in the doctor-patient relationship. But we don't have the data to come down on it. I would think that given the present atmosphere in the level of the science, I would certainly favor an effort to put inserts in with a lot more drugs than we have them in with now.

FOURTH PHARMACEUTICAL MANUFACTURER: We keep talking about the present atmosphere. The present atmosphere is a self-generated thing. The doctor-patient relationship, I think, is a long, traditional, very comfortable thing. I'd hate to see it disturbed.

PROFESSOR NESSON: I'll tell you what I'm driving at. On the one hand, we hear the drug companies saying that the newpapers pander to public interest, and the public is very much concerned with these side effects. Is it an airplane that's gone down? Is it a new side effect for a drug?

There's no question there's a good deal of public ignorance on the subject on which you say every science reporter gets in 101, right?

FIRST SCIENCE REPORTER: I'm not saying that the message gets across.

PROFESSOR NESSON: In fact we're pretty sure that the message, generally speaking, doesn't get across. In fact, the drug companies are in the business, are they not, of selling drugs, and one of the ways they sell them is to suggest that they're safe drugs. That's got to be true.

If one of the problems for the drug companies is the newpaper pandering to a—let us call it an ignorant public, why isn't it the responsibility, why isn't it in the interest of the drug companies to start educating the public much more completely than they are now educated about this very proposition?

FOURTH PHARMACEUTICAL MANUFACTURER: Well, that's a self-answering question, obviously. We should. How is quite another matter again. I'm not clear on that.

PROFESSOR NESSON: (*Turns to the second health official*) The reason why your patient is going to be asking you a lot of silly questions, and coming up with a lot of hypochondriacal symptoms, is because they don't understand the risks. Isn't it quite possible that if they understood a lot more of the risks, they wouldn't be quite so hypochondriacal about them?

SECOND HEALTH OFFICIAL: It's possible, but it's still a difficult thing. I think we don't know how to do it well yet, but I don't think we're going to find out until we start doing it. I believe, probably, on balance, that we have to do much more than we're doing in this regard. What I hear our fourth pharmaceutical manufacturer saying is sort of the same thing, but maybe coming down on the other side of the fence a little bit. But maybe I'm wrong.

PROFESSOR NESSON: Whenever you give somebody antibiotics, the proper thing to do is to make a throat culture at the time you give him the drug, or maybe even defer giving it to him until you see whether there is some particular reaction. Am I right about that? That's good medical practice.

SECOND HEALTH OFFICIAL: Right.

PROFESSOR NESSON: So what the FDA says is that we're going to put an insert into every little package, so whenever a patient gets any antibiotic, he also gets a little note that says, if your doctor hasn't taken a throat culture, he is incompetent. (*Laughter*)

SECOND HEALTH OFFICIAL: Well, I think that you're hitting on something here, which is the fact that there are very, very few black-and-white issues in medicine, and sometimes the gray area is very large. That would probably be an inaccurate insert, and unacceptable to any knowledgeable person, because there are circumstances under which a physician would be not doing a good job for his patient if he didn't proceed with the administration of an antibiotic, despite the lack of a throat culture.

PROFESSOR NESSON: No, understand me, I agree with you. That is, if it's a virulent thing, and he's got to get right on top, and he makes a good guess—but the smart doctor, the good doctor will not only make the best guess, he'll also take a throat culture.

SECOND HEALTH OFFICIAL: It may not always be possible. There are circumstances under which it is not always possible.

PROFESSOR NESSON: To take a throat culture?

SECOND HEALTH OFFICIAL: To take a throat culture.

PROFESSOR NESSON: The person doesn't have a throat?

SECOND HEALTH OFFICIAL: The facilities to do a throat culture are not available throughout the United States—wherever a doctor comes in contact with a patient.

PROFESSOR NESSON: You get my drift?

SECOND HEALTH OFFICIAL: Yes.

PROFESSOR NESSON: That is, there are some things that aren't quite so black-and-white.

SECOND HEALTH OFFICIAL: That's right. You mean there are some things that aren't so black-and-white as what?

PROFESSOR NESSON: There are some things on which a patient could be advised as to this is good and this is bad. Are you in favor of advising him?

SECOND HEALTH OFFICIAL: Yes.

PROFESSOR NESSON: (*Asks first health official*) Why isn't the FDA in that business?

FIRST HEALTH OFFICIAL: I thought I just explained that it is, and I think we've all learned something in the last five minutes about why the FDA has to proceed step by step and why it's difficult. There's very substantial opposition in organized medicine to patient inserts for just the reasons that our second health official gave to your hypothetical labeling suggestion. There are a lot of members of the private bar who are willing to help eat up resources in court every time there is an attempt to make a label compulsory.

PROFESSOR NESSON: Lawyers representing whom?

FIRST HEALTH OFFICIAL: This time around, they're representing the pharmaceutical manufacturers association and the college of ob-gyn.

PROFESSOR NESSON: Why are the pharmaceutical manufacturers against it?

FIRST HEALTH OFFICIAL: You have lots of them here to ask. (*Laughter*) I really wouldn't venture to speak for them. My reasoning, and I've tried, from time to time, to use it, is that just as you suggest, it is in the long run beneficial for that industry to have greater public understanding of therapeutic practice. I think inserts are a good idea for most drugs.

PROFESSOR NESSON: Well, let's hear from our first pharmaceutical manufacturer. Are you pro or con on this one?

FIRST PHARMACEUTICAL MANUFACTURER: Well, I've always thought the patient is entitled to more information relative to medical therapy than is usually given. I think that goes beyond the matter of drugs into the matter of day-to-day care by internists and also into the matter of what is performed.

I think the problem in this regard is what should be in the insert, and I think our health officials have both responded to this question already. Does one educate the patient by terrifying the patient? If any patient today should look at the professional package insert, which by requirement must list all of the side effects that have ever occurred—or had been presumed to have occurred—I think there are many patients who would not take any drugs at all, and therefore would defeat their own therapy. The problem is to educate people to the fact that, as our first science reporter said at the very beginning of this: there is no drug that's completely safe. The very name "drug" means it cannot be completely safe because it interferes with some sort of biological mechanism. Therefore, it's going to cause a problem for somebody, and it's going to cause problems in varying degrees.

Anybody who says "Give us safe drugs" is talking about a paradox that cannot be resolved. There is no such thing as a drug that is safe for everybody. You know that. The salt on your table this morning is not safe for everybody. The sugar on your table this morning is not safe for everyone. Now, how, as a teacher, do we get those bits and pieces of information together so that the patient can be better informed?

That's what we're trying to do.

PROFESSOR NESSON: I can tell you one way to start: it's to tell them.

FIRST PHARMACEUTICAL MANUFACTURER: Yes, but not the way you do. (*Laughter*) I don't think a patient would take that from you. The only reason some of us do is that you're smiling while you do it. (*Laughter*)

PROFESSOR NESSON: Wait until tomorrow. (*Laughter*) (*Turns to the third pharmaceutical manufacturer*) How do you stand on this?

THIRD PHARMACEUTICAL MANUFACTURER: Well, to make it very clear, the very first patient package insert was developed and put into use with a joint cooperative effort involving all the parties of interest, including the drug industry. So I think there is an interest and a concern about delivering this kind of information to patients. It's a question of how the information is delivered and who decides what the information is.

Everyone should appreciate that the FDA's information isn't going to be provided by the doctor, but by the pharmacist. Personally, I think this is a very undesirable way to do it, for reasons that I think our health official made clear.

The only person who can really interpret what that patient needs, in the way of information, and can really respond to the inevitable questions that are going to arise is the physician, not the pharmacist. I think there is a fundamental flaw in the way the insert is being visualized.

Second, the question of who shall decide is in the insert. The present litigation has to do with insert language that is being asserted unilaterally by the regulatory agency. The reason that a number of physicians' groups are suing the regulatory agency in court is that they believe—and I think rightly—that they should participate in deciding what should be said and how it should be said.

PROFESSOR NESSON: (*Asks the second pharmaceutical manufacturer*) Your position?

SECOND PHARMACEUTICAL MANUFACTURER: Well, I'm not really as close to it as some of my colleagues, but my position is very similar to theirs.

PROFESSOR NESSON: (*Turns to the second businessman*) Your position?

SECOND BUSINESSMAN: I think we've come a long way from the media and the customer, in talking about the regulatory agency and industry. Our business is dealing with the media, on one hand, and the customer on the other. We live with this every day, not theoretically.

PROFESSOR NESSON: Is that a position?

SECOND BUSINESSMAN: Our position is, the consumer, the customer, should be told as much as possible, as accurately as possible, because otherwise they are going to come and ask us, and we usually don't know.

PROFESSOR NESSON: (*Returns to the first company official*) Let us suppose that this story about Prothorin has come out, and it's, according to your judgment, a slanted story, an unfair story to your company. It overstates the risk, it overemphasizes the risks. Do you feel you have any course of redress at that point?

FIRST COMPANY OFFICIAL: Yes, there are several things that we might do. Starting with the simplest, you can put out a press release that would answer it, which probably would not get very much play, but it might.

PROFESSOR NESSON: (*Asks the second editor*) Would it get any play? You're going to include in your press release all the good that this drug does, the very few instances of baldness that have been reported, stuff like that? Is that going to get play the second day after the story?

SECOND EDITOR: I think it will. Let me just take quick issue with the earlier statements that the papers are pandering to some sort of perverse public interest in the side effects of drugs. I can't imagine that anybody could make a case that the public shouldn't be intimately concerned about the effects of drugs. In fact, if the FDA and the pharmaceutical agencies aren't going to make this information available, then perhaps the lay press is the only other resource for this information.

PROFESSOR NESSON: Exactly the opposite side of the point we were just discussing, yes?

SECOND EDITOR: Yes.

PROFESSOR NESSON: But let's stick with this one. The company puts out a press release. It's now touting Prothorin. It's now saying, basically, that this risk is overstated, that your story was inaccurate. Are you going to print that?

SECOND EDITOR: Well, to the same extent that we tried to verify the original statement of the doctor, by a variety of means that may or may not have been successful, I think it would behoove us to try to establish the veracity of the rejoinder by the drug company.

PROFESSOR NESSON: (*Turns to the first company official*) What do you expect? Where is it going to run, if it runs?

FIRST COMPANY OFFICIAL: Based on past experience, it's not likely to receive the prominence of the first story, if it receives any attention at all. It is the same kind of thing as indictments and dismissals. Indictments receive very large publicity; dismissals, little or no publicity.

PROFESSOR NESSON: What's your next option?

FIRST COMPANY OFFICIAL: Well, the next option would be either to call a press conference, to see what that produced, or the answer you're looking for, to go to some advertising.

PROFESSOR NESSON: I'm interested in both. Is your press conference going to be any more successful than your press release?

FIRST COMPANY OFFICIAL: Yes, it is likely to be a little bit more successful than the release, I think, based on my past experience. You're likely to get more attention because the press will think you have a more serious situation than a piece of paper that just comes across the desk.

PROFESSOR NESSON: They are actually going to send somebody there.

FIRST COMPANY OFFICIAL: It is likely that some press will show up, yes.

PROFESSOR NESSON: And if they show up, they've taken some time, they may have to have a little product out of it.

FIRST COMPANY OFFICIAL: They have an investment in the situation.

PROFESSOR NESSON: Now tell me about ads. What's your strategy on ads?

FIRST COMPANY OFFICIAL: Well, I'm making an assumption that we have done all of our homework, and we found that there is no merit to the claim of Dr. Fine, and that the reports in the press and on radio and television have not reflected those circumstances. We would then proceed to take an ad that set the record straight, and thus try to undo the damage and try to reassure the consumer.

PROFESSOR NESSON: *(Asks the second editor)* Would you take that ad?

SECOND EDITOR: I would certainly take the ad. I would hope it wouldn't be necessary, myself.

PROFESSOR NESSON: *(Asks the third editor)* Would you take the ad?

THIRD EDITOR: I missed a step here. Didn't we go to the company official and ask him, in the first place, for these kinds of answers, before we printed the story?

PROFESSOR NESSON: It took a little time, the story got ahead of you.

THIRD EDITOR: I don't think it would take that much time.

PROFESSOR NESSON: At this point, where we are, the story has been printed and the company official, at least, thinks it's unfair. I wouldn't be surprised that even if you'd come to him and gotten the answers, he might think the story you eventually run is unfair. *(Laughter)*

THIRD EDITOR: My point was, the answer should have been in the story, but we're assuming then that the answer was not in the story, for whatever reason.

PROFESSOR NESSON: You're going to take his ad and set the story straight.

THIRD EDITOR: It all depends. Yes, if the ad is not fraudulent, untruthful, and all the other things that advertising is not supposed to be. We'd use the company's press release, too, if it had some germane information other than just a blanket denial of any misdoing.

FIRST COMPANY OFFICIAL: Are you going to require me to document the truthfulness of my ad?

THIRD EDITOR: No, but if you're making—

FIRST COMPANY OFFICIAL: You said it had to be true.

THIRD EDITOR: If you're going to accuse people of things in ads, we don't take that, so I'll leave that out.

    If the ad simply says: "Look, this is our story," there's no reason not to run the ad. My question was, what took so long to get that story? Why didn't we have it when we asked them the first time?

PROFESSOR NESSON: If they accused your paper of having made a factual error, would you run the ad?

THIRD EDITOR: Not without very careful checking, no, we wouldn't run the ad. If he accused us of making a factual error, and indeed there was no way we could disprove his allegation, then he wouldn't require an ad; there would be a story.

PROFESSOR NESSON: You would put a little box: "We're sorry, we made an error."

THIRD EDITOR: Yes, at least, and if it were a serious error, we'd play it very prominently.

PROFESSOR NESSON: The company then takes an ad that blows up your little statement saying you made an error to a full page. Are you going to take that? (*Laughter*)

THIRD EDITOR: (*To the first company official*) Would you do that?

PROFESSOR NESSON: Would you do that?

FIRST COMPANY OFFICIAL: Yes, sir. (*Laughter*) There's no question at all about that.

PROFESSOR NESSON: (*To the third editor*) Would you take that ad?

THIRD EDITOR: I suppose we probably would, to tell you the truth. It's a circumstance I really can't envision.

PROFESSOR NESSON: Which: The retraction? The ad? Or both?

THIRD EDITOR: All of this parade of circumstances: that the company had no answers when we asked, or that we rushed into print before the industry had a chance to answer. That's very unlikely.

Then he comes up later with some truly significant data that requires publication. Then he finds out that we made a factual error concerning something he was asked to comment on in the very first instance. All these things are very unlikely. If all these things took place, we behaved irresponsibly, and we'd have to take the consequences—whatever they are.

PROFESSOR NESSON: You make it sound as if there were never errors in any story.

THIRD EDITOR: No, no, no, don't say that.

PROFESSOR NESSON: You always check them out.

THIRD EDITOR: Always check them out.

PROFESSOR NESSON: It just never happens that anything goes wrong.

THIRD EDITOR: It happens once in a while, but not before we check them out, as a rule.

FIRST COMPANY OFFICIAL: You have to understand, we're limited in our rebuttal through the advertising—only in print. We can't do that electronically.

PROFESSOR NESSON: You go to the TV executive and ask him for the same privilege. (*Turns to the first TV executive*) What do you tell him?

FIRST TV EXECUTIVE: It depends. We're not on the same kind of deadlines.

I think we would have checked and we probably would have waited for his response to the fourteen interrogatories. If we had gone with the story, and by now, we were doing more than ten seconds—we were now doing a minute forty-five—if we had gone to that length and we had made a mistake, it is our policy to do a retraction. I'm talking about a factual mistake, a factual error.

SECOND BUSINESSMAN: Did you say you were not operating under a deadline in broadcasting?

FIRST TV EXECUTIVE: On this kind of a story, I wouldn't find myself, in terms of an evening news program, as competitive as, for example, a newspaper might be in this regard.

PROFESSOR NESSON: Take it two ways. First, you put out a story, and the company official thinks the slant is wrong. He's not prepared to say that you have an error on such and such. He just says that you didn't tell the full story. We want to tell *our* story. We want to say what a great drug Prothorin is, and all that kind of stuff. We want our lead to be what a great drug it is, rather than "Drug causes baldness," and we're willing to pay for two minutes of time on your air to get the message across. Do you take it or not?

FIRST TV EXECUTIVE: No.

PROFESSOR NESSON: Why not?

FIRST TV EXECUTIVE: You know, there's somebody sitting here who can answer that better than I can.

PROFESSOR NESSON: (*Turns to the second TV executive*) Do you take it or not?

SECOND TV EXECUTIVE: What's the question again?

PROFESSOR NESSON: The company official doesn't like some story that your network runs. He thinks it's got a bad slant to it, giving his company short shrift. He wants to buy two minutes of ad time, pay a lot of money for it, in order to get the right slant across. Do you take it or not?

SECOND TV EXECUTIVE: No.

PROFESSOR NESSON: Why not?

SECOND TV EXECUTIVE: We don't sell commercial time for the purpose of having a company or any point of view presented in commercial time.

PROFESSOR NESSON: What is the matter with presenting a point of view in commercial time? These fellows present points of view all the time. Aspirin is terrific for you, jam as much Bayer down your throat as you can get. Feel better fast, quick. Anacin, zip, zip, zip.

SECOND TV EXECUTIVE: This is a news story about the effect of a drug, a factual question, and if we were to start selling time, not only on an issue like this but in the case of the company official, he would perhaps want to present issues on other questions relating to the drug industry. Our time would be taken up with conflicting messages and various points of the law, and under the law, if we were to sell—

PROFESSOR NESSON: It sounds good to me. (*Laughter*)

SECOND TV EXECUTIVE: The answer is no, we wouldn't sell him the time.

PROFESSOR NESSON: You won't even sell him any time. Four o'clock in the morning, we'll put it on. What do you say? We'll put it on instead of the old Bugs Bunny cartoon. Why not?

SECOND TV EXECUTIVE: We will cover it in our news programs, and we will attempt to get the facts accurately in that. If there are two points of view, we will put those two points on in the morning and evening or whatever it is. But we will not sell time for contending parties to present their points of view. The exceptions are political commercials produced traditionally . . .

PROFESSOR NESSON: How do you answer our third editor who sells space? He says terrific.

SECOND TV EXECUTIVE: I can answer him this way. First of all, he's not subject to the Fairness Doctrine, which says that if we present a point of view, whether the time is paid for or not, we must present a contrasting point of view and give the time away free, if we have to.

PROFESSOR NESSON: I see, it's a money problem you've got.

SECOND TV EXECUTIVE: No, no, no. We have a limited amount of time. We can't expand the schedule the way a newpaper can. A newspaper can add pages, and so forth and so on. Television has a limited number of availabilities, and if we permitted time to be sold for people to present one specific point of view, we would find the airways cluttered with different points of view—

PROFESSOR NESSON: Oh—terrible! (*Laughter*)

SECOND TV EXECUTIVE: We would really be selling the points of view of people who have the most money to spend. We think the better way to do it is to do it on our own news programs, and to try to present, on those, all points of view on any controversial issue.

FIRST COMPANY OFFICIAL: I just want to rebut. I don't want to buy for a question of issue in this case. All I want to do is rebut something that they have already presented the case on.

PROFESSOR NESSON: (*Says to the second TV executive*) Let's take it step by step. You say, something called the Fairness Doctrine. If you put on the Prothorin piece, for example, you've got to offer time to somebody on the other side, whether they could pay or not.

SECOND TV EXECUTIVE: Right.

PROFESSOR NESSON: Sounds like a money problem, at least to start with. There's money in it anyway, huh?

SECOND TV EXECUTIVE: It's not a money problem.

PROFESSOR NESSON: You just mention that to educate us?

SECOND TV EXECUTIVE: The point I'm making is if I offer it to the company that makes Prothorin, then I've got to offer it to Toyota when they come in, because they want to go on the air to tell us about why—

PROFESSOR NESSON: Small cars are better than big cars.

SECOND TV EXECUTIVE: Right.

PROFESSOR NESSON: What's the matter with that?

SECOND TV EXECUTIVE: Because, as I've indicated, you'll find a great deal of your time taken up by partisans presenting a point of view they're trying to push, and paying money to push. We feel the better way to do it, because our system is different from the printing system, is to get those issues out on the regular news programs we have, and to seek to have a balance on those programs of all points of view.

PROFESSOR NESSON: (*Asks the fifth editor*) Does this make any sense to you?

FIFTH EDITOR: Well, it makes sense to permit the greatest diversity of opinion as possible to be published, it seems to me. That's part of the primary principles of communication. I sympathize with their problem, but it seems to me that they have not got a very good solution.

PROFESSOR NESSON: Do you have anything to recommend?

FIFTH EDITOR: In my opinion, they *should* permit people to buy commercial time to respond or reply to charges with which they disagree.

PROFESSOR NESSON: (*Turns to the first TV executive*) How does the explanation of your colleague in television sound to you?

FIRST TV EXECUTIVE: Now you're getting back to what we do. First of all, in fairness and balance, I would think that any report that we put on the air would include, within it, both sides; and in giving the opportunity, even if we had to edit it down—and we are all in the editing business— we would get the salient attack and denial, if that was the two sides, on Prothorin.

To come to a point about advertising, you know there's a commercial that's currently running on the air in which a man plays the role of a television correspondent. He's standing in front of a building in Washington and appearing to be a reporter. In fact, it happens to be placed on some news programs. And the illusion that advertiser is trying to create is that their product is being endorsed in some way by the journalistic profession. In a way, there's a confusion there, a deliberate confusion. If you can do that in advertising, it calls into question the total credibility of everything else that is put on television. This is so because what advertising is doing there is using the visual credibility, the devices that we, on the journalistic side, use to present information with fairness and balance. I am sure that if Rothwell tried to buy time and was sold time, they would go out at a hundred thousand dollars a minute or more, and create an ad that used every possible technique to confuse the audience.

PROFESSOR NESSON: As opposed to what they do during their regular commercial advertising? (*Laughter*)

FIRST TV EXECUTIVE: There, mind you, they are selling a product flat out. They can do whatever they want, given good taste and all of that. But they are not under any restraints in ads or in commercials about fairness or balance. If in fact they chose, as I am sure they would, to confuse rather than to inform the audience—because they would not give both sides. You yourself could probably be a good copywriter for Prothorin because you undoubtedly have already stated that it's the greatest thing since sliced bread. They would use it, and it would appear on news programs or it would appear elsewhere, as if it *were* a news broadcast. I think that we would find that the public, instead of being informed, was being misinformed.

PROFESSOR NESSON: (*Turns to the first company official*) Now you understand the Fairness Doctrine, right? (*Laughter*) You've got a clear picture of the justification for this thing, right?

FIRST COMPANY OFFICIAL: Right.

PROFESSOR NESSON: (*Now addresses the second TV executive*) Let me ask you a question. If I offered you a deal, you can get rid of the Fairness Doctrine if you want, all you've got to do is say yes, would you take it or not?

SECOND TV EXECUTIVE: Sure.

PROFESSOR NESSON: You don't want that doctrine, do you?

SECOND TV EXECUTIVE: We can live with it. We prefer not to have it. We'd get rid of it if we could, yes.

PROFESSOR NESSON: Let me ask you another question. Why aren't the media, the great shapers of public opinion, an industry, a great source of all sorts of powers, why haven't they gotten together to get rid of the damn thing? It doesn't make a bit of sense, the way I hear it.

SECOND TV EXECUTIVE: I don't think the industry can do anything. It's essentially a political, Congressional problem. It's a regulatory provision that we see little chance of getting rid of. Certain people are against it. Senator Proxmire would get rid of it. I think Senator Javits might. There is such a background of regulation, case law, that it's very tough to get rid of something like that after all these years.

PROFESSOR NESSON: Do we have anyone here who defends the Fairness Doctrine?

FIRST TV EXECUTIVE: I'll talk to that on one level. It's not a network level, but it's a local station level. The problem there is that I know for a fact that many local stations' managements interfere quite deliberately because of business decisions. They tell their news directors at local levels what to put on or what to leave off. If it were not for the possible threat that the other side, on whatever issue we're talking about, could cite Fairness Doctrine, I think you would see in too many local stations around this country a marked diminution of both sides being heard on controversial issues in those areas.

PROFESSOR NESSON: I hear it right. The Fairness Doctrine is a doctrine to defend the news management of stations against the owners of stations.

FIRST TV EXECUTIVE: Could be.

FIRST LAWYER: Well, it could be. One could make exactly the same argument for the Fairness Doctrine for newspapers. I wouldn't make it for either. I'm very disappointed to hear a TV executive make it for television or radio broadcasting. There's no doubt that having the government out there making sure the press, of one sort or another, is fair might indeed make it fairer, and indeed, keep it in line. It seems to me not worth anything like the risks of having the Fairness Doctrine, let alone the costs that the company official is just finding himself having to pay, and that is a major reason why his ads can't run. It would be very useful, I would think, if the company official and others who find the Fairness Doctrine offensive, outside the television industry, would say so publicly some time.

PROFESSOR NESSON: Well, before we pass it, let's just stop and mark it. In this area of conflict between media and business—unless I'm wrong, this is one where there isn't a conflict. This is one where there's a community of interest. As far as I can tell, all of you here are against the Fairness Doctrine.

VOICES: No, no.

PROFESSOR NESSON: Where have you been? Where have you been?

FIRST COMPANY OFFICIAL: What happens in terms of the behavior of the television networks if you eliminate the Fairness Doctrine? Fairness is not necessarily the issue. It's become a cover for a lot of other issues that we've been told can't be handled *because* of the Fairness Doctrine. But access is more the issue than fairness.

    If you told me that, with the Fairness Doctrine, television stations would conduct themselves as newspapers do and allow freelance journalists in, and allow an op-ed page type of thing, and would commit themselves to a spectrum of experimentation, I'd say let's try it. But I have not seen any evidence on the part of network television to experiment in the access area, and that's the basic problem.

PROFESSOR NESSON: (*Acknowledges the fourth editor*)

FOURTH EDITOR: I agree with the last speaker.

PROFESSOR NESSON: (*Acknowledges the first pharmaceutical manufacturer*)

FIRST PHARMACEUTICAL MANUFACTURER: I'm just not certain that I know what the Fairness Doctrine is that we're discussing.

PROFESSOR NESSON: Our first company official will tell you. (*Laughter*) It's the doctrine that keeps him from having access to the broadcast media.

FIRST PHARMACEUTICAL MANUFACTURER: I don't think that's true. I don't believe I got an answer to my question.

FIRST COMPANY OFFICIAL: Let's understand that the television networks could take my ads tomorrow without violating the Fairness Doctrine in any way. That's a corporate decision that networks have not to take the ads. There's nothing in the Fairness Doctrine—indeed, the FCC has suggested to the networks that they try some experimentation in the advocacy advertising area, but they have not tried it. So let's understand, it's not the Fairness Doctrine that prevents my ads.

PROFESSOR NESSON: (*To the second TV executive*) Do you want to respond?

SECOND TV EXECUTIVE: Yes. Our decision not to take his ads is not because of the Fairness Doctrine. The point I was trying to make was that if we were to sell time for his ads and Mr. X's ads, Mr. Y's ads—all of which present a partisan and specific point of view —we would then be required to give to those who wish to answer that specific partisan point of view time to do so, whether they buy it or not. We could convert television into a medium where those who have the most dough could get on the air to buy what they want. We feel a better way to do it is to do it in our regular news programs.

Now, the subject of access. You have programs like *Meet the Press, Face the Nation*, the *Today* show, and many other programs. We get every kind of point of view on those programs, and on the local level you not only have editorials presented by the local stations, but you have responses to those editorials.

So access does exist in the sense that there are many places on the air where you do have spokesmen for different points of view. You have the Israeli ambassador and the Egyptian ambassador. You have the drug companies and you have the people who answer them. You have the oil companies and the people who think they're not doing a good job. So access exists, but it exists within the forums that we set up, and it doesn't exist by selling time to people who want to present their specific points of view.

PROFESSOR NESSON: (*Acknowledges the sixth editor*)

SIXTH EDITOR: Have you finished with the Fairness Doctrine? I just wanted to say on the area of the drug question—while I agreed entirely with all my colleagues about this story, and the way it ought to be checked—I *am* slightly uneasy about the idea that there is something terrible—and everybody is very defensive here—about publishing this story about the side effects of drugs. Perhaps this will provoke a hostile reaction, but I think we're overlooking the very positive aspects of newspaper publication, of which the most important is feedback from people.

Just take the instance of thalidomide. In the thalidomide case, there were side effects of peripheral neuritis when this drug was taken. They were not reported. Newspapers were frightened by it. They wanted to be cautious. Doctors were persuaded to write favorable papers. There was a whole series of events like that. So the warning signals of peripheral neuritis, which was the first indication that we were about to produce the biggest drug disaster of all time, never got into the newspapers. Therefore, other people with peripheral neuritis never got in touch with their doctors, and the whole thing multiplied.

In June 1960, an Australian doctor discovered that thalidomide caused birth defects. He sent an article to a medical journal. It wasn't printed. Pregnant women kept on taking this drug, and a vast number of deformed babies were born from June 1960, conceptions which might have been prevented if that doctor had felt he could trust the newspaper.

The drug was not withdrawn until 1960. International publication of that story in a sensible way would have told people in Germany that things they didn't know were going wrong *were* going wrong and somebody would have put two and two together. I think the press is being too defensive this morning. I think there's been too little recognition of the beneficial influence the press can bring to bear. The drug companies should keep that in mind. But don't let's lose sight of the fact that free flow of information is a benefit.

PROFESSOR NESSON: (*To the sixth editor*) Let me ask you this. Free flow of information is a benefit. Would you expect a businessman to agree with you?

SIXTH EDITOR: I find it's the message of my life to try to persuade them. I think it's easier to persuade the businessman than it is the government, but there's not much difference between the two.

PROFESSOR NESSON: Might you expect a businessman to say that control of information is control of power to some extent?

SIXTH EDITOR: Yes.

PROFESSOR NESSON: Free flow of information, according to my agenda?

SIXTH EDITOR: Yes.

PROFESSOR NESSON: Then why do we leave it to the newspapers? If we want to put something out, we'll put it out.

SIXTH EDITOR: Well, I'm not pretending that we do a perfect job. I'd just like the more positive side recognized. We don't like being used, but we don't like being lied to or delays. They get a raw deal. We get a raw deal. It's bad at the moment. I just think we're all lovey-dovey here, but the situation is that press inquiries get shunted aside. You get lied to. You get distortions, and so on, and drug companies and business companies get pressure put on them, and all sorts of tricks are played, and the whole situation is not particularly good. I think it's a pity that at the end of the day we lose sight of what could come from the beneficial side of the free flow of information.

As a result of thalidomide the drug industry, I feel, has suffered ever since, because now, in some senses, it is probably overregulated.

PROFESSOR NESSON: (*Recognizes the fourth editor*)

FOURTH EDITOR: The point is that it's a duty of the media not to suppress the story of an allegation like this. You only publish the fact of the allegation. You check it out, you work out how much emphasis you give it, but you must not suppress it. You can't, because there will be a rumor started anyway.

PROFESSOR NESSON: (*Now recognizes the second pharmaceutical manufacturer*)

SECOND PHARMACEUTICAL MANUFACTURER: Could I just hypothesize a different set of facts for the story? We call up Rothwell, the answer is: "Yes, we are aware of this. As a matter of fact, we were first aware of it back around 1972. We've been in touch with the FDA over a period of time. We've done some work. There seems to be, perhaps, a relationship, and the relationship is that somewhere in the neighborhood of one per one million treatments. There's even, in the package insert, if you'll read it, a little statement that says that this is a possible contra-indication, and that's our story."

Now, what happens to that one?

SIXTH EDITOR: Then it's not news.

SECOND PHARMACEUTICAL MANUFACTURER: Well, that could be an answer which nobody suggested, which I suggest might well be an answer with these facts.

SIXTH EDITOR: You're saying it's an old story—

SECOND PHARMACEUTICAL MANUFACTURER: No, I'm saying we know about it, it exists, here's what we've got, and the one thing that, let's say, I'll give is that in a certain number of cases—one per million or one per half million—it's possible that you can have total alopecia.

SIXTH EDITOR: You've already said this in your packet.

SECOND PHARMACEUTICAL MANUFACTURER: Let's say, just to really nail it down, in the professional insert, down there in all that fine print, you will find it.

FIRST SCIENCE REPORTER: Could I answer that? First of all, I think I said the first thing I would do with this drug is go to the PDR, the *Physician's Desk Reference*. The PDR is a compilation of all the package inserts. So that would have a bearing on it.

But I would also like to say that there have been many instances in which, indeed, the drug company has known for five, ten, sometimes twenty years that there is something harmful about a drug. And it has gone to all kinds of lengths to suppress that information. One thing that a science writer learns—because if you are any good you become quite knowledgeable scientifically and technically about what you are doing—is when you are being lied to. It is very, very easy to tell on most occasions. There is a lot of lying that goes on.

If you want me to be specific about some cases, I'd be happy—

PROFESSOR NESSON: I'd just as soon you wouldn't.

FIRST SCIENCE REPORTER: Let me say something else. There are a lot of first-rate companies who have been guilty of what I would consider less than ethical behavior, although this is an industry that calls itself the ethical drug industry. It is one of the great ironies in the language.

PROFESSOR NESSON: Well, let's explore it a little bit. (*Turns to the fourth pharmaceutical manufacturer*) This story has come out in the paper. It's not a big story, but it's something that's going to cause you trouble. It indicates that a drug which is a high flyer for your company has got some side effect that the public hadn't really focused on before, that is not described in your insert.

FOURTH PHARMACEUTICAL MANUFACTURER: It is not described.

PROFESSOR NESSON: Not described in your insert. As the leader of the company, what's your fear at that point? What's your list of worries about the possible bad things that can happen to you in the future?

FOURTH PHARMACEUTICAL MANUFACTURER: Well, if you've given me the fact that the story is now out—

PROFESSOR NESSON: The story is out.

FOURTH PHARMACEUTICAL MANUFACTURER: The story is out. My fear, obviously, is is the story accurate? Just what are the proportions that should be attached to the story, which usually are not in the stories that

I've read. It comes out as a bald fact that Prothorin causes baldness. It doesn't say anything about the one in ten million. Maybe they don't know. So my fear is that at that point the objectivity of the story—

PROFESSOR NESSON: Do you have any worries about what the FDA is going to do?

FOURTH PHARMACEUTICAL MANUFACTURER: No, not in the slightest, because so far as I'm concerned, the very first thing—and this has not been mentioned at all, and I'm astounded to hear our first science reporter make the statement that was made—we are, under law, obligated to report to the Food and Drug Administration any side effect or any *any*thing that comes down the pike that seems to us to be different or unusual. Particularly if it's not in the package insert. Isn't that true?

FIRST SCIENCE REPORTER: That's true, but it's been observed in the breach on several occasions.

FOURTH PHARMACEUTICAL MANUFACTURER: Well, you know some things I don't know. And I'm not denying it.

PROFESSOR NESSON: Here's what I'm asking you to do.

FIRST SCIENCE REPORTER: May I just add one thing, and I'll do it very quickly. One thing that drug companies have not been likely to do is to do the kind of retrospective studies, to go back and find out on a systematic basis what the incidence of certain side effects has done, and the classic example of this has been the use of estrogens to treat menopausal women. Several doctors on the West Coast, for very little money, surveyed some patient populations and came up with some data.

Now, I submit that the companies have been in the business of selling menopausal estrogens for what—thirty years, at least? Whatever kinds of research had been done, no one in those companies has ever made an attempt to go back and look at what had happened along the way. That's not the kind of research that drug companies have been prone to get into.

PROFESSOR NESSON: Why do you think that's true?

FIRST SCIENCE REPORTER: Well, I think it's quite obvious that the responsibility of the drug company is to its stockholders. Therefore, you want your drug, for whatever condition it is, to be relevant or suitable for as many patients as possible. It often turns out, when something goes wrong with a drug and it turns out to have side effects, that the real problem is not with those relatively few patients who really need this drug, because for them the benefits outweigh the risks. It's what happens when you give that drug to an enormous universe of patients, for many of whom the risk is not less than the benefit. We've seen that over and over again. Again, I could be specific.

PROFESSOR NESSON: (*Turns to the fourth pharmaceutical manufacturer*) Do you have an answer as to why that kind of research isn't done?

FOURTH PHARMACEUTICAL MANUFACTURER: Well, in the first place, the assumption is not correct. These studies *are* being done—at least at our company they are. I suppose a reason that you don't do retrospective studies is that you have no cause to suspect that something may be a problem.

PROFESSOR NESSON: Let me put the question a little differently. What is your incentive to do that kind of research?

FOURTH PHARMACEUTICAL MANUFACTURER: Normally, you get some slight indication that there is something that is being observed in the widespread use of your product that you haven't known about. To be very honest, I would not know how to set up a retrospective study to find out what's going on. What would you ask a doctor to look for? Everything? Anything?

When we *do* do these retrospective studies—and we *are* doing some right now, as I think you know—it is because there's been some signal that you've gotten that there is something that may not be quite right here; now, with that as a clue, let's go back and look.

PROFESSOR NESSON: (*Asks the second lawyer*) What is the incentive of the drug companies to do research on their drugs?

SECOND LAWYER: It arises partly out of a fear of lawsuits, that if they injure enough people, either the cost of their premiums or their excess of suits over premiums are going to make it cost more than any benefit they would have gotten from the sale of the drug.

PROFESSOR NESSON: Is it your experience that if the company hasn't done some research, and there's some injury, you're going to be able to collect?

SECOND LAWYER: Certainly.

PROFESSOR NESSON: So their incentive is the tort incentive, saving money in the long run?

SECOND LAWYER: I don't know how heavy it is, but I know it influences their scientific procedures, yes.

PROFESSOR NESSON: (*Turns again to the fourth pharmaceutical manufacturer*) Is he talking to you?

FOURTH PHARMACEUTICAL MANUFACTURER: No, he's not, because he's going to recover from me whether I do the retrospective study or not, as he well knows. (*Laughter*) I feel that the reason we do it is because we believe in our products. If there's something wrong about it, dammit, I want to know about it. I want to know about it now, and I want to be the first to know about it.

PROFESSOR NESSON: All right, let me just follow up on it. You've gotten some indication from this story that there's a question about one of your drugs. You want to know about it, you want to know about it fast. Do you give any consideration to changing the marketing of your drug right away?

FOURTH PHARMACEUTICAL MANUFACTURER: I suspect we would, if for no other reason than the automatic provision. We would notify the FDA of this study, even if they didn't know about it. The FDA would come back and say, okay, put a black box in your package insert, and that would change the marketing within a month.

PROFESSOR NESSON: (*Turns to the first health official*) Is that what the FDA is going to do?

FIRST HEALTH OFFICIAL: I would hope that the FDA would know about it first, but restriction in labeling certainly would be the first step. The FDA would also take two or three others. It would start to go to places where it thought it had a handle on epidemiological data that would indicate, in a much firmer way than the scenario does, whether in fact there's a causal association.

I think one of the reasons for the press hesitance on this story is that the scenario limps badly at that point. I think what you really want is a much firmer indication that there really is a problem here.

PROFESSOR NESSON: That's what I'm curious about. The FDA is not about to put a black box on their drug right away, on what you've got here.

FIRST HEALTH OFFICIAL: On the data that's in here, absolutely not.

PROFESSOR NESSON: The FDA is going to call in Dr. Fine, for starters. It's going to check out his method, do a bunch of other tests. It's going to do a lot before it gets to the point where it tells them to change the way they market. No?

FIRST HEALTH OFFICIAL: Yes, a good deal. Not the things you mentioned, but a good deal.

PROFESSOR NESSON: (*Turns to the fourth pharmaceutical manufacturer*) And you're going to be fighting him all the way, aren't you?

FOURTH PHARMACEUTICAL MANUFACTURER: We are going to try to make him more reasonable than he otherwise would be. (*Laughter*)

PROFESSOR NESSON: (*Asks the third lawyer*) If you're representing our fourth pharmaceutical manufacturer, what options does he have, as you see it?

THIRD LAWYER: It's obviously gone to the Food and Drug Administration. I'd want to take a look at that professional insert in the box, to see what it says on this subject. I'm concerned about that insert, because there may not be enough information to include this. On the other hand, he may be including matter for which he has just a little information, and I know that that piece of paper in the box is going to become a problem if it turns out that baldness becomes quite prevalent. Obviously, I'm going to want to know how many incidents of baldness have been reported. I'm going to want to have some judgment as to whether or not this is a fact that's got to be disclosed to the shareholders. On the basis of what I know here, the answer to that would be emphatically no. I'd be telling him to go about his own business, looking into these indications, the way they would when other indications are brought to their attention.

PROFESSOR NESSON: Would you have any hesitance at all about using your skills to buy the company as much time as possible in his dealings with the FDA?

THIRD LAWYER: Well, there's an implication in that. (*Laughter*) I would have absolutely no problem at all in advocating that he be given as much time as necessary in order to do the type of research that's required. On the other hand, I have no difficulty at all, very frankly, with putting out a warning to the medical profession, along with the three thousand other things that are contained in the professional insert. You know, they read like the plagues of Egypt, and—

PROFESSOR NESSON: You feel it doesn't make too much difference, anyway.

THIRD LAWYER: I think that ultimately you rely on the doctor to make the judgment, in the case of the patient, as to whether his problem requires this particular drug, taking into account the fact that there may be side effects. I would like to try this case because it seems to me, particularly if it is a male, that I could make the plaintiff talk about all the discomfort and burning and pain that he had with the urinary infection, and maybe conjure up the image of Telly Savalas or some other well-known person without hair. It seems to me that it is not the end of the world if one of the side effects is baldness.

PROFESSOR NESSON: I'll tell you what I'm interested in. (*Asks the first health official*) You say FDA's process is measured in epochs and eons. It's got some little thing that comes on the horizon. FDA doesn't know exactly what it is yet. FDA is going to figure it out or not figure it out, according to the agenda of how important it thinks it is. Does their response, in any way, affect a sense of importance?

FIRST HEALTH OFFICIAL: I think it's not likely to in a case like this. I think the FDA would take a look at the merits and Dr. Fine's paper, and try to sketch out the magnitude of the problem. Then it would have to make what amounts to a resource allocation decision. How much of its time, which the FDA has to invest in worrying about various public health problems, does it spend worrying about this one?

PROFESSOR NESSON: Suppose that our first editor has made the judgment that this is a big story. We're going to go after it, and we're going to keep on it, so the FDA is under constant pressure from the press. Does that affect the resource allocation at all?

FIRST HEALTH OFFICIAL: It probably does so more than it should. (*Laughter*)

PROFESSOR NESSON: Why does it have the effect?

FIRST HEALTH OFFICIAL: A lot of people who have a lot to do with FDA's job read papers. (*Laughter*) Public media pressure means Congressional pressure. It means a lot of things happen that, in turn, exert commands on resources. So whenever the FDA gets a public issue on which there is media pressure and Congressional pressure, FDA knows it's going to have to make investments. If it doesn't make them at the front end, Congress is going to get FDA to make them at the back end.

PROFESSOR NESSON: (*To the first editor*) You've just had a big effect on this fellow.

FIRST EDITOR: I'm glad to hear it.

PROFESSOR NESSON: He changed his schedule all around. He's made a rational resource allocation that has this little problem about baldness way down the list. But you, by dint of your paper, have now switched it to the top of the list. Do you congratulate yourself, or not?

FIRST EDITOR: Well, if it's valid to put it at the top of the list. I'm taking your assumption. I would not put this at the top of the list.

PROFESSOR NESSON: Well, not at the top of the list, but we're going to get to it pretty damn quick. That is, at least before [Senator William] Proxmire gets to it. We've moved it up.

FIRST EDITOR: I have no embarrassment whatsoever about putting a little pressure on him.

PROFESSOR NESSON: (*Recognizes the third businessman*)

THIRD BUSINESSMAN: I'd like to make a point, from the business point of view, about how the press treats the story, as distinct from whether they publish it or not. That is, looking around this room, it is obvious that the incidence of baldness is not unusual in the population. Perhaps our average age here is above the average age of the population, but there are, I dare say, more people suffering from baldness in this room than from urinary infection. (*Laughter*) To me, the thing that would really count about the way the media handles this story is whether they bring that point out. It's not only how many of the people who take the drug suffer from baldness, but also the relative values, and I think that's what we're overlooking in this discussion.

PROFESSOR NESSON: You want a story that describes just how much it hurts. (*Laughter*)

THIRD BUSINESSMAN: Exactly, to be bald as compared with having a serious urinary infection, I certainly think so. I think this is, from the businessman's point of view—

PROFESSOR NESSON: A first-hand account of George Jones who pees twice a day with his urinary infection.

THIRD BUSINESSMAN: No. Our resident guru keeps telling me that we don't have a riskless society, and I agree with him.

PROFESSOR NESSON: I think that's something he learned from you.

THIRD BUSINESSMAN: Well, perhaps. (*Laughter*) But in any case, it seems to me that the fundamental attitude of the press toward this story should be one of balance. Frankly, I haven't heard very much of that.

FIRST EDITOR: May I respond to that? I think the whole thing is out of whack here. I think if there's any fault of the press in the reporting of science, it's been for going overboard in favor of new drugs—new wonder drugs. We've exaggerated. We've gone along with the enthusiasm of the first investigators on the basis of very little experimental data, and time after time, as any science reporter will tell you, we have found ourselves caught, hooked, dragged along by the enthusiasm of the scientific community for a drug that blows up a few years later. "Mer 29" is a good example. That was supposed to be a great drug for lowering cholesterol. It turns out it causes baldness, the very thing we're talking about here today. Later, it turned out it caused a lot of other serious effects, and as far as I know, it's off the market now.

PROFESSOR NESSON: It turned out there's a little suppression in there, too.

FIRST EDITOR: Generally speaking, I would say that we underplay, are slow to catch on to, and do very little to correct the bad effects of drugs, after the first onrush of very favorable publicity. I think our papers probably cured cancer two or three times. Other papers have probably cured it even more times.

PROFESSOR NESSON: Let me play out the scenario just a little bit here. (*Turns to the fourth pharmaceutical manufacturer*) This isn't your drug company. This is one of your competitors. Instead of delivering his paper, Dr. Fine came to one of your competitors, early on in his research process, and he said: "Gee, I'm getting some results here that may affect your drug." Could you imagine any of your competitors, at that point, saying: "Gee, that's very interesting. I want to know everything there is to know about this drug. I'll put you on my payroll as a consultant, and you continue with your research." Can you imagine one of your competitors doing that?

FOURTH PHARMACEUTICAL MANUFACTURER: Why, yes.

PROFESSOR NESSON: Do you imagine yourself doing it?

FOURTH PHARMACEUTICAL MANUFACTURER: Yes.

PROFESSOR NESSON: (*Turns to the first science reporter*) You get a call, somebody inside Rothwell Labs wants to talk to you privately. He says: "I have some information that's very interesting, but you're going to have to protect me. I want total source protection. Can I talk to you in total confidence?" Yes.

FIRST SCIENCE REPORTER: You mean you want me to say just yes?

PROFESSOR NESSON: What would you say?

FIRST SCIENCE REPORTER: I will say just yes, but I also— (*Laughter*) Wait a minute, but I will also say that I am going to reserve the right as to (*a*) whether I will use this material, (*b*) I will check it out six days from Sunday.

PROFESSOR NESSON: Absolutely understood. The only thing I want is to be absolutely sure that nobody finds out I talked to you.

FIRST SCIENCE REPORTER: We all do that in the newspaper business.

PROFESSOR NESSON: You're going to say yes. So what this source now tells you is, something very bad is going on at Rothwell Labs. This fellow named Fine came to the head of the company two years ago with information about a side effect. He was immediately put on the payroll and has been dawdling along with the research ever since. The company has not contacted the FDA about this. It is basically suppressing the data about this drug. That's an interesting story for you, yes?

FIRST SCIENCE REPORTER: Yes.

PROFESSOR NESSON: This source says: "In fact, I've seen a précis of the tentative findings of Fine that points out this side effect." Is that document interesting to you?

FIRST SCIENCE REPORTER: Yes, I was going to say I really need that document.

PROFESSOR NESSON: You really need that document!

FIRST SCIENCE REPORTER: And I need to have some indication of how I can verify its authenticity.

PROFESSOR NESSON: The source says to you: "Well, I might be able to get the document to you, but it would mean stealing it out of the files."

FIRST SCIENCE REPORTER: That's his decision. (*Laughter*)

PROFESSOR NESSON: That's his decision.

FIRST SCIENCE REPORTER: Yes, I'm not telling him to either steal it or not to steal it. I am telling him—I am going to receive it.

PROFESSOR NESSON: Say it again, I can't hear you.

FIRST SCIENCE REPORTER: I said I am telling him that it's up to him, as to whether he's going to take it out of the files or not. I am telling him that I am willing to receive it, if he's willing to provide it, but it is his decision as to whether to take it out of the files or not.

PROFESSOR NESSON: I suppose if he said to you: "I'll tell you where it is and you could steal it," you wouldn't have any doubt. You wouldn't do that.

FIRST SCIENCE REPORTER: Well, let's be practical about it. How could I? (*Laughter*) I once dealt with a story not involving drug companies, but with surgeons, with certain similarities, and somebody left it in a hole in a hollow tree, but that kind of thing doesn't happen very often.

PROFESSOR NESSON: Suppose the source says to you: "I could get it for you, but there's a risk involved, and frankly, I'd like to be paid for my services."

FIRST SCIENCE REPORTER: I am in no position to pay for that news information.

PROFESSOR NESSON: Would you ask your editor?

FIRST SCIENCE REPORTER: Possibly, I would . . .

PROFESSOR NESSON: All he wants is five hundred dollars, if we like the information. Would you ask him?

FIRST SCIENCE REPORTER: Well, because I know my editor pretty well, I might talk it over with him. I am very leery of that sort of thing, I'll be very frank with you.

PROFESSOR NESSON: (*Calls on the first editor*)

FIRST EDITOR: I'd tell her we couldn't afford it, probably. We're over our budget already.

FIRST SCIENCE REPORTER: I think it would have to be an extraordinary situation.

PROFESSOR NESSON: It's a pretty good story, worth five hundred bucks. We were ready to go out and hire a consultant to check this out, before. That would cost at least a couple of thousand.

FIRST SCIENCE REPORTER: Frankly, I wondered about that, because if you have a good science writer on your staff, he or she will know where to check it out.

PROFESSOR NESSON: Suppose only fifty bucks? Just a couple of Xerox costs.

FIRST SCIENCE REPORTER: I don't think it's the amount of money that is at issue here. I think it's the whole principle.

FIRST EDITOR: To answer your question. Normally, I would be opposed to paying for that kind of information, but I would not rule it out, ever. In other words, I could imagine circumstances in which the story involves the safety of a large population, or other circumstances where there are compelling reasons for public knowledge of something, and I don't think paying for *that* information would necessarily violate some great ethical rule.

PROFESSOR NESSON: *(Returns to the first science reporter)* You get the précis. You look at it. You want to check it out. You ask your source: "Who could I check it out with?" And you're told: "You can check when Fine came to work, you can check what he's working on, and I'll even put you in touch with the assistant director of research, who I think feels terrible about this. He'll be able to confirm it for you. Maybe he'll talk to you, maybe he won't."

You go to the assistant director, and lo and behold, he asks for a total confidence, and tells you that's exactly what's happened. You've got a pretty good story here, right? It's a good one. You print the story, and the FDA now wants a copy of that précis. You've described it in your paper. The FDA gets in touch with you and says they would like a copy of that.

FIRST SCIENCE REPORTER: That kind of thing happens all the time. I never provide copies to—incidentally, it isn't only government agencies who want copies of things. It's sometimes congressmen, sometimes other journalists.

PROFESSOR NESSON: You never provide a copy of anything?

FIRST SCIENCE REPORTER: Not if it's a copy given to me on a confidential basis, no, I do not.

PROFESSOR NESSON: You're not telling them who gave it to you. You're just giving them a copy of the document.

FIRST SCIENCE REPORTER: No, but that copy was given to me, and it was given only to me. It was not given to me to give to everybody else. I do not provide copies. They can read what I've written about it.

I just had a recent instance of this.

PROFESSOR NESSON: You are super-scrupulous about this source business.

FIRST SCIENCE REPORTER: I am. Now, that doesn't mean that everyone is. It's just the way I do it.

PROFESSOR NESSON: *(Turns to the first editor)* Do you print this story?

FIRST EDITOR: Oh, sure.

PROFESSOR NESSON: How do you verify that her story is accurate?

FIRST EDITOR: All I have to do is ask my reporter whether it's accurate; I know the reporter.

PROFESSOR NESSON: You take the reporter's word for it.

FIRST EDITOR: I think that's a very important point. I think if you work with a reporter over a great many years, you come to recognize the ones that are very solid, that you trust. I would not have to ask a lot of extra questions as to whether that story is true or not.

PROFESSOR NESSON: Would you ask any questions of the reporter?

FIRST EDITOR: Absolutely. Sure. I'd ask the reporter all sorts of questions.

PROFESSOR NESSON: Suppose it was another reporter? Would you ask the new reporter any questions about this story?

FIRST EDITOR: Yes, sure.

PROFESSOR NESSON: Do you ask this reporter who the source is?

FIRST EDITOR: Yes, in many cases, I do ask the reporter for the source, who the source is, and I've never had that rejected yet but I suppose it could happen.

PROFESSOR NESSON: (*Turns again to the first science reporter*) When the editor asks you, do you tell him?

FIRST SCIENCE REPORTER: Yes, but I think that's based on the knowledge that we know each other. I'm not sure that I would tell everybody who my sources are. I recently had an example of this with a leaked memo.

PROFESSOR NESSON: So when you tell that source that you'll protect the confidence absolutely, you mean absolutely except for your editor.

FIRST SCIENCE REPORTER: Well, I think I would tell the source—in fact, I know I would—that I would very likely have to tell my editor. I should have said that.

PROFESSOR NESSON: Your source talks to you and says, "Will you treat it in confidence?" "Yes, of course, except for my editor."

FIRST SCIENCE REPORTER: That's what I would answer.

PROFESSOR NESSON: (*Turns to the first editor*) Does it end there? You're the only one that's going to find out the source.

FIRST EDITOR: I think so.

PROFESSOR NESSON: You don't worry at all that maybe Rothwell Labs is going to feel upset about this story and they sue you. You don't want to talk to your lawyer, or anything like that?

FIRST EDITOR: Obviously, I would weigh all of the consequences, and if there's a possibility of a tremendous libel suit or something, we might actually not run it for that reason. But I would weigh all of those considerations myself, and make a decision.

Occasionally, we call a lawyer if we can afford it.

PROFESSOR NESSON: (*Calls on the first lawyer*) Do you want to find out what the source of that story is? You're representing the paper. They want you to check through the story a little bit.

FIRST LAWYER: I generally wouldn't ask for the source. No, I would give them libel advice based on the assumption that they would not reveal the source at any point during the case. But it wouldn't be very important for me to know who the source is. As a general matter, I don't see any reason to increase the list of people who know the source.

PROFESSOR NESSON: *(Turns back to the first editor)* You'd go with this story. Here it is, a story about suppression at Rothwell Labs. It comes out. It's big news. It implicates Fine. It implicates some people at Rothwell Labs.

(Addresses the first company official) You're upset about this story. It hurts your company a lot. What are your options?

FIRST COMPANY OFFICIAL: Well, the first thing I have to find out is the accuracy of the story, as best I can, within the company. That's number one.

Number two, I have to find out if there were subsequent reports that went on beyond this one particular report. I have to find out a lot more information before I decide what ought to be done.

PROFESSOR NESSON: What are you interested in?

FIRST COMPANY OFFICIAL: Well, I'm interested—

PROFESSOR NESSON: Not facts. I mean, what tactics are you considering?

FIRST COMPANY OFFICIAL: Well, the tactics would be determined after I find out exactly what the situation is. Based on what you've given me so far, that may or may not be the whole story. I would also point out that nobody has yet called us to ask for our comment on this report. I think that one of the newspaper people would have said, "Before we go to print, we will call the company and ask for a comment about it."

PROFESSOR NESSON: *(Turns to the first lawyer)* Suppose you're advising this company. They are outraged by this story. They look at it. They don't think the facts are too good. They think they're doing what our fourth pharmaceutical manufacturer was doing. This fellow comes along interested in exploring this thing. They put him on the payroll; provide him research. We're interested in finding out the facts here. They want to sue for libel. Do you have any advice to them?

FIRST LAWYER: Well, first, I would tell them that, the libel law being as it is now, the drug company, at least in this case, would surely be held to be the same as an official of the government, a public figure, and a public official. Therefore, I would tell them that the only way they can win is if they can prove that the story was printed with malice, as the law defines it, which means that the newspaper printed it knowing it was false, with serious doubts that it was true.

I would tell them that is very hard to do, and why. I would tell them that a newspaper could also defend on the grounds of truth. So if there are any problems in terms of the truth of this story, that's another problem area. I would tell them that the newspaper could go into their files and conduct extensive discovery. That's another problem with suing.

PROFESSOR NESSON: It sounds like you're telling them: "Geez, there are a lot of problems here."

FIRST LAWYER: Well, yes, that's where I'd start.

PROFESSOR NESSON: (*Asks the fourth lawyer*) Are you in agreement with our first lawyer on that?

FOURTH LAWYER: I agree with our first lawyer, that to advise the client to start libel action here would be a very serious piece of advice.

PROFESSOR NESSON: You're going to list all the things that can go wrong. You're going to say, this is a hard suit to win—public figure, reckless disregard, tough standard to make. You're going to say: "Your company is going to be open to discovery on all this stuff from the newspaper." Yes?

FOURTH LAWYER: Yes.

PROFESSOR NESSON: You're going to say: "Got any others?"

FOURTH LAWYER: Yes, in bringing the action itself, you may increase the amount of attention.

PROFESSOR NESSON: Fuel the controversy.

FOURTH LAWYER: That's right.

PROFESSOR NESSON: Another big story.

FOURTH LAWYER: And for a long time.

PROFESSOR NESSON: Every time another pleading is filed, we're going to live with this damn thing.

FOURTH LAWYER: Especially if our first science reporter were really on the case. The reporter might take a look at all the depositions. We could have a devil of a time.

PROFESSOR NESSON: (*Asks the third lawyer*) Are you with him on that?

THIRD LAWYER: Yes, except I'd want to know a little bit more about what the fact is. There are some times when even though your natural reaction is to say "For God's sake, don't sue," you really have to stand up and say: "We are going to sue now, because if we don't we're going to be just flooded with this kind of story, over and over again, and if it's irresponsible, this is the only way we're going to be able to make our point."

FIRST COMPANY OFFICIAL: The act of suing per se shouldn't be a deterrent if you have the facts, and if you're really sure of your facts in your own mind. The possibility of suing should be seriously considered, but the problem of the standard of the burden you have under malice is so heavy and so difficult that your chances of winning a suit are very, very slim, even if you have the facts on your side.

THIRD LAWYER: I don't care about winning.

FIRST COMPANY OFFICIAL: I agree with you.

THIRD LAWYER: I will settle for the decision of the court that says I can't win because there's no malice, but that newspaper shouldn't have printed it.

FIRST COMPANY OFFICIAL: I completely agree with that.

PROFESSOR NESSON: (*Calls on the third pharmaceutical manufacturer*) Did you ever find yourself in a situation of wanting to sue and having your lawyer tell you no, it's really not well advised?

THIRD PHARMACEUTICAL MANUFACTURER: Yes, often, and I wish I'd listened to him. (*Laughter and applause*)

PROFESSOR NESSON: (*Turns to the third editor*) Let's just suppose you've been sued. The story has come out and the reaction has been sue. And you're now facing a libel suit alleging reckless disregard—the whole thing, absolutely false story, $50,000,000 damages. And now your science reporter comes up with something else on this story—another little tidbit.

THIRD EDITOR: Can it help the suit?

PROFESSOR NESSON: Are you going to closely look at it?

THIRD EDITOR: Sure, I looked at it closely the first time.

PROFESSOR NESSON: Are you going to show it to your lawyer now?

THIRD EDITOR: As a matter of fact, I would have showed it to the lawyer the first time, too.

PROFESSOR NESSON: Ah-hah.

THIRD EDITOR: As a matter of fact, I would have done a lot of things the first time.

PROFESSOR NESSON: Are you going to be any more cautious because you've got a libel suit in front of you?

THIRD EDITOR: Certainly. I think that caution should have been there in the first instance.

PROFESSOR NESSON: Well, we recognize that. Every newspaperman is supercautious at all times. There's never any default along that line. But the question is, are you more cautious because you've got that lawsuit facing you right in the face?

THIRD EDITOR: Yes, you're talking about a story related to this story.

PROFESSOR NESSON: Yes. You're worried that if you keep after this story in a dogged fashion that that's going to fuel the company's ability to show you're really after these people. This is a malicious thing.

THIRD EDITOR: Sure. So you examine the story, but if the story is legitimate, I see no reason to hold back. As a matter of fact (*addressing the first lawyer*) it would probably help the case, wouldn't it?

PROFESSOR NESSON: Well, that would depend a little, wouldn't it?

FIRST LAWYER: Yes, it would depend. I would tell you to look at it, or have me look at it with special care.

THIRD EDITOR: You would want to look at the first one.

FIRST LAWYER: I know that. (*Laughter*) But I would have to tell you that if the second story is inadvertently wrong, you're in more trouble on the issue of ill will, which would go to punitive damages. And so I would have to tell you to be especially careful.

PROFESSOR NESSON: (*Turns to the third lawyer*) How are you going to proceed with this lawsuit? What's your first step going to be after you file it?

THIRD LAWYER: You mean for the drug company, now?

PROFESSOR NESSON: Yes, you're representing the drug company. You're a plaintiff in this libel suit.

THIRD LAWYER: I'm going to try to get discovery of the files of the defendant and put that newspaper reporter on the spot. The reporter is trying to protect the confidentiality of the sources and won't tell me what was done. That's what I'm going to do.

PROFESSOR NESSON: You're going to put the reporter in the chair and say: "Where did you get this story?"

THIRD LAWYER: Yes.

PROFESSOR NESSON: The reporter is going to say: "I got it from a confidential source." You're going to say: "Show me the précis of which you printed excerpts." The reporter is going to say: "No, I don't give out précis to anybody."

THIRD LAWYER: I'm going to say: "Judge, tell her to give it to me."
(*Laughter*)

PROFESSOR NESSON: Judge? (*Laughter*)

FIRST JUDGE: I wouldn't like to do anything to embarrass the reporter. (*Laughter*) At the moment, looking at the courts in general, I think that they are rather respectful of the confidential source in civil litigation, as contrasted with criminal litigation, where it has worked the other way. It seems to me that there's a difference between the confidential source and the document. When someone has really given a narrative account of the document in the column of a newspaper, the residual confidentiality seems to be very weak. I don't think there would be many judges who would hesitate to call for the document. The identity of the source would not be granted at an early stage of the litigation. The thing would have to shape up in such a way that you could say that unless this is revealed, there's already enough evidence of recklessness, inaccuracy, and lack of care presented by the plaintiff. Now all we can say is that if you don't produce the document, the judgment will likely go against you.

THIRD LAWYER: I think that's exactly the way the trial is going to shape up. The reporter accused my company of suppression. I'm going to be proving that we suppress nothing. I'm going to present the case as one of suppression—suppression by the newspaper. Here they are, defending on the grounds that they didn't have malice or recklessness when they had all of these inaccuracies because they had information from a confidential source. But who is that confidential source? No, they won't tell you or the jury *that*.

PROFESSOR NESSON: "Sore Throat." (*Laughter*)

FIRST SCIENCE REPORTER: Let me just say this about "Sore Throat." None of us who covered "Sore Throat" ever knew who he was.

PROFESSOR NESSON: Let's suppose the litigation has gotten to the point—

THIRD LAWYER: I don't want to put the reporter in jail.

FIRST SCIENCE REPORTER: Thanks.

THIRD LAWYER: I don't want the judge to rule that the reporter has to serve time if the information isn't turned over.

PROFESSOR NESSON: You're content to get your $50,000,000 judgment?

THIRD LAWYER: As long as I don't have to defend it in the Supreme Court.

PROFESSOR NESSON: (*To the first science reporter*) Let's suppose the litigation has developed to the point where the judge is somewhat interested in your source. There's been some inaccuracy shown. He's already forced you to give up the précis. Are you going to turn it over when he tells you to?

FIRST SCIENCE REPORTER: If I have a court order to do so.

PROFESSOR NESSON: Okay, it gets to the point where the judge says: "We've got to know your source if we're going to find out whether this story that you printed is a firmly based story or whether you acted in reckless disregard. We've got to know what kind of information you relied on."

FIRST SCIENCE REPORTER: I'm not going to turn over my source to him. I will tell him how I cross-checked it, but I am not going to turn over my source to him if I gave that person my word.

FIRST JUDGE: I think it's very hard to decide these questions except in the atmosphere of the case, and you're on the touching point of the tensions there. As someone just said, the Supreme Court hasn't really given us the word. But my inclination is that if the reporter does show that a careful check of some sort was made then it seems to me that there's less requirement for turning over the source.

PROFESSOR NESSON: One of the major ways the reporter checked was by getting a second confidential source.

FIRST JUDGE: No, that won't do. (*Laughter*) I mean, an infinitesimal plus an infinitesimal doesn't yield the real number.

PROFESSOR NESSON: (*Asks the first lawyer*) What's going to happen here?

FIRST LAWYER: First, if I can just answer an earlier question very quickly. The prepublication advice I would have given the editor is that if this story is based just or almost entirely on two confidential sources, and if there's no one that we're going to be able to show up with in court to vouch for the story, this is a very questionable thing. There are very severe libel risks. That's what I would have told him in advance.

What's going to happen in this case is that I would try to keep the judge happy by giving him other ways and other things to do rather than require the confidential source. For example, maybe we could prove truth, and I would argue to him: let us try to prove truth first so we don't have to reach the issue of confidential source. Maybe there's some other privilege out there which governs. I would argue let's do that first before we get to confidential source.

PROFESSOR NESSON: You're in a real tussle at this point, right? You're worried.

FIRST LAWYER: Yes.

PROFESSOR NESSON: Can you give me a ballpark figure of what it's likely to cost the newspaper to defend this suit, even if they win?

FIRST LAWYER: Against our third lawyer and . . .?

PROFESSOR NESSON: The third lawyer representing Rothwell Labs—big-money corporation.

FIRST LAWYER: That is seriously pursuing this lawsuit.

PROFESSOR NESSON: They want you to spend as much money as they can make you spend. They want you to pay for that story in dollars. One way they can make you do it is by defending a libel suit. What's the bottom line, ballpark?

FIRST LAWYER: I have some people in the room I wish would close their ears. (*Laughter*)

PROFESSOR NESSON: Would you rather I ask another lawyer? (*Laughter*)

FIRST LAWYER: Yes, as a matter of fact.

PROFESSOR NESSON: (*Turns to the fifth lawyer*) I don't have anything particular in mind, but just a ballpark figure?

FIFTH LAWYER: I think it could cost easily a quarter of a million dollars. Probably a lot more if the company's lawyer really turned loose with the resources he had available.

PROFESSOR NESSON: (*Asks the fourth lawyer*) Is this suit sounding a little better for you? I mean, we've got a big payoff and haven't even won it yet.

FOURTH LAWYER: So far, you know, we don't have any facts. We've been talking about the pressures on the various parties, but on the basis of the facts in the text, this is a very questionable lawsuit.

PROFESSOR NESSON: But what you just heard, I think, is that if you've got some facts, you may not need to have an absolutely firm case. You may not need to be able to go to the mat to prove reckless disregard. You may even lose, in the end. But the fact is, you can still exact a lot of pain out of somebody you regard as an adversary—i.e., the newspaper that published this story. What is more, you can slow them up from publishing more stories. They are going to look even a little more carefully.

FOURTH LAWYER: You asked the first lawyer the price tag on his services, but you didn't ask the third lawyer the price tag on his. This works both ways, you know.

PROFESSOR NESSON: (*Turns to the first company official*) You've listened to this. You've experienced this. Is it worth it for companies—big companies—to go after newspapers and punish them for tough stories when you think they're wrong, even though you may not be able to win?

FIRST COMPANY OFFICIAL: When you say "punish," I assume what you're saying is that you're convinced that the story is 100 percent inaccurate and it is going to do very severe financial damage to your company.

PROFESSOR NESSON: Let's say so. You may not be able to prove it, but you're convinced of it.

FIRST COMPANY OFFICIAL: As our third lawyer pointed out, that one way of establishing the accuracy of our position in the public's mind is to get a jury to at least acknowledge that the story was inaccurate, even if you can't get malicious damages. That has some merit. Really, I don't think the motivation is to punish. The motivation is to find a vehicle to correct the damage that has been done, and I don't believe in punishment. I believe in balancing the situation.

PROFESSOR NESSON: A little deterrence, no?

FIRST COMPANY OFFICIAL: Not primarily.

PROFESSOR NESSON: You mess with me—you're going to get a lawsuit down your throat. None of that.

FIRST COMPANY OFFICIAL: Primarily to correct the record.

PROFESSOR NESSON: But if they happen to get the deterrent message you're not upset.

FIRST COMPANY OFFICIAL: Well, I don't see anything wrong with putting people on notice that if they're going to engage in reckless behavior, action will be taken against them.

PROFESSOR NESSON: This drug has been out. We've had stories back and forth. We have some people who have been injured. (*Calls on the sixth lawyer*) They come to you. You have this woman who has come to you. She took the drug not knowing about the risk and is now bald. She's not just bald on her head. She is *bald*. (*Laughter*) What do you tell her in your initial interview?

SIXTH LAWYER: I'd try to evaluate the liability, compute the damages, and tell her how much it is going to cost her.

PROFESSOR NESSON: What do you think it might be worth to her?

SIXTH LAWYER: First, I'd ask her how she reacted to her condition.

PROFESSOR NESSON: Oh, terrible, terrible! (*Laughter*)

FIRST JUDGE: How old is she?

SIXTH LAWYER: That's a good question.

SECOND SCIENCE REPORTER: Can I ask one question I think is pertinent here? Is this alopecia reversible or not? In other words, is she bald for the rest of her life, or if she quits taking the drug, will her hair come back in six months?

FIRST COMPANY OFFICIAL: They'll make it appear that it's irreversible. (*Laughter*)

PROFESSOR NESSON: I suspect that if our third lawyer is on the other side of the suit, before the suit is concluded, we may find out.

SIXTH LAWYER: A four-year delay in the court will find out what happened.

PROFESSOR NESSON: What do you tell her? Here is what she wants to know: "What kind of money can I get out of this?"

SIXTH LAWYER: She's got at least a $100,000 injury, I think.

PROFESSOR NESSON: "How long is it going to take me to get it?"

SIXTH LAWYER: A four-year delay in the court, and it's not likely to get settled by the company until we get to trial.

PROFESSOR NESSON: "What's it going to cost me to bring this suit?"

SIXTH LAWYER: Nothing.

PROFESSOR NESSON: "Oh, nothing! How? What a miracle! [*Laughter*] Did a public welfare organization subsidize these kinds of suits?"

SIXTH LAWYER: I'll handle it on a contingent fee. If I win, I'll keep a third of what I get. I don't even make it sound as though it costs her anything.

PROFESSOR NESSON: Tell me how you do it. Here I am, what's it going to cost me?

SIXTH LAWYER: I'm going to put up the expenses, as we go along, and if we win, I'm going to pay myself back the expenses and I'm going to keep a third of whatever I collect. If we get a jury verdict or settlement, I'll keep a third. If we get nothing, I get nothing.

PROFESSOR NESSON: Very good, very good. How much are those expenses likely to be?

SIXTH LAWYER: If yours were the only case, and I have to investigate Rothwell Laboratories, it will be about $10,000 to do the proper discovery—to get an expert to testify—court costs.

PROFESSOR NESSON: So you figure, maybe $50,000 for me and $50,000 for you.

SIXTH LAWYER: No, I'm willing to take a third.

PROFESSOR NESSON: Plus expenses.

SIXTH LAWYER: $10,000 plus expenses. I have a whole group of cases, and we have a national group of lawyers. The expenses might be $500.

PROFESSOR NESSON: If you do it on a mass production basis, you lower the overhead.

SIXTH LAWYER: Sure. Why not? (*Laughter*)

PROFESSOR NESSON: This is a business investment for you. You're going to lay out money.

SIXTH LAWYER: Right. I tell that to the client. It's not just a professional question; whether I take the case or not depends on whether I think I can succeed and what I'll get out of it.

PROFESSOR NESSON: Suppose there are now a hundred people across the country who have this baldness. How do you get them as your clients?

SIXTH LAWYER: I don't get them as my clients. I work with other lawyers who are representing them.

PROFESSOR NESSON: You'd like to get them for your clients?

SIXTH LAWYER: Well, certainly.

PROFESSOR NESSON: Is there any way of rattling the cage to see if you can get a few to come in? (*Laughter*) Here, here, nibble, nibble, nibble; free lawsuits right here—low overhead.

SIXTH LAWYER: We're allowed to advertise now, though no one has gone as far as advertising for specific cases, nor would they ever.

PROFESSOR NESSON: Would you consider it?

SIXTH LAWYER: No.

PROFESSOR NESSON: Why not?

SIXTH LAWYER: Out of professional training.

PROFESSOR NESSON: Professional training. (*Asks the second TV executive*) Would you take an ad from this fellow? (*Laughter*)

SECOND TV EXECUTIVE: No. (*Laughter*) I'd speak to my lawyer first. This is a new area.

PROFESSOR NESSON: You've got to talk to your lawyer first.

SECOND TV EXECUTIVE: I'd have to check that out, because this is an ad with an obvious point of view.

PROFESSOR NESSON: *(Turns to the seventh editor)* Would you take an ad from this fellow?

SEVENTH EDITOR: We'd probably run it editorially and not even charge him for it.

PROFESSOR NESSON: And say go see the sixth lawyer.

SEVENTH EDITOR: Yes. Say, do you know if there were any other instances of this case with this kind of result, and if we thought that it was really doing serious damage to a number of people? It was done with DES daughters, for instance.

PROFESSOR NESSON: Specifying lawyers to whom they can go?

SEVENTH EDITOR: No, just asking them to write letters if they have experienced this symptom.

PROFESSOR NESSON: And then what?

SEVENTH EDITOR: In that case, the answers were turned over to a public interest law firm.

PROFESSOR NESSON: That's not our sixth lawyer. *(Laughter)* *(Asks the third lawyer)* How do you handle these suits? There are a bunch of them that begin to crop up—$100,000 here, $100,000 there. The figures could get pretty tough.

THIRD LAWYER: Yes, they can, and you are not in a rush to go to trial.

PROFESSOR NESSON: Not in a rush to go to trial. *(Laughter)* What's your theory?

THIRD LAWYER: The theory of defense—the theory as to why I don't want to get to trial in a hurry?

PROFESSOR NESSON: The theory of why you don't want to get to trial in a hurry.

THIRD LAWYER: Because the first decision that we get adverse to us may very well be a binding decision and a collateral estoppel principle against us and every other case. It will increase the price of all of the cases.

PROFESSOR NESSON: Feather in the wind. The first one that gets $100,000— that's the floor?

THIRD LAWYER: That's going to be the floor, and it's going to inflate the prices of all of the others.

PROFESSOR NESSON: *(Turns to the sixth lawyer)* What do you expect the tactics that you will face on the other side to be?

SIXTH LAWYER: I think they're stalling as much as possible, but not for any specific reason. They're just putting off the day when eventually they'll have to pay.

PROFESSOR NESSON: If you haven't paid $100,000 today, you haven't paid $100,000.

THIRD LAWYER: I'd want to try to settle them as a group as much as possible, so that I don't have to face the proposition of a bare precedent and everybody else jacking the price up.

PROFESSOR NESSON: Is it a matter of any interest to you, how much you think our sixth lawyer is good for? After all, he's financing these suits. He must worry a little bit when he sees money going out for the suit.

THIRD LAWYER: If you want to know what the conversation is going to be, I'm going to tell him what the risks are—that he's going to lose—

PROFESSOR NESSON: Have the conversation with him.

THIRD LAWYER: (*To the sixth lawyer*) Well, I want to explain to you what kind of discovery we have in mind. We're going to have thirty witnesses.
    We're going to be taking this testimony all over the country. I'm talking about responsible testimony. Obviously, I know that you can afford any kind of discovery that we can, and I think that at the end of it, we've got a very substantial chance of winning. In addition, look at the history of your client and what her doctor told her. There's an opportunity now for a quick settlement at a fair price.

PROFESSOR NESSON: A cheap price. I'll give you a good deal. (*Laughter*)

THIRD LAWYER: At a fair price.

PROFESSOR NESSON: (*To the sixth lawyer*) Are you interested?

SIXTH LAWYER: Whatever figure you've got, you tell me, and I'll pass it along to my client. She may want to settle.

THIRD LAWYER: I don't want to negotiate that way—about passing it on to your client, and she may settle. I want to get a reaction from you.

PROFESSOR NESSON: After all, you are the main investor in this lawsuit. (*Laughter*)

SIXTH LAWYER: Well, I've heard this talk before. I'm not afraid of this. I'll expend the effort and pick up some more cases along the way, and the costs will start dropping.

PROFESSOR NESSON: Do you think you have any shot at punitive damages against this company? Here we've got suppression of all the data and stuff like that?

SIXTH LAWYER: Certainly. If there was failure to tell the Food and Drug Administration information, or physicians, certainly.

PROFESSOR NESSON: Certainly.

SIXTH LAWYER: It's borne out by verdicts. There have been numerous punitive damage verdicts against drug companies.

PROFESSOR NESSON: So that all the hundred people who have this baldness are likely to get punitive damages?

SIXTH LAWYER: The first ones will. After that, the judges may say that they've been punished enough.

PROFESSOR NESSON: So suddenly you've got an interest to get in there quick with your first one.

SIXTH LAWYER: Correct, for many reasons.

PROFESSOR NESSON: (*Turns to the first judge*) Does it seem right to you that the first one in should get some punitive damages and the rest of them not, because the company already has been punished enough?

FIRST JUDGE: Well, I think you deserve a premium for being first. Why not? It doesn't seem shocking to me, and there is the principle, as our sixth lawyer put it, that if you're giving the civil equivalent of a fine, a person should only be fined once for the malefaction. So it doesn't seem illogical or unjust in any way.

PROFESSOR NESSON: (*Turns to the sixth lawyer*) Will these cases be litigated just once on the key issues of whether they suppressed? Is that the way it works?

SIXTH LAWYER: No. I don't think collateral estoppel would apply generally, so we would have to try each case except in the instance when enough were tried; both sides understand where they stand, and the settlements occur.

PROFESSOR NESSON: But it is perfectly possible that out of the first ten cases, Rothwell could win five and you could win five.

SIXTH LAWYER: That doesn't bother us, because the five are likely to be large verdicts. If one lawyer had all ten, which would be unusual, he'd still probably come out ahead. Five clients would have gotten nothing, and five may have been overpaid. But from the lawyer's—

PROFESSOR NESSON: From your point of view, terrific, what the hell. Does it make any sense to litigate that ten times?

SIXTH LAWYER: Not when the legal issues are so close. Collateral estoppel would be a good idea. For the nonlawyers here in the audience, that means it's been decided, so we won't litigate the same legal issue again.

PROFESSOR NESSON: (*Turns to the fourth pharmaceutical manufacturer*) Tell me, how does it enter your decision-making, that there is a possible lawsuit way down at the end? Is that something you worry about, day to day, when you're making decisions about do we do this research, or do we not do this research? Do we tell the FDA or not—or is that simply an irrelevance to you?

FOURTH PHARMACEUTICAL MANUFACTURER: Well, I can hardly say it's an irrelevance, but I'd like to think that the decisions that I'd be making about whether we do or do not do research or advise the FDA are based on what I understand my responsibilities and obligations to be, and not because somebody may wind up and sue me for something.

PROFESSOR NESSON: It's not money that counts.

FOURTH PHARMACEUTICAL MANUFACTURER: Well, now, I didn't say that. (*Laughter*) I don't think the possibility of a suit is something that I think about on a daily basis, no.

PROFESSOR NESSON: There's not a calculation going on in your mind—how much am I going to make by selling this drug, how much is it going to cost me to pay for the injuries?

FOURTH PHARMACEUTICAL MANUFACTURER: I'm hoping that if I decide to market a drug, or whatever, I'm confident it's a safe and effective product. Therefore, it doesn't cross my mind that something of that nature may happen.

PROFESSOR NESSON: (*Acknowledges the first business reporter*)

FIRST BUSINESS REPORTER: I hate to be a Johnny-one-note, but I think we're overlooking a major consideration, and that is, what's going to happen to the stock? That really is a very important consideration.

    Back in the early 1970's when all stocks were going down, a number of corporate executives were having very serious personal problems. The idea of a stock going down has a physical effect.

PROFESSOR NESSON: So you want to ask a pharmaceutical manufacturer if that interests him? (*Turns to the first pharmaceutical manufacturer*) Two questions for you. I'm interested in your decision-making process. I want to know if—as you sit in your office making the judgments about hiring Mr. Fine, reporting to the FDA, putting a warning on our package, withdrawing this drug, changing our detail men, and sending a letter to doctors—it is a consideration in your mind what's going to happen to my stock. What's going to happen if there are lawsuits down at the other end?

FIRST PHARMACEUTICAL MANUFACTURER: No, it's not. I think the business reporter ought to know that. I think Wall Street is schizophrenic anyway.

    Let me say this, and it's not been mentioned. You have in your presence four executives who operate under the criminal penalties of a statute whereby they can suffer criminal penalties without having been negligent or willfully guilty of misconduct if only one of their people did something wrong; even if they knew something about it.

    Those are rather excessive burdens to carry. I think that's the only statute that does not say that you have to be negligent.

PROFESSOR NESSON: How many of your colleagues have gone to jail on that?

FIRST PHARMACEUTICAL MANUFACTURER: We've had some that have been fined.

PROFESSOR NESSON: Some that have been *fined*.

FIRST PHARMACEUTICAL MANUFACTURER: Yes. It's not a laughing matter.

PROFESSOR NESSON: I'm not laughing. How many of your colleagues have gone to jail on that?

FIRST PHARMACEUTICAL MANUFACTURER: I don't think, at the moment, any. None.

PROFESSOR NESSON: None.

FIRST PHARMACEUTICAL MANUFACTURER: But I think that's an extraordinary statute under which to operate. I'm telling you that under those circumstances, and in my instance, even without those circumstances, those things would not be taken into account.

I believe that if we have any information, the Food and Drug Administration should have it too for the benefit of our company and for the protection of people who might have taken our medicines. I believe that strongly.

PROFESSOR NESSON: Answer me a question that's been bothering me for a long time. You talk to people who run drug companies, and everyone believes you have to tell the FDA everything. You have to play everything fair and square and there money matters never count. Yet our science reporters can list instances in which that didn't happen. A lawyer deals with "Mer 29." Somebody who is the head of a big drug company made a decision different than yours.

Now, I presume that that fellow wasn't crazy. I presume he had some logic in his mind, when he made those decisions. He didn't just fall into them. Can you tell me what the logic was that must have been going on?

FIRST PHARMACEUTICAL MANUFACTURER: No, I don't think I can speak for them. I don't think I can tell you what was going on in anybody else's mind.

PROFESSOR NESSON: You can't imagine what the logic would have been for them?

FIRST PHARMACEUTICAL MANUFACTURER: No, I don't choose to examine the logic of other people. As a matter of fact, I haven't heard the facts, Mr. Nesson. You said we didn't want them here, and I guess they shouldn't be here. I would hope that my company was not involved in any of those things.

PROFESSOR NESSON: *(Calls on the fourth businessman)* Could you imagine the logic that might lead the head of a drug company to suppress data?

FOURTH BUSINESSMAN: I do not believe that heads of responsible drug companies make decisions to suppress data.

PROFESSOR NESSON: *(To the first business reporter)* Can you imagine?

FIRST BUSINESS REPORTER: I don't know.

FOURTH BUSINESSMAN: And to answer one point obviously, which is implicit, it's probably not even remotely correct.

PROFESSOR NESSON: (*Acknowledges the sixth lawyer*)

SIXTH LAWYER: And the discovery we've had in some cases indicated that officers of drug companies participated in or directed nondisclosure of information which related to side effects of drugs.

PROFESSOR NESSON: Why? Any idea?

SIXTH LAWYER: Sure, because it was the best-selling drug in their company, and if adverse information came out, it would affect the sales of the drug. They developed a steamroller belief that the product was good for the public and had relatively few side effects, and they couldn't adapt their thinking to new information.

FOURTH BUSINESSMAN: At what level were these officers?

SIXTH LAWYER: President and vice-president.

FOURTH BUSINESSMAN: A responsible company?

SIXTH LAWYER: Yes.

PROFESSOR NESSON: Thank you very much; it's time to go to lunch. (*Applause*)

   (*Whereupon this session was concluded*)

Case Study
2: Precision Dynamics

Professor Schmidt

The Case:

I

Precision Dynamics Corporation is a manufacturer of military and commercial aircraft, missiles, radar, and related equipment. About one-third of Precision's sales are to foreign countries, divided, as are domestic sales, about equally between commercial and military orders. Precision's fortunes have improved dramatically over the past three years, due largely to increases in foreign military orders. One important recent foreign sale by Precision was to Olay, an oil-rich country in the Middle East, which bought fifty Panthers, supersonic fighter-aircraft which are also purchased in substantial numbers by the United States Air Force. Each Panther fighter costs ten million dollars. Precision has also benefited from very large development contracts with the Pentagon for a top-secret, long-range, air-launched missile capable of such course changes and elusive maneuvers that it would be virtually invulnerable to existing Soviet air defense and anti-ballistic missile technologies. If this new missile becomes operational, the United States could drastically reduce other offensive missile systems, such as the cruise missile. Such reductions could produce dramatic progress in SALT negotiations with the Soviets. A prototype missile has been built, and in extensive testing it has met all specifications.

Code-named "Broken Field," the new missile depends on highly sophisticated airborne guidance systems, which are separate from the missile itself and code-named "Hydra," and which can read defenses deployed against the Broken Field missile and instruct it to take diversionary action. For the guidance process to work, it is necessary that at least two Hydra surveillance and computer systems be airborne along geographical vectors north and south of the general target area. These systems are highly complex, utilizing recent breakthroughs in surveillance, data processing, and transmission technologies. Each Hydra system is housed in a large aircraft, an adaptation of a long-range bomber which Precision manufactures for the United States Air Force.

The Pentagon has adopted plans to deploy Broken Field missiles on fifty aircraft in various parts of the United States, and to keep two Hydra systems airborne in each vector north and south of the Soviet Union at all times. Aircraft based at SAC airfields in the United States can easily maintain the vector position to the north of the Soviet Union. However, the vector south of the Soviet Union (roughly the area from the Philippines to Saudi Arabia) presents strategic problems. The guidance aircraft are to be camouflaged as SAC bombers. These bombers regularly occupy airspace to the north, east, and west of the Soviet Union, but not to the south. Thus, even disguised, the Hydra aircraft would excite Soviet curiosity along the southern vector.

To meet the need for airborne southern guidance systems, the Pentagon has proposed an ingenious solution: a country located along the southern vector should be induced to purchase six or more guidance systems on the supposition that the systems are to be used solely for its own defense. The buyer-country would not be aware of the additional Hydra guidance function in relation to the Broken Field missile. Rather, other equipment would be included and the systems would appear to the buyer-country to be advanced surveillance and communications systems, useful for spotting land or air incursions into largely uninhabited border areas. The highly sophisticated devices necessary to guide the Broken Field missiles would be hidden. Only routine surveillance systems would normally be operational. On a signal from the United States during testing sequences or during an actual launching of the Broken Field missiles, the Hydra systems would be activated to provide guidance for the Broken Field missiles. Even when activated, however, the Hydra function would not be apparent to the buyer-country.

With this plan in mind, the Assistant Secretary of Defense for International Security Affairs called on Andrew Josephs, the president and chief executive officer of Precision, to discuss the possibilities of persuading Olay, which is located south of the Soviet Union, to purchase the guidance systems. Olay seemed a logical choice not only because of its strategic location, but also because of its recent purchase from Precision of the Panther fighters. The Assistant Secretary suggested to Josephs that Olay be induced to buy six (disguised) Hydra systems. The United States was also planning to purchase six systems. If the Pentagon approved the sale to Olay, and endeavored to persuade Olay that the disguised Hydras would be useful for Olay's security, the Assistant Secretary inquired, would Precision use its contacts among Olay's military leaders to try to make a sale? The Assistant Secretary pointed out that successful deploying of Hydra systems in the airspace over Olay would make it possible for the United

States to give up several missile systems that have been stumbling blocks in SALT negotiations with the Soviet Union.

For Josephs, the matter of Precision's contacts in Olay currently happens to be one of acute sensitivity. Josephs took over as head of Precision about twelve months ago, after the former president of the company resigned under pressure due to disclosures of widespread questionable payments in several foreign countries. One of Josephs's first steps as the new president of Precision was to order a confidential audit by outside counsel of all payments and commissions paid by Precision to foreign consultants. He has just received a report on payments made in connection with the sale of Panthers to Olay which disclosed that two million dollars was paid about eighteen months ago to an unnamed "high official" of the Olay Defense Ministry. The Panther sale was finally closed about six months ago, although negotiations had been in the works for more than a year before the deal was closed. At present, about half of the fifty Panthers have been delivered to Olay; the remainder are to be delivered within the coming six months. Precision's chief sales agent in Olay has said that he will not disclose the identity of the recipient of this money to anyone other than Josephs in person, claiming that the official could be executed if his receipt of money from Precision is revealed. Josephs has summoned the agent to meet with him. He is due to arrive in two days.

Some Questions for Josephs

1. If Josephs learns the identity of the Olay official to whom the two-million-dollar payment was made, should he reveal that fact, or the questionable payment generally, to the outside counsel conducting the investigation, to the board, to the company's general counsel, to his personal lawyer? Does it matter if any of these lawyers is also a member of the board?

2. Should Josephs notify the SEC, the Justice Department, or any other agency of the federal government? How much should he reveal?

3. Suppose Precision proceeds with a public offering of a $250 million bond issue in order to tool up for production of the Broken Field/ Hydra program. How much should Josephs disclose in the prospectus about the Broken Field/Hydra project? Should he disclose the prospects for sale of Hydras to Olay? Should Josephs disclose the possibility that a bribe in Olay might be revealed which might threaten the sale of Hydras to Olay?

4. How should Josephs respond if a reporter calls and asks whether Precision is planning to sell advanced airborne surveillance-computer systems to Olay?

Some Questions for Reporters

1. Suppose a reporter is telephoned by an anonymous caller who claims that he is a Precision employee, and who says he has confidential corporate documents which show that Precision bribed a high military official in Olay in connection with the sale of Panthers. Should the reporter pay for the documents? Should the reporter be concerned about how the documents were obtained?

2. What should the reporter do if he gets the documents and believes them to be true? Should he contact Josephs? The Defense Department? The SEC? Anyone else?

3. If the reporter believes he knows the identity of the Olay military official who received the questionable payment from Precision, should he reveal the official's identity in a story? Should the reporter contact any government agency beforehand? Should he notify the official in Olay beforehand?

4. Suppose the anonymous caller offers the reporter a copy of a memorandum from the Assistant Secretary of Defense for International Security Affairs describing a potential sale to Olay of communications equipment which would have a hidden function relating to guidance of American missiles. Should the reporter accept the copy of the memorandum? What if the memorandum is stamped: *"Top Secret—Classified Defense Information.* Unauthorized Possession Punishable by Federal Espionage Statues"? Should the reporter reveal this memorandum in a story?

II

Wellington Duke is an investigative reporter for the *New Angeles Post*, one of the leading newspapers in the United States. For several years, Duke has covered news relating to defense contracts, the defense budget, weapons technology, disarmament, and foreign arms sales. It was Duke who broke the story of bribes paid to officials in countries of Western Europe by Precision Dynamics Corporation, a leading manufacturer of military and commercial aircraft, missiles, radar, and related equipment. He has since written follow-up stories about other American companies that made questionable payments abroad, about new governmental regulations designed to prevent questionable payments, and about the steps Precision and other American firms have taken to prevent corruption in future dealings with foreign countries. Duke also wrote several stories about Precision's recent sale to Olay, an oil-rich country in the Middle East located south of the Soviet Union, of fifty Panther fighters, advanced supersonic aircraft also purchased in large numbers by the United States Air Force. He covered the bitter condemnation of the sale by Israeli leaders and the intense, but unsuccessful, Congressional opposition to the sale.

One morning Duke receives a telephone call from an anonymous caller who asserts that Precision is continuing to bribe foreign officials abroad and that the recent sale of Panther fighters to Olay was accomplished by the payment of a two-million-dollar bribe to a high official in the Olay Ministry of Defense, whom the caller says he might be persuaded to name. The caller claims that Precision's president, Andrew Josephs, knows about the payment but is trying to hide it both from his board of directors and from the SEC, each non-disclosure constituting a violation of a standing agreement entered into by Precision and the SEC. The caller claims to have copies of documents that prove his allegations. He offers to meet with Duke if Duke will give him an absolute guarantee that his identity will not be revealed. He also says that he wishes to discuss whether Duke can reimburse him for certain expenses incurred in getting the documents.

A few days later, the managing editor of the *Post* is told by the Israeli ambassador to the United Nations that the Pentagon is secretly considering the sale to Olay of airborne computer-communications systems manufactured by Precision, the primary use for which is to coordinate land military operations. The ambassador asserts that Israel is the only logical target of Olay in a land war, and that the sale of these advanced systems to Olay will upset the balance of power in the Middle East.

Some Questions

1. Should Duke promise the caller that his identity will be confidential? Should Duke try to get the documents allegedly proving that Preci-

sion bribed a high military official in Olay? Does it matter how the documents were obtained? Should Duke pay for the documents?

2. How should Duke proceed if he gets the documents and believes they are probably true? Should he contact Precision's president, Andrew Josephs? Should he contact the Defense Department? The SEC? Anyone else? At what point does he have a story worth printing?

3. If Duke learns the identity of the Olay official who received the questionable payment from Precision in connection with the Panther sale, should he reveal the official's name in a story?

4. Should the information about the Pentagon's consideration of the sale of the computer-communications systems to Olay be a part of any story about questionable payments in connection with the Panther sale? Should this planned sale be an independent story?

III

Casper Bump has recently become director of the Central Intelligence Agency after a distinguished career in the United States Air Force, including four years as Chief of Staff. Yesterday his chief of intelligence for the Middle East told him some bad news. The CIA's best source of intelligence in Olay, a high official in the Ministry of Defense, has communicated to Washington that he will be removed from office and probably killed if it is revealed that he received two million dollars from Precision. The chief of intelligence told Bump that the agent in Olay had notified the CIA of his intention to accept the payment during the previous director's tenure (and during the previous administration). The CIA did not block the payment because the Olay official had said the payment was essential to offset bribes being paid by French aircraft companies. The Precision payment was said to have been distributed to a number of high-ranking military officials. Now, according to the message from Olay, the new management of Precision is in the process of uncovering the payment and might make the information public.

The chief also points out that the revelation of Precision's payment in connection with the Panther sale will probably trigger a reaction in Olay that could jeopardize the planned sale of Hydras to that country.

The Seminar:

PROFESSOR SCHMIDT: Good afternoon. The hypothetical case that is before you involves, essentially, a series of conflicts between disclosure and secrecy. Before we get started, there is something that I should disclose about it. There are three different parts of this hypothetical case. The people that we've categorized as business, or their advisors, have received a business version. The reporters and their advisers have received a journalistic version, which I would call "the business," if that wouldn't create confusion. Then there are some highly privileged members of the group who are taking on essentially governmental responsibilities, who have both the business version and the reporters' version, as well as a small but juicy additional piece of information about this problem.

Now, when we planned this session, the votes were about evenly divided between those who said that all these various sets of facts would break down in chaos and confusion and, on the other hand, those who thought, "Well, it's worth a try." After all, that's more or less the way it is in the real world.

So if confusion seems to be setting in, I'll give everybody all the information that everybody else has at some point that I think is appropriate.

You are now veterans, after this morning, of this curious method of pedagogy. I propose to moderate a somewhat more loosely textured discussion than we had this morning. I would like to encourage people to butt right in. I'd like to encourage people to converse directly with others at the table. All comments need not be routed through me. I will, however, interrupt, make you be quiet, declare you out of order, if there is some point that I think is worth pursuing at the moment. But in general, I think perhaps we're ready for a more relaxed and open-ended discussion.

(Addresses the first reporter) I'd like to start with the journalistic

perspective on this hypothetical case. I would like you to suppose that you have reported in the past on questionable payments made by the Precision Dynamics Corporation to various foreign officials in connection with arms sales to foreign countries.

You know that a scandal rocked Precision, to such an extent that its chief executive officer was forced to resign. He was replaced by a new chief executive, Mr. Andrew Josephs, who was pledged to a policy of disclosure and no more questionable payments. One day, you are called by someone who refuses to identify himself to you, and who claims that Precision paid an official of the Middle Eastern country of Olay two million dollars, in order to get that country to buy fifty rather expensive advanced fighters. Panthers, as they are known; that the existence of this payment has come to the attention of the new executive, Josephs; and that he is trying to cover it up. He has not disclosed it to his own board, nor to the SEC. What do you do at that point? You're on the telephone.

FIRST REPORTER: One thing I'm not clear on in this case. Do I have to suppose that this guy is asking me for confidentiality and that I've already agreed to give it to him? The case states that I've done that, and that's the last thing a reporter wants to do.

PROFESSOR SCHMIDT: Well, let's take it step by step. What would you say?

FIRST REPORTER: The first thing I want to do is find out who's calling. I don't want to go far at all without first knowing who it is.

PROFESSOR SCHMIDT: So you say, "Let's get together."

FIRST REPORTER: Well, yes. I'd try to find out over the phone who's calling. Also, very much a part of the first conversation is, "How do you know these things?" I mean, who's going to know this?

PROFESSOR SCHMIDT: He says, "I have valid reasons for not wanting to get together with you, and not wanting to disclose my identity to you. However, I can provide you with documents which should prove to your satisfaction the truth of what I am alleging about Josephs and this two-million-dollar payment to Olay."

FIRST REPORTER: Well, we've got to get together to get the documents.

PROFESSOR SCHMIDT: Well, not necessarily. It can go over the transom or be left in the baggage locker at La Guardia, or whatever, if they still have them there. I guess they don't.

FIRST REPORTER :   I don't know, I might spin out a conversation in which I'd start assuming, maybe, the source of this information and try to get it that way, for a start. Two things that I might assume come to mind immediately. Who's going to know this? There's maybe somebody in the company who hates Josephs, his enemy. It probably has to be somebody in the company, anyway.

PROFESSOR SCHMIDT: Or maybe in a different company.

FIRST REPORTER: Or in a different company, although it's not my impression that contractors share their payoff information with one another.

PROFESSOR SCHMIDT: Maybe another company working in the same territory in Olay couldn't come up with a high enough bid and lost out on the contract, but learned about their competitors. Why does any of that matter?

FIRST REPORTER: Well, the credibility of the source is crucial. For a start, since I don't have the documentation—the documents may be so incredible that they would discredit whoever gave them. But while it's just a phone conversation—you get a lot of nut calls—I'd want to know who it is. That would be my first effort. I might ask whether the caller had been in the Middle East or—

PROFESSOR SCHMIDT: All right, you run into a stone wall on that.

FIRST REPORTER: Okay, say I get nowhere.

PROFESSOR SCHMIDT: Let's suppose the caller says, "I'll drop off these documents or I'll make them available to you, but I've incurred certain expenses in getting copies of these documents. I need to be reimbursed for those expenses to the tune of five thousand dollars."

FIRST REPORTER: Forget it.

PROFESSOR SCHMIDT: Why?

FIRST REPORTER: I'd check with my managing editor before coming over here. (*Laughter*)

No, frankly, believe it or not, I've never been asked for money.

PROFESSOR SCHMIDT: I'm supposed to do the rigging. What does your managing editor say?

FIRST REPORTER: It is a firm and clear policy to pay nothing for any information, ever, under any conditions.

PROFESSOR SCHMIDT: Is there a reason for that firm, unconditional policy?

FIRST EDITOR: Well, there's an ethical reason that we don't pay for information. There is also a very practical reason, because we would than encounter a situation in which everyone would expect to be paid, and we'd go out of business.

PROFESSOR SCHMIDT: So there's a practical business judgment. Why pay for it when you can get it free?

FIRST EDITOR: No, first there is an ethical question.

PROFESSOR SCHMIDT: First an ethical question.

FIRST EDITOR: In any case, under no circumstances do we pay for information.

PROFESSOR SCHMIDT: What is unethical about paying for it?

FIRST EDITOR: We consider ourselves to be operating in the public domain, with certain responsibilities to our readers. The very fact that a payment is involved means that we inject an element of motivation on the part of the person supplying the information, which might very well tend to distort the information, or produce information that is deliberately misleading.

PROFESSOR SCHMIDT: May I try to break that answer down a little?

FIRST EDITOR: Yes.

PROFESSOR SCHMIDT: Your duty to the public—why wouldn't that duty to the public be taken care of by a policy of disclosure on your part? Here's the story and here's what we paid for it, public, and you can draw your own conclusions about whether the fact that we paid for it undermines the credibility of the story or raises questions about the source's motivation.

FIRST EDITOR: When we pass on information, we take responsibility for the character of that information, and our compact with the public is a compact between the staff of our newspaper and the public. We're giving the public certain assurances as to what the nature of that staff is.

PROFESSOR SCHMIDT: Suppose, by paying, you can be more certain of the truth of the story? The source comes to you and says, "Here it is, this company, two million dollars, and so on," and you don't know for sure, but that's what the source says. But the source then says, "I'll give you documentary proof. You can publish the documents that will prove the existence of this bribe, so your readers will have a chance to see the actual documents." Now, isn't that a case in which your higher obligation to the readers might call for buying the documents, so you could give them the most concrete, verified story?

FIRST EDITOR: In practical terms, we have found that, with the kind of reportorial resources we have, once we become aware of a given situation, we can dig it out without paying a price for it.

PROFESSOR SCHMIDT: (*Asks the second editor*) Is that your impression? Is it ever necessary to pay for a story? Is it ever justifiable to pay for a story?

SECOND EDITOR: I don't suppose you could rule out absolutely every extreme possibility. I suppose if we're on the brink of World War III, or something like that, or a plague epidemic, one might consider it. But in any ordinary situation, certainly in any that I've come across, our policy is the same. We do not pay for information, and the reason is that if you do pay for information, you totally undermine the credibility of your material. If you set up a monetary incentive for people to come to you with stories, the public would not really believe you.

PROFESSOR SCHMIDT: You pay your reporters.

SECOND EDITOR: Certainly.

PROFESSOR SCHMIDT: You reward your reporters with raises when they uncover a good story?

SECOND EDITOR: Certainly.

PROFESSOR SCHMIDT: The public knows that. Aren't you paying for news that way?

SECOND EDITOR: No.

PROFESSOR SCHMIDT: You're rewarding people.

SECOND EDITOR: I'm paying for work.

PROFESSOR SCHMIDT: You're paying for work. So our first editor has an unconditional, never, never a payment policy. Your position is, in the event of a cataclysm, bubonic plague, you might pay.

SECOND EDITOR: I might add that I would consider an airplane ticket tourist from, let's say, Los Angeles to New York, if my informant wanted to come here.

PROFESSOR SCHMIDT: How about a couple of weeks at the Plaza?

SECOND EDITOR: No. (*Laughter*) At the Dixie, yes. (*Laughter*)

PROFESSOR SCHMIDT: That might be even better. How about a book publishing contract? The guy says, "I've got a good story, and by the way, my autobiography is pretty good, too. If you'll give me a ten-thousand-dollar advance, I'll let you have the first crack at it, the first little glimmer of what I've got, documents showing that Precision Dynamics has just paid two million dollars and that they are in the process of covering it up, and so on."

SECOND EDITOR: I would have to say that a book contract is, of course, an entirely different matter. I'd have to be convinced that there really is a book there. I would try to separate that one piece of information from the entire book proposition.

PROFESSOR SCHMIDT: May I ask one more question? What if you could buy the missing eighteen and a half minutes of the Watergate tapes? (*Laughter*) How many weeks at the Plaza would that be worth?

SECOND EDITOR: I would again have to say, choking (*Laughter*) —I would not want to pay for it, no.

PROFESSOR SCHMIDT: Maybe, perhaps, a comparative perspective would be of interest. You're a newspaper editor. Do you ever pay for stories?

THIRD EDITOR: Quite frequently. And many newspapers pay for memoirs.

PROFESSOR SCHMIDT: Oh, but there's a book there.

THIRD EDITOR: But not something in hard covers.

PROFESSOR SCHMIDT: What about the two points that our first editor made? Doesn't that raise your cost of doing business?

THIRD EDITOR: One rule I have is, never do something you can't admit in public—in terms of journalism, that is. (*Laughter*)

PROFESSOR SCHMIDT: We'll work on a definition of journalism in just a moment.

THIRD EDITOR: Second, I'd never induce anybody to commit an offense.

PROFESSOR SCHMIDT: Do you mean admit in public or volunteer in your paper?

THIRD EDITOR: I mean volunteer in the paper. We always explain the method by which we got information. If we paid for it, we always come clean with with the reader. And we never induce anybody to commit an offense. You can wrap this up, either seriously or otherwise, in a number of ways. When I bought some documents, it cost me ten thousand dollars, and the story would not have come out unless I had paid for the documents, period. I believed we had something secret within those documents. We bought the documents for technical and scientific knowledge, which the man selling the documents was going to put into a book, which we were going to help him to write.

PROFESSOR SCHMIDT: Has he written that book yet?

THIRD EDITOR: He's dead. (*Laughter*)

Let me say this: we don't pay criminals for their memoirs, and we don't part with money to induce people to commit an offense of any kind.

PROFESSOR SCHMIDT: I was just going to ask that. Supposing this fellow called you up, instead of our first reporter, and said not "I *have* these documents," but "I can *get* documents if you will pay me, because it's going to cost me to get them." He describes the documents, gives you a good enough description so that you think it has the ring of truth. What do you say?

THIRD EDITOR: If it's a sensational first draft of a very important story— (*Laughter*) I'd be inclined to say, "I'm sorry you put it that way, because if you had the documents, I would have been prepared to consider paying you." (*Laughter*) I'd say, "Why didn't you ring me up later?" (*Laughter*)

PROFESSOR SCHMIDT: But to pay in advance, that would be wrong, that's for sure.

THIRD EDITOR: I have cases where we've been asked to pay people to get information that they haven't got, and we've refused.

PROFESSOR SCHMIDT: What's so important about paying before or after?

THIRD EDITOR: Well, it's difficult. If the informant is going to steal, then we don't want to be caught with our hands in the till.

PROFESSOR SCHMIDT: Why are your hands any more or less in the till, depending on whether you pay him before he steals or after? In one case, you're buying stolen goods, and in the other case, you're buying goods that aren't stolen yet, but will be, because you're willing to pay.

THIRD EDITOR: I think there's a difference.

PROFESSOR SCHMIDT: (*Asks the first lawyer*) Is there a difference?

FIRST LAWYER: I think there probably is. I think, if you pay in advance, you may be participating, aiding and abetting, participating in a conspiracy—there are lots of ways to phrase it—in a sense that you might well not be if someone comes to you afterwards and says, "I have some documents, and I'd like to sell them to you." I think there's a kind of active participation on the editor's part if he pays in advance, which certainly puts him a lot closer to potential criminal liability.

PROFESSOR SCHMIDT: He's an accessory before the fact if he pays first.

FIRST LAWYER: I mean, as a legal matter, I would say it's just a lot riskier to pay in advance when you have any kind of knowledge that the money is going to be used for this, than it is to buy the documents afterwards.

PROFESSOR SCHMIDT: (*To the first reporter*) Okay. We've gotten over this money hurdle, one way or the other. Either you work for an editor willing to pay, or you talk your source into giving it to you without pay. And the source provides the documents and is willing to tell you why, in general, he's interested in the story coming out.

Let me give you a couple of variations and see if it makes a difference. The source is an executive of Precision, who was passed over when Josephs was made the chief executive officer. He's mad at Josephs, thinks maybe he'll be tapped now if he can force Josephs out because of a scandal. Does that alter the newsworthiness of the story at all?

FIRST REPORTER: That would be the most predictable person to offer the information.

PROFESSOR SCHMIDT: The source is someone who works for a competing plane-manufacturing company that would like to mess up Precision's relationships with Olay and thinks that if this bribe is publicized, the government of Olay will say, "We're not going to deal with Precision anymore," and so they'll buy the whatever-it-is of this competing company. Does that alter the newsworthiness?

FIRST REPORTER: No, I don't think so.

PROFESSOR SCHMIDT: The source says he's a member of some sort of Israeli intelligence operation. His interest is in throwing up roadblocks in the relationship between American arms manufacturers and Middle Eastern countries that are hostile to Israel. Does that alter the newsworthiness?

FIRST REPORTER: No, it's still the same story. Your decision is whether that is a newsworthy story or not.

PROFESSOR SCHMIDT: Would you reveal all three of those things in your story?

FIRST REPORTER: That's why I wouldn't want to promise this confidentiality we talked about, which I had to promise in the first place.

PROFESSOR SCHMIDT: You would want to reveal the fact that you got this from a competitor, that you got it even from Israeli intelligence?

FIRST REPORTER: Sure.

PROFESSOR SCHMIDT: Do you think if you reveal the fact that you got it from Israeli intelligence, you'll get many more stories from them? Or does that enter your thinking?

FIRST REPORTER: No, it doesn't. I just don't imagine that they are a regular leaker to the American press. If they are, well—the decision is whether this is a newsworthy story, not the motives of a—

PROFESSOR SCHMIDT: And whether it's newsworthy depends on whether it's true and on its importance. But newsworthiness is not tainted by the motive of the source.

FIRST REPORTER: This is where we talk about the money. Too much payment taints, I think, more than—

PROFESSOR SCHMIDT: Well, the source is tainted if he demands five thousand dollars, but not if he's trying to get Mr. Josephs fired or—

FIRST REPORTER: No, the principle of payment can lead to, I think, messy situations in the future. In this case, the question of how good the documentation is will be the first question.

PROFESSOR SCHMIDT: The documentation looks pretty good. It's some sort of a report to Josephs from somebody who seems to be a sales agent or something in Olay. It identifies the person in the Olay Defense Ministry who is alleged to have received this two-million-dollar bribe. It identifies the date. It identifies the source of the money. But you're not sure, I mean, it could be forged, right? Particularly if you're dealing with, say, Israeli intelligence, there would be that possibility; whether they would do it, I don't know. Would you call up Josephs or someone at Precision?

FIRST REPORTER: Absolutely.

PROFESSOR SCHMIDT: Who'd you call?

FIRST REPORTER: I'd do some nosing around to see if there's anybody else around town or in the world who knows this kind of information, who might substantiate it, indirectly or in other ways, before I go immediately to the principals involved.

PROFESSOR SCHMIDT: It doesn't work.

FIRST REPORTER: No way.

PROFESSOR SCHMIDT: Well, let's just say it doesn't work. Would you go directly?

FIRST REPORTER: So in other words, if all I have is this material, and I can't get anything else on this subject, and I call Josephs, then what do I say? I tell him exactly what I have.

PROFESSOR SCHMIDT: Do you describe the document?

FIRST REPORTER: No, but I say I understand—

PROFESSOR SCHMIDT: What do you say, exactly?

FIRST REPORTER: Well, we have information. I wouldn't tell him I had a document, for a start. I'd say, "We have information that on such and such a day, in such and such a contract, so much and so much was paid to a prominent official." I'd leave some of it out, to see how much he's filling in, and so forth.

PROFESSOR SCHMIDT: Mr. Josephs— (*Calls on the first businessman*)

FIRST BUSINESSMAN: Where did you get that kind of information? (*Laughter*)

FIRST REPORTER: I can't reveal the source.

FIRST BUSINESSMAN: Then I don't have anything to talk to you about.

PROFESSOR SCHMIDT: Nothing at all.

FIRST REPORTER: You don't deny it.

FIRST BUSINESSMAN: No comment.

FIRST REPORTER: No comment, okay, I'll talk to—I mean, that's—

PROFESSOR SCHMIDT: And then what happens? Do you run the story?

FIRST REPORTER: No, no, no, no. I mean, I'd call the guy in Olay, first, for a second phone call.

PROFESSOR SCHMIDT: Aha, what do you say to him?

FIRST REPORTER: I'd suggest that we know certain things about moneys received, and leave a few of them out, and see what he says.

PROFESSOR SCHMIDT: Stonewall, denial.

FIRST REPORTER: He denies.

PROFESSOR SCHMIDT: Yes.

FIRST REPORTER: You wouldn't let me call all these people. There are more people around who probably know something about the situation. I'd call the Israelis. I'd call anybody who might be involved.

PROFESSOR SCHMIDT: Okay, I'll get back to you in just a second. (*To the first businessman*) Would you do anything after you received this call from the reporter? Supposing the reporter happens to be right and you know that there was a two-million-dollar payment. You don't know to whom the payment was made, let's suppose, but you have information that two million dollars was paid to a high defense official in Olay. Now, you've got a reporter who is on your track.

FIRST BUSINESSMAN: I'd do everything I could to find out any additional information as quickly as I could, assuming that I had reason to believe that there was some possible truth to the story.

PROFESSOR SCHMIDT: Would you check with the State Department?

FIRST BUSINESSMAN: Not necessarily.

PROFESSOR SCHMIDT: You wouldn't be concerned, at this point, about possible foreign policy implications?

FIRST BUSINESSMAN: Well, I guess if I knew who the person in Olay was who got money and that the company had actually paid it, I might be. Yes.

PROFESSOR SCHMIDT: If you undertook your own investigation and you learned the identity of the official in Olay who received this money, would you reveal that fact to your board of directors?

FIRST BUSINESSMAN: Sure.

PROFESSOR SCHMIDT: Would you reveal it to the reporter who called you?

FIRST BUSINESSMAN: No.

PROFESSOR SCHMIDT: Why not?

FIRST BUSINESSMAN: For, I guess—

PROFESSOR SCHMIDT: Let me remind you that you are the new reform candidate, who is at the head of this company. This bribe did not take place under your leadership, but that of your predecessor. I use the word "bribe." I don't mean "bribe." "Questionable payment." It might be in your interest, might it not, to disclose this?

FIRST BUSINESSMAN: I'm assuming that the company hasn't made any disclosures of a general nature.

PROFESSOR SCHMIDT: That's correct.

FIRST BUSINESSMAN: No, if we were going to make a disclosure, I'd go ask my lawyer whether I had an obligation to disclose, under the securities laws or any other laws.

PROFESSOR SCHMIDT: (*Asks the second lawyer*) Does he have an obligation under the securities laws?

SECOND LAWYER: Well, three years ago, I would have answered this differently. Today, I would tell him that we're going to have to follow 350 other companies and put out a general statement about the fact that we, like our 350 brothers, have made questionable payments in connection with our foreign business. I would tell him, if we're talking about today, that the military export sales act, or whatever it's called, is going into effect, so that we're going to have to be on the record as having reported this to the State Department, and we'd better report it to the Defense Department. I think that would probably be the friendliest arena to start in. (*Laughter*)

PROFESSOR SCHMIDT: The Defense Department.

SECOND LAWYER: The Defense Department. We would ultimately end up with the Securities and Exchange Commission, whether we like it or not. But there are two things that I would not want to make public. One is the name of the country. The other is the name of the recipient. I would hope that my president was not burdened with the name of the recipient, which I frankly think is an irrelevancy in terms of his responsibilities.

PROFESSOR SCHMIDT: Would you want to be burdened with that knowledge: If he said, "Yes, well, I happen to know it."

SECOND LAWYER: Who am I? Am I corporate counsel or am I one of these fifth columnists that the SEC has put in the company? (*Laughter*) I have to understand who I am in answering that question.

PROFESSOR SCHMIDT: You are a senior partner of the law firm that does most of the really difficult legal counseling on financial matters for Precision, and you sit on the board. (*Laughter*)

SECOND LAWYER: Okay. Maybe I ought to get off that board. But if I'm their counsel and he knows the name, then I want him to tell me the name. His communication to me is going to have more privilege than the communication that he had that gave it to him. As far as I'm concerned, I was at least to give him some ear that he can talk to and give some sound advice, hopefully.

PROFESSOR SCHMIDT: What if he asks you, "Do we have to disclose the name of this recipient, the name of the country, the transaction in connection with which this payment was made?"

SECOND LAWYER: I'm going to tell him that we're going to try a general disclosure, in terms of SEC responsibility, in terms of our overall sensitive payment problem. We will institute a sensitive payment inquiry and we'll report that over the last five years, we paid thirty million dollars in questionable payments in connection with five billion dollars of business, or five hundred billion dollars, or whatever the figure is, over a long period of time. But I would have to tell him that there is no privilege and that there might come a time when we would have to make a public disclosure of the name of the country and the name of the individual, if we have it. I could not give him the assurance that that would not become public.

The question, from our point of view, is whether we should resist disclosing the name of the country and resist disclosing the name of the individual.

PROFESSOR SCHMIDT: (*Asks the first ex-government official*) Are you satisfied with that? Would you believe that the fact that over the last five years in the aggregate, Precision had paid thirty million dollars in connection with five billion dollars of orders, and so on? Is that sufficient to inform investors and to inform Precision's shareholders about their franchise, corporate governance questions?

FIRST EX-GOVERNMENT OFFICIAL: I should disclose that the company is one of my stockholders, and say: "Yes, I think so." I think the issue, however, is one you could spend a whole day on. If no other facts are present, what you're trying to tell the stockholders is that there is a risk that some part of the business of this company may be discontinued because it was obtained by means which may make it impossible for this company to do business with somebody else. The question, insofar as the securities laws are concerned, ought to be, in my judgment, nothing more than that.

PROFESSOR SCHMIDT: What if a shareholder says, "Well, gee—"

FIRST EX-GOVERNMENT OFFICIAL: There's one other question, and that is, who knew and what has anyone who was elected by stockholders done—is there anything here that reflects upon the quality of existing management? Is there some person who was elected to the board at the last stockholders' meeting, who authorized these payments?

PROFESSOR SCHMIDT: No.

FIRST EX-GOVERNMENT OFFICIAL: And if there's not, if those people have been thrown out with the wash, then you can say, I think, with some candor, that the risk to this company is of losing future business.

PROFESSOR SCHMIDT: What about an investor who says, "Look, I will invest to the hilt in a company that pays bribes in Country X, because in Country X, that is just as traditional as shish kebab, and everybody does it, and everybody knows about it."

FIRST EX-GOVERNMENT OFFICIAL: I don't want my money to go someplace that doesn't participate in that market.

PROFESSOR SCHMIDT: "But in Country Y, if the fact of this payment comes out, that will be the end of future deals for a while, and could be a big loss." So another investor says, "Me, I'm trying to decide whether to buy Precision stock or stock in a rival company. And if I know that Precision has got this questionable-payment problem in Olay, I might want to buy the rival stock because the rival company has got questionable-payment problems only in Shish Kebab, or some other country where it doesn't matter so much."

FIRST EX-GOVERNMENT OFFICIAL: You run the risk of losing a good investor.

PROFESSOR SCHMIDT: You run the risk of failing to inform an intelligent investor of something very material.

FIRST EX-GOVERNMENT OFFICIAL: It's a long argument, obviously, but it seems to me that the sense of the securities laws is satisfied if you disclose the risk of future profit and loss.

SECOND REPORTER: Even though a company has already signed a consent agreement with the SEC and has just violated that?

FIRST EX-GOVERNMENT OFFICIAL: Well, they haven't violated it, if the first time the person in charge learned of the payment, he took whatever action was necessary to make the required revelation. Some consent decrees do preclude the company from making the payments. But most of them preclude the company from making material payments without disclosing them.

PROFESSOR SCHMIDT: I'll take one more comment on this.

SECOND BUSINESSMAN: I want to ask a question. It seems to me you've moved very rapidly from the term "questonable payments" to what appears now to be "bribe." My question is, is it illegal in Olay to have made the kind of payment you're referring to or not, because the term "questionable payment" is a very fuzzy thing. A bribe is something very clear.

PROFESSOR SCHMIDT: Yes, it is illegal in Olay.

SECOND BUSINESSMAN: It is illegal in Olay.

PROFESSOR SCHMIDT: It's not the first time it's happened.

SECOND BUSINESSMAN: But it's illegal under the laws of Olay.

PROFESSOR SCHMIDT: That's right. Does that matter to you?

SECOND BUSINESSMAN: Very much so.

PROFESSOR SCHMIDT: Why?

SECOND BUSINESSMAN: Because if you're doing something that is legal in Olay, you may have a very different situation than if it's illegal in Olay. Indeed, it may not be illegal even under United States laws. For example, you may be using a person who holds a government job in a country, but you may be paying him a sales commission. If that's legal in Olay, there may not be a problem.

PROFESSOR SCHMIDT: But the question is, it is illegal in Olay, and the question is what level of detail you need to get into in disclosing to the SEC and to prospective investors—

SECOND BUSINESSMAN: You have a much heavier burden when it's illegal in the other country.

PROFESSOR SCHMIDT: I have not heard a dissent from the opinon that a very general level of disclosure is appropriate, that it's not necessary under the securities laws to identify the country or to identify the recipient.

FIRST EX-GOVERNMENT OFFICIAL: I don't think it has anything to do with whether it's legal or illegal—quite honestly.

PROFESSOR SCHMIDT: (*Asks the second ex-government official*) You're the director of the CIA and you get some bad news from the chief of your Middle Eastern desk, who comes in one morning and says, "Our best source of intelligence in Olay has a serious problem. He took a two-million-dollar questionable payment from the Precision Dynamics Corporation and now they're nosing around. If that fact is revealed in Olay, he will lose his head and you will lose an extremely productive source of intelligence." This is a guy well up in the defense ministry. And you hear, because you know it, that the Precision management is looking into this, and that a reporter is looking into it. Now, how would you proceed if you wanted to try to bottle up that story?

SECOND EX-GOVERNMENT OFFICIAL: It sounds like it's a little hard to get it back in the bottle right now. But I think the first thing I'd do is to make sure that my friend over in Olay was aware of this danger, and that we had a little extra airplane around to filch him out of the country and resettle him in Brazil with a new name, pretty soon.

In the meantime, on the off chance that we might be able to sit on his identity—as distinct from the rest of the story—I think I might, depending upon the government's relationships with Precision, go through someone who did a lot of business with Precision and its new management. I'd just say that we had a report that there had been some kind of questionable payment over in Olay, and that it was of considerable importance to us to know whether or not they knew who was involved.

PROFESSOR SCHMIDT: And you ask that of Olay and they say, "No, I don't know the identity."

SECOND EX-GOVERNMENT OFFICIAL: I say, "Well, in that case, I would just as soon leave it at that. You go ahead and do whatever you have to do, but if you do learn who is involved, then I would deeply appreciate a chance to make a pitch to you."

PROFESSOR SCHMIDT: Then he says, "You know, I've had this reporter bugging me, who keeps calling me up and giving me the name of the minister of defense. Now, it surprises me to think that he is taking bribes, but the reporter claims to have some documents. I don't know where they might have come from." What do you do then?

SECOND EX-GOVERNMENT OFFICIAL: What paper does the reporter work for? (*Laughter*)

PROFESSOR SCHMIDT: Oh, let's say for a leading newspaper.

SECOND EX-GOVERNMENT OFFICIAL: Well, I think I'd probably take a look at the problem, make a rough guess as to how many people the reporter had talked to and whether this had been nosed around elsewhere.

PROFESSOR SCHMIDT: You've dealt with the reporter before. This reporter plays it pretty close to the vest.

SECOND EX-GOVERNMENT OFFICIAL: If the reporter had a tradition of keeping the story quiet and not checking it with half the management, then it might be worth an appeal to the publisher or someone in the senior leadership.

PROFESSOR SCHMIDT: Let's try that and see how it works. What would you say?

SECOND EX-GOVERNMENT OFFICIAL: What I would say is that "I understand your reporter is nosing around on a story and apparently has some elements of a story and apparently has some names. I'd be very interested in knowing just exactly what names, because depending upon the names it might be terribly important that I have some chance to react and to try to convince somebody to leave a name out of whatever action is taken on the story."

FIRST PUBLISHER: Are you asking me what I'd do? I'd call up my editor. (*Laughter*) Seriously, I would confer with the editor.

PROFESSOR SCHMIDT: Well, our ex-government official hasn't told you why the story concerns him. All he's asked for is information that the reporter has or is in the process of developing so he can know how much of his cat is out of the bag. Now, do you need to call your editor?

FIRST PUBLISHER: Yes, I would call my editor, seriously, in any event, because we would discuss this together.

PROFESSOR SCHMIDT: (*Calls on the fourth editor*) What would you say when your publisher called you? Would you advise—

FIRST PUBLISHER: Well, there are certain principles that newspapers operate on. For instance, and our government official hasn't told us this, if he came to us and said an agent's life is in danger—

PROFESSOR SCHMIDT: He hasn't said that yet.

FIRST PUBLISHER: He hasn't said anything. He just wants to know names, but we're not going to tell him.

PROFESSOR SCHMIDT: All he said is "I have some information that your reporter is working on something that may be very important to me. Would you let me know what the reporter has?"

FIRST PUBLISHER: Well, I would ask my editor to confer with the government official, and I would be in on it.

PROFESSOR SCHMIDT: Okay. Confer.

A VOICE: Could I interrupt and ask where that conference would be held?

SECOND EX-GOVERNMENT OFFICIAL: At the newspaper's office, probably.

PROFESSOR SCHMIDT: Okay, you're in the offices of the newspaper.

FOURTH EDITOR: Well, I would tell the publisher the status of the case, if the publisher didn't know already. That's the first thing. The second thing would be to decide whether there is any reason to tell the director of the CIA, and I can't think of one.

PROFESSOR SCHMIDT: Well, he's told you that the story is very important to him and that it may involve risk to someone's life.

FIRST PUBLISHER: No, he hasn't.

FOURTH EDITOR: Has he just added that?

SECOND EX-GOVERNMENT OFFICIAL: I just said it could be very important.

FOURTH EDITOR: I would probably say: "Look, if we know the identity of this person, if we can find it out, you certainly can find it out." And I don't believe—here comes the pitch. I mean, it sounds like the original thing to the reporter about money sounding like a con. This sounds a little bit to me like, "I'm the only person that knows it," and I don't believe it.

PROFESSOR SCHMIDT: Let me put some words into the government official's mouth. He says, "Mr. Editor, I'm going to tell you something in strict confidence."

FOURTH EDITOR: I'd say, right away, please don't.

PROFESSOR SCHMIDT: You mean, he can't tell you something—

FOURTH EDITOR: Not if he's made a big trip down, and you know, he doesn't move out of that office all that often. (*Laughter*)

PROFESSOR SCHMIDT: How is he going to see you otherwise?

FOURTH EDITOR: I'm going to get taken. I can just tell you right now, I'm going to get taken if I listen to him.

SECOND EX-GOVERNMENT OFFICIAL: I think at that point I would say, "Now, wait a minute, I would like to say that there is a very serious threat to human life involved here." At that point, I would drop that. In other words, I'm trying to get away without saying it, but at this point, I'm saying that there is something very dangerous here.

PROFESSOR SCHMIDT: Let me again, if you don't mind, put a few words in his mouth. Since the reporter is just working on one of these run-of-the-mill stories—they are a dime a dozen—

FOURTH EDITOR: Who says this?

PROFESSOR SCHMIDT: The government official. It's another Middle Eastern high official who is bribed. That's happened before and it will happen again. The guy happens to be our best source of intelligence—

FOURTH EDITOR: And you won't let me stop him from telling me this.

PROFESSOR SCHMIDT: No. He says, "Wait a minute, hear me out. This guy is our best source of intelligence. If you print this story about his receiving a bribe, to be sure, a story of some public interest—but weigh that against the intelligence value of this guy. Oh, and by the way, if you print this story, the guy is going to lose his life, too."

FOURTH EDITOR: There are two different things here. The life—I don't like that, and I'd say, "How long will it take you to get him out?"

PROFESSOR SCHMIDT: (*To the ex-government official*) How long?

SECOND EX-GOVERNMENT OFFICIAL: Three days, five days?

PROFESSOR SCHMIDT: Five days. (*Laughter*)

FOURTH EDITOR: No, no.

PROFESSOR SCHMIDT: Why?

FOURTH EDITOR: Because I don't believe it. Where is he?

PROFESSOR SCHMIDT: He's in Olay.

FOURTH EDITOR: You've got planes. (*Laughter*)

SECOND EX-GOVERNMENT OFFICIAL: He can't get on the airplane, I've got to get a guy in there to hide him in a mail sack and carry him out some way. It's going to take three days to get him out.

FOURTH EDITOR: This is a fantasy. We're dreaming, all of us.

SECOND EX-GOVERNMENT OFFICIAL: In fact, three days is quick.

PROFESSOR SCHMIDT: What do you say? Three days.

FOURTH EDITOR: Come on!

PROFESSOR SCHMIDT: What's going to happen in three days?

FOURTH EDITOR: Is the story ready to run?

PROFESSOR SCHMIDT: The story is ready to run. The reporter has verified these documents.

FOURTH EDITOR: He's going to die. Somehow I know he's going to die if I print it.

PROFESSOR SCHMIDT: You know, the government official said—

FOURTH EDITOR: Well, I don't always believe the government official. (*Laughter*) No, I have great respect for him, but he's lied before, and he should have.

PROFESSOR SCHMIDT: Tell me something I don't understand. Slowly. What's the difference between publishing it today and publishing it three days from now?

FOURTH EDITOR: Well, it's there, and I don't believe that nothing will happen if I don't run it for three days.

SECOND EX-GOVERNMENT OFFICIAL: The king of the country said he'd execute anybody who was accused of receiving bribes. It's a statement and he did execute somebody.

PROFESSOR SCHMIDT: I·still want to know the difference between tomorrow and three days from now.

FOURTH EDITOR: It's all the difference in the world.

PROFESSOR SCHMIDT: Three days' difference.

FOURTH EDITOR: If you wait three days, something will happen.

PROFESSOR SCHMIDT: It's not an election tomorrow. This isn't a question of whether you reveal the fact that the candidate for office is a Soviet agent.

FOURTH EDITOR: My competitor is on this story. So is another newspaper. I tell you, every time somebody has said it doesn't make any difference, they're wrong.

PROFESSOR SCHMIDT: It's competitive pressure.

FOURTH EDITOR: It *is* competitive pressure.

FIRST TV EXECUTIVE: Wait a minute. I've got the story, too. (*Applause*) I'm going with it tomorrow. (*Laughter*)

PROFESSOR SCHMIDT: That competitive pressure is more important to avoid—

FOURTH EDITOR: Okay, if I've got the story alone, and an impassioned plea by a very skillful advocate, I suspect—

PROFESSOR SCHMIDT: He's not on his knees. He's just telling you.

FOURTH EDITOR: We might hold our breath and wait, and then listen to it on television the next day. (*Laughter*)

PROFESSOR SCHMIDT: Now I'm going to put some words in the government official's mouth that I know he wouldn't utter, but I just want to see how you'd react. He says, "Look, I'll do some horse-trading with you. This isn't that big a story in terms of the public interest. If you will sit on this one, I'll give you a really big one that doesn't happen to jeopardize my intelligence methods. I've got something on Idi Amin that you wouldn't believe." (*Laughter*)

FOURTH EDITOR: You can't have anything on Idi Amin I wouldn't believe. (*Laughter*)

FOURTH EDITOR: And he shows it to me?

PROFESSOR SCHMIDT: Well, he says, if you'll make this deal—

FOURTH EDITOR: No, I've got to see it.

PROFESSOR SCHMIDT: Make this deal with me. If I can provide you with a story that you think is ten times as valuable—

FOURTH EDITOR: "What's the story?" I would ask.

PROFESSOR SCHMIDT: He says, "I'll let you decide. I want to make the deal first. I don't want to give you the story unless you tell me you'll kill the other one."

FOURTH EDITOR: No, I'm not going to kill the other one unless I see the story.

PROFESSOR SCHMIDT: All right, supposing you see it and it is ten times more interesting.

FOURTH EDITOR: And the guy's life is still in danger? I think I'd make the deal. (*Laughter*)

PROFESSOR SCHMIDT: Supposing you couldn't make a deal with him. Would you print what he told you, namely, that the guy who received this bribe is also a CIA agent? Now, your reporter didn't find that out. That's what the government official told you in the effort to persuade you not to print.

FOURTH EDITOR: And he was dumb enough to come in with no ground rules? He hadn't said anything?

PROFESSOR SCHMIDT: He said, "In strictest confidence, I have to tell you something—"

FOURTH EDITOR: Well, no, the "in strictest confidence" is an implied "off the record," and I don't betray that. But if he hadn't said that—

PROFESSOR SCHMIDT: So that form of words is more important than this guy's life?

FOURTH EDITOR: No. Now, wait a minute, I've already made the deal, I thought. I'm waiting for this other one.

PROFESSOR SCHMIDT: But you're saying you would withhold the story that the CIA had an agent who was the minister of defense of Olay, because—

FOURTH EDITOR: I've got one ten times better.

PROFESSOR SCHMIDT: The government official said "in strictest confidence."

FOURTH EDITOR: No, I've lost you. I thought I withheld it because I was getting one ten times better.

SECOND EX-GOVERNMENT OFFICIAL: No, we didn't make that deal.

FOURTH EDITOR: We didn't make that deal.

PROFESSOR SCHMIDT: I'm saying that you didn't make the deal. (*Asks the first TV executive*) What about you? If the government official came in to you and said, "In strictest confidence, you've got hold of something and you don't realize how damaging it is to our interests. This guy is not only pocketing some questionable payments, but he's also our agent." What would you do?

FIRST TV EXECUTIVE: I'd go.

PROFESSOR SCHMIDT: Go with what?

FIRST TV EXECUTIVE: I'd go with the story up to the point that I knew it.

PROFESSOR SCHMIDT: Including the fact that he's a CIA agent?

FIRST TV EXECUTIVE: He told me that in strictest confidence, which again is what we just said, that's off the record.

PROFESSOR SCHMIDT: So again, the words "in strictest confidence" justify withholding that story from the public.

FIRST TV EXECUTIVE: There are certain terms of art in this business of journalism, which we, in our trade, craft or skill, accept as binding upon us, and in fact, there are gradations of that. There are "on the record," "off the record," "on background," "deep background," and several others that Henry Kissinger made up when he used to call himself a "government spokesman" and things of that sort. If somebody came into my office and applied those rules, we would operate under them. Indeed, if I have a story, it seems to me that journalism, both broadcasting and print, is filled with examples of cases in which people have come to us and, not in strictest confidence, but appealing to all kinds of higher duty, have convinced us that we should not go with various stories.

The Bay of Pigs comes to mind, as an opener. The *New York Times* has yet to live that one down. And the prestige of an individual who comes to us is meaningless; for example, we recently had a man who, for a long time, insisted that there was a third-rate burglary somewhere, and that, indeed, was a very prestigious office.

I don't believe any of that.

PROFESSOR SCHMIDT: Let me try to frame the question. Why is it more important for you to abide by your own internal standards of what terms of art mean, like "in strict confidence"? You abide by that rule, even if the consequence of that is to keep from the public a story of tremendous interest, right? That's your craft, that's what you said. Those are the rules of the game.

SECOND EDITOR: I think, if I may, he's withholding only the fact that this man is with the CIA. He's not withholding the story itself.

PROFESSOR SCHMIDT: That is correct. I understand that.

SECOND EDITOR: Professor Schmidt, I think if you changed the question— the real problem that our government official has when he comes in is that he's given a lead. When you say "off the record," then the question is—well, it may be off the record, but if I could get the information from somebody else—or if the reporter then comes in and says: "Gee, you know, this guy is going to be executed, and I've got a hint that he may be working for the CIA," then the managing editor is in a hell of a spot because he's sitting there knowing full well it's a CIA man. His own reporter has come up with the lead, and he's got to decide how to handle that question. Those are the kinds of real problems you get into. These things you've been talking about, I think, we all have handled very easily.

PROFESSOR SCHMIDT: But as I understand our TV executive, he would not run the fact that this man is a CIA agent.

SECOND EDITOR: No, no, that's not it. You have two points here. One point is, his reporter gets the story on his or her own.

PROFESSOR SCHMIDT: Of the questionable payment.

SECOND EDITOR: No. The reporter's got a hint that he belongs to the CIA or is an agent. The second issue is, he goes home that night and he says,

"I wish I hadn't gotten that off the record," and he picks up the phone and tries to develop separate information to prove independently of the government official's visit.

PROFESSOR SCHMIDT: He comes in and he says, "I'm going to tell you something in the strictest confidence, and you—"

FOURTH EDITOR: You shouldn't listen. That's why you should stop him right there.

FIRST TV EXECUTIVE: That's right. He shouldn't come in the first place. If you're really talking about this kind of a life-and-death situation, you are dealing with probably the leading edge, the thin edge of a problem that doesn't happen all the time. What does happen, if I can come back to the media and business, is that we're never confronted with life-and-death situations. In the real world, it is not very often that the head of the CIA is going to come into my office, or that the head of a major company is going to come into my office and say, "Hey, off the record." It's just not going to happen that way.

PROFESSOR SCHMIDT: All right, we've opened up a subject that I want to pursue from some various directions—you might call it "cooperation with the CIA." What I would like to do for a few minutes is back away from the hypothetical case and pursue a detour that aims at developing some parallel questions about the willingness of business to cooperate with the CIA and the willingness of the media to cooperate with the CIA.

PROFESSOR SCHMIDT: (*Calls on the first banker*) If your business took you to foreign countries and, in the course of that business, you had interviews with leading governmental officials in foreign countries, and if the director of the CIA came to you and said, "We value your judgment very highly. We would appreciate it very much if you would share with us your evaluations of the foreign officials whom you see when you get back. Now, we don't want you to do anything that you wouldn't do in the normal course of your business. But, when your business brings you in contact with the Chancellor of the Exchequer, if it does, we'd like your impressions of him—his physical health, his mental health, his attitude to the world, his attitude to the United States." Would you make your knowledge available to the CIA under those circumstances?

FIRST BANKER: I think the question in today's value system would be whether or not you want to act as an "agent" for the CIA, rather than whether or not you want to make that information available. I would make that information available to a newspaper reporter who asked me. I would make it available to a member—

PROFESSOR SCHMIDT: They didn't happen to ask, though. The CIA happened to ask and you're not an agent. They don't pay you. They don't make it easy for you to get an exit visa. They don't do anything for you.

FIRST BANKER: I see nothing the matter with that, whatsoever, whether it's the Department of State or whether it's the secretary of the treasury. I'm an American citizen. I live here. My government asks me not to be a spy, not to subvert my integrity, not to do anything, as you phrase the question, but to tell what I think of Denis Healey. I don't see anything the matter with that, and I would do it, of course.

PROFESSOR SCHMIDT: (*Calls on the fifth editor*) Is that a newsworthy story? If you learned that the banker went down to the CIA on the day after his return from foreign travels and shared his impressions?

FIFTH EDITOR: I doubt it.

PROFESSOR SCHMIDT: Why not? How about this: "Banker Cooperates with CIA?" ? (*Laughter*)

FIFTH EDITOR: I haven't had a chance to think about it, in terms of putting it into any categories, but my instinct is that the fact that this banker goes in and talks with somebody from the CIA is probably not a story.

PROFESSOR SCHMIDT: Would you be free about disclosing to a journalist the fact that you had agreed to provide this service for the CIA?

FIRST BANKER: Well, I didn't agree to provide a service. What you said to me is that if I went abroad, and they asked me for my impressions when I came home, would I tell it to the CIA, the Treasury, or anybody else. Now, if you change the ground rules and say, "Will you be their agent?" that's an entirely different ball game.

PROFESSOR SCHMIDT: That comes in a minute. (*Laughter*) But now I'm simply asking whether once you have agreed to share your impressions with the CIA, you'd share them with me if I called you. I don't happen to call; the CIA does. Are you at all reticent about making that information available to the press? You haven't done anything wrong; you think you've done your patriotic duty.

FIRST BANKER: As the gentleman says, it would cause a lot of yawns in the press. It's not a story. It's possible that somebody in the press would ask you. The consultations that go on between government officials and the private sector are almost continuous.

FOURTH EDITOR: I think it is a story.

PROFESSOR SCHMIDT: You do? What does it say?

FOURTH EDITOR: If major bank presidents and industrialists are routinely reporting to the Central Intelligence Agency what they hear from foreign officials, of course it's a story.

SECOND EX-GOVERNMENT OFFICIAL: Would it be a story if it was reported to the State Department?

FOURTH EDITOR: Probably less important.

PROFESSOR SCHMIDT: Why?

FIRST BANKER: A lesser headline, but just as important. The question you said, routinely—

PROFESSOR SCHMIDT: What's the difference?

FOURTH EDITOR: The difference is the use to which this information might be put.

PROFESSOR SCHMIDT: To wit?

FOURTH EDITOR: I don't know.

PROFESSOR SCHMIDT: The CIA is trying to figure out what's going on over there. The State Department is also trying to figure that out.

FIRST BANKER: Newspapers are trying to figure it out. I'd tell you, too.

PROFESSOR SCHMIDT: I want to move on to the next step. (*Turns to the third businessman*) Supposing the CIA came to you and said, "Look, you have a lot of foreign operations in your company. We're very anxious to get a certain agent into the country of Olay." Now, forget about the questionable payments and all that stuff. We're on a detour.

"You have an operation in Olay, chemical refining, I don't know what. We would like you to provide this CIA agent with cover. It happens to be a woman. Would you set her up as a secretary in your operation in Olay? That's all you have to do, just give her the cover. You don't even have to pay her. We will reimburse you for whatever it costs, whatever her salary is." Would you do that?

THIRD BUSINESSMAN: The answer is no in today's world.

PROFESSOR SCHMIDT: What would it have been yesterday, and what's the difference?

THIRD BUSINESSMAN: If you go back far enough into yesterday's world, the answer might have been, "If it's important enough, we'll think about it."

PROFESSOR SCHMIDT: What's the difference?

THIRD BUSINESSMAN: The difference is that the country today perceives the CIA and its operation in a different way. In yesterday, we would have started from the premise that as citizens we have an obligation to assist the government in proper ways. In today's world, we would walk away and say, "The country won't stand for it, and if it wants to solve this problem, it will have to do it in a different way."

PROFESSOR SCHMIDT: (*Asks the fourth businessman*) Is that your reaction? You're asked to provide cover, now, for a CIA agent.

FOURTH BUSINESSMAN: It's a tempting reaction, but I guess I'd want to satisfy myself about the nature of the mission of this agent.

PROFESSOR SCHMIDT: Well, we'll try that two ways. First, it's to read whatever public information is published in the country. It's to collect facts, to keep her eyes open and just to inform us about a lot of things.

FOURTH BUSINESSMAN: I'd want to know why the CIA can't get that from just going and talking to employees that we already have there.

PROFESSOR SCHMIDT: Well, they need a trained person to do that.

FOURTH BUSINESSMAN: Well, I think I'd be more inclined to be willing to do it than the last speaker.

PROFESSOR SCHMIDT: Okay, supposing they need someone in place to handle transactions between agents inside the country and agents outside the country—a kind of a drop-off point or a bag woman or whatever it would be called.

FOURTH BUSINESSMAN: Could it jeopardize our operations over there?

A VOICE: I didn't hear that question.

PROFESSOR SCHMIDT: He wants to know if it will jeopardize his operations over there, in case it becomes public. The headline you don't want to see, your company provides cover for the CIA. Why don't you want to see that headline? For the same reason that the last speaker indicated?

FOURTH BUSINESSMAN: I think so, but I think I'd be prepared to accept a little bit of that headline if I were satisfied that all we were doing was assisting in gathering information.

PROFESSOR SCHMIDT: Because any association with the CIA these days is—the CIA is the tar baby, as far as the American public is concerned.

FOURTH BUSINESSMAN: I think the second case you have, though, in which the agent is actively in contact with spies, let us say locals, is more serious. One of them could be arrested. She could be arrested. There's no question about it—she wouldn't have diplomatic status. Then the company would be involved in some fashion in an espionage action, which is illegal under their laws. Then it does blow back on the company.

PROFESSOR SCHMIDT: So you're concerned not only about the American public's reaction, but about the fact that you might run into penalties abroad. You might be declared *persona non grata* in some countries that don't like the CIA.

FOURTH BUSINESSMAN: Yes.

PROFESSOR SCHMIDT: Those are essentially business judgments?

FOURTH BUSINESSMAN: Well, I think it's a balancing of the responsibility to assist one's government and the consequences of that assistance.

PROFESSOR SCHMIDT: (*Asks the fifth businessman*) Suppose the CIA came to you and said, "You are the only person in the United States with the scientific training, the engineering knowledge, and the organization to build us a special kind of vessel that could drag up a Russian submarine from the deep waters." And let's suppose that it happens that you are the head of the only company in the United States that builds this class of vessels—deep-sea drilling vessels or mining vessels. They're willing to pay for this extraordinary vessel, but it has to be kept completely secret. Indeed, there has to be a cover story. There has to be, for public consumption, a claim that you're not building this for the CIA, you're building this for Howard Hughes.

Would you do it?

FIFTH BUSINESSMAN: I wish you hadn't brought up Howard Hughes. That stretches the imagination a little too much. (*Laughter*)

PROFESSOR SCHMIDT: Well, I want to give the story a sort of family resemblance.

FIFTH BUSINESSMAN: Until you said that, I was thinking that the moment the CIA contacted me and began the very first sentence in connection with this, I would make a quick assumption in my mind that very likely I'm going to be doing this. I'm going to do it. I would make that assumption because I would say that bringing up that Russian submarine is a sensible thing for the United States to do. And they're right—my organization is the right one to do it. I'd concern myself with doing it right, which includes not only the technical aspects, but the matter of secrecy and other matters that relate to secrecy and the CIA and its other activities.

First of all, I would give them a lot of trouble on the question of being so doggone secret about it. I would argue that it's impractical, it's going to get out. Doing this will require that there be a very large number of specialists involved. They will know what's going on, so there will be a certain amount of leakage to be expected. The leakage will occur in other areas, as well. We will not be the only company that has something to do with this. There will be few repercussions and little evidence built up. One way or another—

PROFESSOR SCHMIDT: May I just interject something? He also wants you to operate this vessel, go out there and actually fish up the submarine, and he says, "That's a risky business because if the Russians know you're out there doing that, they may try to blow you up out there. However, our intelligence sources in the Soviet Union are good enough, we think, that if they find out that this plan is in process, we'll know that they find out, and we'll scratch the whole thing."

FIFTH BUSINESSMAN: Well, you anticipated something I was going to shift to. When I said I'd want to see that they do it right, one of my concerns was the aspect of secrecy. The other had to do with dangers of the kind that you're talking about. In this instance, I wouldn't trust the Defense Department or the CIA to have an adequate evaluation of what could happen if and when the Soviet Union finds out about it, as I assume would certainly be the case, perhaps before we were finished. I therefore would say we need a plan in which we do certain things and the Defense Department, possibly the Navy, takes over at a certain point, in order to try to police or minimize or reduce almost to zero the chances of my company's being involved in a war. (*Laughter*)

Now, having talked about both of these things, if you want a quick guess, without a very long dissertation, which I'm sure you do, I think it would be possible to so arrange the project that there would be a reasonably good chance that the part that my company should do could get done, and the transfer be made, before it becomes public knowledge, before it becomes known to the Soviet Union.

PROFESSOR SCHMIDT: How do you write the headline, five years down the road? "XYZ Industries Engages in Secret Project with the CIA, Operates Secret CIA Naval Recovery Project."

FIFTH BUSINESSMAN: To me, that's trivial—the negative public relations resulting from association with CIA: I'm cocky enough to think that our reputation would survive it. The real question is, is it a good thing to do?

Is it a sensible thing to do? Is it in every way defensible as we would see it from the standpoint of ethics and every other consideration. This is one reason I suggest that the CIA announce that they're going to bring up the submarine.

PROFESSOR SCHMIDT: Let me ask a couple of other questions. The CIA says you may not share this information with your board of directors.

FIFTH BUSINESSMAN: Then I can't accept the project.

PROFESSOR SCHMIDT: You could tell two members of your board.

FIFTH BUSINESSMAN: Not enough.

PROFESSOR SCHMIDT: You'd have to tell your whole board?

FIFTH BUSINESSMAN: I have to be able to tell the board—

PROFESSOR SCHMIDT: Even if you have a fifth columnist, whom the SEC has forced you to take on your board?

FIFTH BUSINESSMAN: Well, first of all, I'm assuming that I would ask my chief outside counsel, who is the best in the world for this type of thing, and who incidentally would never be allowed to be a member of our board, about that question. I'm guessing that he would suggest that I go to the board and say: "We have a special, highly classified project. I cannot tell you any more. Naturally, we can't do it without permission from the board. Would you, the board of directors, be willing to appoint a small committee of the board that would be cleared and have full access? If they agree to do the project, would you then go along with it, and in effect, cause the majority of the board to go with it?"

PROFESSOR SCHMIDT: How much of this do you think you'd have to disclose to the SEC?

FIFTH BUSINESSMAN: Initially, I would again, of course, go to the attorney, and I'm only guessing—

PROFESSOR SCHMIDT: (*Turns to the second lawyer*) What would you say?

SECOND LAWYER: Well, there's a national security provision in the securities law, so that classified information gets protection, and—

PROFESSOR SCHMIDT: Do you have to tell the SEC, though, even if you don't publicize the information—do you have to say, "We have classified—"

SECOND LAWYER: The process, as I understand it, is that you go to the Defense Department and you get a letter from the Defense Department with respect to the project. You do not impart that information to the SEC.

FIRST EX-GOVERNMENT OFFICIAL: Let's put that in a more realistic context. You don't have to say anything to the SEC ever. The issue is whether or not your cover is misleading your stockholders as to the kind of business you're in. If, for example, you go around and say, "We're about to go into the mining of nodules in the ocean floor, and it's the greatest thing since sliced bread, and we're going to make a lot of money on it," and that's your cover, and if people say, "We have always wanted to invest in nodules," then you've got a problem—not with the SEC, not with the defense contractors, but with stockholders and prospective stockholders, because you've misled them as to material facts.

PROFESSOR SCHMIDT: Suppose you don't say anything about this project?

FIRST EX-GOVERNMENT OFFICIAL: The only requirement is not to misrepresent the earnings of the company. If there's a chance that your whole company is going to be pinpointed for a special strike by the Soviets, then of course you've got a few worries. But that isn't a realistic worry in the case that you've given.

FIFTH BUSINESSMAN: Realistically, we would not take on the project unless we felt the combination of these factors was right. I'm saying that I would initially be optimistic that the right combination could be worked out. That would include, for all practical purposes, no cover story because we have a perfect right to be out there with various ships.

In fact, making an announcement about doing something as technologically spectacular as building a special ship to bring up nodules from the deep ocean floor would get more interest from the Soviet Union than announcing that you're going to bring up their submarine.

PROFESSOR SCHMIDT: What would happen if you announced that the *Glomar* was being built in order to bring up a Russian submarine?

SECOND EX-GOVERNMENT OFFICIAL: They'd have a Soviet destroyer follow it all through the sea, every day.

PROFESSOR SCHMIDT: And then what would happen?

SECOND EX-GOVERNMENT OFFICIAL: As soon as it stopped and started to operate, the destroyer would nudge against it and push it away and make it impossible to continue with the operation.

PROFESSOR SCHMIDT: It would ruin the project.

FIFTH BUSINESSMAN: Meanwhile, you'd have the real ship in another location. (*Laughter*)

SECOND EX-GOVERNMENT OFFICIAL: Let me say one thing. We have a very important job in mind for you. (*Laughter*)

PROFESSOR SCHMIDT: What I hear, I believe, from the business people present, is that they are willing to cooperate with the CIA so long as an objective assessment of the business risks and public-relations risks of that cooperation is taken and measured against the values of that cooperation—they assess that, and if they're satisfied that the pluses outweigh the minuses, then they cooperate.

Now, I'd like to ask our first editor what his reaction would be if he engaged in a series of foreign trips during which he interviewed the heads of foreign governments and so on, and the CIA came to him and said the same thing to him that they said to our banker, which was, you remember, "We don't want you to do anything you wouldn't otherwise do. We're not paying you. We're not doing anything. Would you share with us your impressions of these foreign people; that is, any impressions that you don't get around to putting into your stories."

FIRST EDITOR: No.

PROFESSOR SCHMIDT: Why not?

FIRST EDITOR: Absolutely not.

PROFESSOR SCHMIDT: Absolutely not.

FIRST EDITOR: Apart from any other consideration, it would undermine my professional capacity as a newspaperman. It would give me a double role and I think that, journalistically, I could serve my society a lot better by sticking to journalism than by acting in a double role.

PROFESSOR SCHMIDT: The CIA representative says, "We'll talk to you on Sundays, when you're not working. We won't take up your time at the paper." How does it undermine your role?

FIRST EDITOR: Because you enter into an understanding with your readers that you are a journalist, and also with your sources, and you don't play a double game with them.

PROFESSOR SCHMIDT: I'm not suggesting that you should disclose any confidences. I'm just saying that all the CIA wants is to read your stories and then talk to you about any further impressions that you got. "He looked a little sick." You wouldn't put that in a story because you didn't know it, but you might mention that to the CIA, as a kind of hypothesis of yours.

FIRST EDITOR: Yes. Well, both reporters and editors follow a policy which we regard as ethically and practically important: we do not play a double role; we don't pose as being something that we are not.

PROFESSOR SCHMIDT: (*Asks the first banker*) Were you playing a double role, posing as being something you were not, when you agreed to share your impressions?

FIRST BANKER: No. I was asked when I returned, according to your question.

PROFESSOR SCHMIDT: That's right.

FIRST BANKER: I would share the impressions with the CIA, and I said I would share them with anybody. In the editor's case, he can sell them, because he's a newspaper editor. I can't sell them, so I don't see why in one it's playing a double role and in the other it isn't. I'm baffled.

FIRST EDITOR: Well, I'm not questioning what a banker might do. As far as he is concerned, I think that if he and his organization were routinely providing information to the CIA, it would be a story. I would hazard to say society as a whole would regard it as a questionable practice.

PROFESSOR SCHMIDT: More of a story than a bank's cooperating.

FIRST EDITOR: Journalistically, I would not, under any circumstances, consider it.

PROFESSOR SCHMIDT: (*Asks the fourth editor*) Is that the way you see it?

FOURTH EDITOR: I don't see anything wrong at all with a banker's providing information to the CIA.

PROFESSOR SCHMIDT: How about you?

FOURTH EDITOR: It's a fine line of work, but it's not the one I chose.

PROFESSOR SCHMIDT: Well, neither did he. He's not working for the CIA. He's not being paid by the CIA.

FOURTH EDITOR: A newspaper must avoid all official connections with government. In a communist society, there are very close connections. Absence of such connections is a very complete definition of democracy.

SECOND EX-GOVERNMENT OFFICIAL: Would you talk to the American ambassador or to the chief of station?

FOURTH EDITOR: Yes, and routinely. Every newspaperman routinely talks to CIA station chiefs in remote countries, where they eat together and they drink together.

SECOND EX-GOVERNMENT OFFICIAL: And they exchange information.

FOURTH EDITOR: Well, yes.

PROFESSOR SCHMIDT: Why isn't that a much closer connection than providing the CIA with your impressions? We've now moved to the next stage in this, which is the question of whether a journalist would trade information with a CIA agent in a foreign country.

FIFTH EDITOR: I think there is one point that has to be clarified. As you put the question originally, the CIA was asking the banker before he went, whether he would agree to share his impressions. I think there's a little bit more of an implication—

PROFESSOR SCHMIDT: I'll make it any way you want. They don't ask you until you get back from the trip. Is your answer that there should be absolutely no connection? The definition of democracy is that I have no connection with you, unless you have some information that I want, in which case maybe we can make a deal that I'll tell you what I know if you'll give me something good.

FOURTH EDITOR: Well, realistically, I think what is likely to happen is that somebody with whom you had some contact in the CIA, maybe someone you had interviewed out in Saigon or something like that, would call up and say, "Let's go to lunch."

PROFESSOR SCHMIDT: (*Asks the first editor*) What would you say at that point?

FIRST EDITOR: I would say no.

PROFESSOR SCHMIDT: There's free lunch. (*Laughter*)

FIRST EDITOR: As an editor, I would say no.

PROFESSOR SCHMIDT: Undermines your credibility—it's playing a double role if you have lunch with a CIA agent who may have some good information for you.

FIRST EDITOR: As an editor, that's true, I wouldn't do it.

A VOICE: What about a KGB agent?

FOURTH EDITOR: Yes, I'd have lunch with him.

PROFESSOR SCHMIDT: Is this still a democracy if your fourth editor is willing to have this lunch and trade information? That sounds like a connection to me.

FOURTH EDITOR: Yes, but he's going to get the short end of the deal. I don't know anything that I haven't written. (*Laughter*)

PROFESSOR SCHMIDT: You don't? Nothing?

FOURTH EDITOR: Very little.

PROFESSOR SCHMIDT: (*Recognizes the second lawyer*)

SECOND LAWYER: (*Addresses the first editor*) I was curious, if Cy Vance were to call and ask "Did Brezhnev seem short of breath?" would you still tell him, "I can't tell you that"?

FIRST EDITOR: If I have a conversation with—

SECOND LAWYER: He calls you, he's on the board of your paper and he's a friend and he calls you, and he says, "I know you saw him. Did he seem short of breath?"

FIRST EDITOR: It would depend upon the nature of the question. (*Laughter*)

SECOND LAWYER: That's the question.

FIRST EDITOR: If it were a question about the shortness of breath, I don't think I'd have any hesitation in replying to it.

SECOND LAWYER: But knowing that Cy Vance was going to report that to Turner of the CIA and every other decision-maker in the government?

FIRST EDITOR: There's a distinct difference between having a direct contact with an intelligence agency and having it through the intermediary of the Secretary of State.

PROFESSOR SCHMIDT: I think I know what the answers to my next three questions are, but I've got these parallels on the brain. The CIA says, "You've got an operation in London. Will you take one of our agents on as a typist and provide her with cover?"

FIRST EDITOR: Of course not.

PROFESSOR SCHMIDT: Of course not. Why not?

FIRST EDITOR: Well, for all the obvious reasons. First of all, the CIA ought to do these things on its own. They shouldn't ask us for help. Second, it would totally undermine our integrity as journalists.

PROFESSOR SCHMIDT: To have a typist?

FIRST EDITOR: Yes.

PROFESSOR SCHMIDT: Why? She's not writing any stories.

FIRST EDITOR: It has nothing to do with whether she's writing stories or not writing stories. We're not in the business of providing cover for intelligence agents, in peacetime, I might add.

PROFESSOR SCHMIDT: I'm glad you said that, because I've got one more set of parallels to try out. (*Calls on the sixth businessman*) I'm now going to lay out a hypothesis even more absurd than all this fanciful stuff in the hypothetical, so get ready.

SIXTH BUSINESSMAN: It couldn't be more absurd than some of the things we get, but come on.

PROFESSOR SCHMDIT: I'd like to suppose that terrorists take over your nuclear facility, and they take some hostages in there, some of your employees. They threaten to blow up a metropolitan city and cause a catastrophic nuclear release unless their demands are met. They've got a long laundry list. You can't show *The Great Mohammed*; that movie has to be killed. There are a whole series of demands. One of them is that you go into that plant with a couple of your colleagues so the terrorists—let's make them environmental weather-people—can show you firsthand that your nuclear facility is made of crappy material and that this plant could blow up at any time.

Now, if you were inclined to go in there, and if the FBI asked, "If you go in there, will you take one of our agents in there and pretend that he's your assistant vice-president in charge of cooling pipes?"—what would be your answer?

SIXTH BUSINESSMAN: I'd take him.

PROFESSOR SCHMIDT: You'd take the FBI man in with you?

SIXTH BUSINESSMAN: Yes, sir.

PROFESSOR SCHMIDT: You don't even need to think about it?

SIXTH BUSINESSMAN: No, I'd take him.

PROFESSOR SCHMIDT: (*Asks the fourth editor*) Let's say the terrorists demand that one of your reporters go in there—let's put you in charge of a broadcasting operation. They want you to send them a big, well-known broadcaster, with a camera crew, so they can show the American people what crap this nuclear facility is made out of—just tin cans that can blow up any time—and let's suppose you are inclined to comply. The FBI comes to you and says, "You know, we have some people who are trained to be cameramen. We've got an agent who can go in there and do just as good a job with the camera as your cameraman. We want to get him in there so he can size up the defense" and so on. What would you do?

FOURTH EDITOR: After he's out, can I write a story about how he went in? (*Laughter*)

PROFESSOR SCHMIDT: No, not right away, because one of the terrorists' threats was they would shoot one of the hostages if any police came in there in the guise of reporters and cameramen.

You're satisfied, though, that this cameraman makes a very good impostor. This FBI agent really looks like a cameraman, so you think, on the whole, it will help the hostages to take this chance, to get a pro in there to size up the terrorists' weapons, to see how many of them there are. Would you do it?

FOURTH EDITOR: I don't know.

PROFESSOR SCHMIDT: Think about it.

FOURTH EDITOR: Yes.

PROFESSOR SCHMIDT: (*Calls on the first editor*) Do you need to think about it before you give me that answer?

FIRST EDITOR: Yes, I've already thought about it. I've been thinking about it while you've been putting my colleague on the griddle. My answer to that is, on the surface, it sounds as if it's a very straitlaced, a very safe position to take.

PROFESSOR SCHMIDT: Even humanitarian.

FIRST EDITOR: But the bottom line on this thing is that, as a journalist you protect the integrity of what you're doing, and you perform your function, which is too important to fritter away in isolated instances—no matter how important assistance of this character might be to the FBI.

PROFESSOR SCHMIDT: And that's because the next time you're asked to send reporters and cameramen into the scene of a terrorist operation, people might not believe you. Suppose you're not asked to do that every day. This is the first time it's ever happened to you. Isolated event. Once in a lifetime. Still, it's the principle that undermines your credibility, not the situation.

FIRST EDITOR: I find principle very closely related to reality.

PROFESSOR SCHMIDT: (*Acknowledges the fourth editor again*)

FOURTH EDITOR: I think I'd probably go ahead and cooperate. I would try to get rid of the silly restriction about waiting for three days. (*Laughter*)

PROFESSOR SCHMIDT: Until they get the terrorists out of there.

FOURTH EDITOR: You'd have to persuade me, because a cameraman is in there, a bona-fide cameraman. He's going to take pictures of the terrorists, which is why the FBI presumably wants to go in there in the first place. They've got the plans. The company man gave them the plans, quite properly, so I'm not quite sure of the purpose of putting the FBI man there.

PROFESSOR SCHMIDT: To get a trained law-enforcement, SWAT team in. They know where to look, more than your cameraman.

FOURTH EDITOR: I would quibble with you, but I'm not allowed to do that.

PROFESSOR SCHMIDT: You can report it all, as soon as they get the terrorists out of there.

FOURTH EDITOR: I think I'd do that.

PROFESSOR SCHMIDT: You would do that?

FOURTH EDITOR: I think so.

PROFESSOR SCHMIDT: (*Asks the second editor*)

SECOND EDITOR: Well, I think I probably would, too, although I would try to persuade you that you could hire some actors to go in instead, pretend—

PROFESSOR SCHMIDT: As long as they work for the FBI.

SECOND EDITOR: Right.

PROFESSOR SCHMIDT: Okay, I want to get back now into the hypothetical. End of this little detour about cooperation with the CIA and the different perspectives that business people have in terms of various problems of cooperation, as contrasted with the perspectives—and it's not a single, monolithic perspective—the different perspectives of members of the press. Pretty stand-offish, on the whole, but our fourth editor is willing to go to lunch with the CIA station manager, whatever he is, and is willing to take in that cameraman-FBI agent in this rare hypothetical situation.

All right, I'd like to come back to our first industrialist. I'd now like to expand the secrecy problem in this hypothetical. It's time now to stop keeping secrets from the journalists. We could play that out, but in the interests of time, let's explain to them what is going on.

There is in prospect a new missile that has the capability of avoiding Soviet anti-ballistic missile interception defense mechanisms. This new missile has been given the code name "Broken Field." I must say, I apologize; this part of the hypothetical case rests entirely on imagination rather than knowledge on my part. I disclaim any knowledge of the weapons capability, guidance mechanisms, or anything else. I ask you to accept the technological and military feasibility of this part of the problem as a given.

This new missile is guided by separate airborne radar-communications processes. So you've got this missile and it's taking directions from planes that are up in the air. What those planes are doing is looking at what comes up to hit that missile and telling the missile to take diversionary action. All right?

It turns out that what is necessary for this project to work is to have the government of Olay purchase some of these airborne guidance systems and to keep them in the air. So, if it turns out that we have to launch these missiles, the guidance system over Olay can steer the missiles when they get into the Soviet Union's airspace.

Now (*To the first reporter*), you get a call from someone who identifies himself as a member of the Israeli intelligence community. He says to you, "Our information is that Precision Dynamics is, with Pentagon approval, planning to sell the government of Olay six airborne communications surveillance systems. As far as we can see, the only function of those systems is to manage a land war. We, Israel, are the only logical targets of a land war, if Olay gets involved in one."

Now, to save time, I'm going to assume that you go to our first industrialist with this information, and he says, "You know, Israel doesn't quite have it all. These things that we want to sell Olay are not just communications systems to help Olay. That's what the Olay people think. There is a hidden function of these things that the Olays don't know about. That hidden function is to guide our missiles if we need to launch them.

"Don't publish the fact that there is this hidden function. The Olay people won't take it, and if the Soviets find out about it, then they'll shoot all these things down. As it is, all they'll think is that these are just AWACS, just regular communications radar surveillance systems."

What do you do with that story?

FIRST REPORTER: I guess the first thing I'd do is go to the Defense Department, go to the government, to confirm what I've been told—to see if this is substantiated by our own authorities.

PROFESSOR SCHMIDT: They say, "Yes, it's true, and it is vital that you do not disclose the hidden capacity of this AWACS system."

FIRST REPORTER: Once again, I'd go to my editor on this. I don't think we'd publish it, but I wouldn't make a decision like that.

PROFESSOR SCHMIDT: (*To the first editor*) What do you think?

FIRST EDITOR: I think we'd probably publish the story. I mean, I'd have to know more about it, but I'd publish it on the basis of the fact that, first of all, the Israelis would be leaking it all over the place. My competitor would publish it, if we didn't. Second, all of our experience in situations of this kind has been that the Russians generally are fully aware of what is happening. When we withhold information it is not from the Russians, but from the American public. So my answer is that we'd probably publish the story.

PROFESSOR SCHMIDT: Let me be clear. The Israelis tell you that a company is about to sell a bunch of AWACS to Olay. The function of those AWACS, the Israelis say, is to manage land war and air fighter conflicts in the Olay airspace. But when your reporter goes to the head of the company, he says, "What about that? That's going to upset the balance of peace." He says, "Look, there's this added hidden function in relation to guiding our missiles, and that function is hidden, not only from the Soviets, but from the Olays."

Now, how much of the story do you go with?

FIRST EDITOR: Well, first of all, we don't really accept everything that we get from the head of the company or from the Israelis. I mean, we check this out ourselves. We would bring in, for example, our Pentagon correspondent. It's already apparent to us that Olay lies south of the Soviet Union and that there is a relationship to the Soviet Union. We understand that.

PROFESSOR SCHMIDT: Not a friendly relationship, but a geographical one.

FIRST EDITOR: That's true, and so the story would probably be written on the basis of taking all of these factors into account. I don't think that we would necessarily publish a specific item of information that would imperil what we regard as the security of the United States.

PROFESSOR SCHMIDT: The specific item of information that would imperil the security of the United States is the fact that these guidance systems have a hidden capacity to guide U.S. missiles. Now, are you going to disclose that?

FIRST EDITOR: We might not disclose that specific point in the story. But I think we would publish the fact of the sale itself, particularly if it was going to affect the balance in the area.

PROFESSOR SCHMIDT: Right. Mr. Brzezinski comes to you. He's the National Security Advisor, and he says, "If you want to publish the fact that we're selling AWACS to Olay, fine. If you want to publish the fact that Israel regards that as upsetting the balance of power, fine. Just please do not publish the fact that these systems have sort of a piggyback, hidden technological function in relation to our own intercontinental missiles." You would accede to his request not to publish that central, secret fact, is that right?

FIRST EDITOR: Very possibly.

PROFESSOR SCHMIDT: All right. (*Turns to the fourth editor*) Do you agree with that?

FOURTH EDITOR: No, I don't, I'm afraid.

PROFESSOR SCHMIDT: Why not?

FOURTH EDITOR: Because I don't believe the given that Mr. Brzezinski told me. I have found that most—really, all—experience shows that the claim of national security doesn't work out. I suspect that—

PROFESSOR SCHMIDT: Whose experience?

FOURTH EDITOR: Mine.

PROFESSOR SCHMIDT: Yours is better than Mr. Brzezinski's on that score?

FOURTH EDITOR: Well, perhaps it's longer in listening to pleas from public officials. I mean, let me suggest something here. It would be perfectly obvious that if a plane had a capacity to manage land war, it would also have the capacity to guide missiles. As soon as this plane is in place, the Soviet intelligence people—they'd know about it in the early issue of *Aviation Week*.

PROFESSOR SCHMIDT: Mr. Brzezinski says, "I know it stretches credulity to imagine, but you wouldn't believe what XYZ Industries has invented— a laser-beam, highly directional communications technology, which, as far as we know, the Soviets can't intercept, so that this—"

FIFTH BUSINESSMAN: We'd better be clear about what your assumption is. There are some classified items in weapons systems that it is reasonable to assume you can keep secret from the Soviet Union for a while. It is to the advantage of our nation. Such a secret may come to the attention of the news media. They may be aware of the fact that it is a secret and they therefore have the problem that you're asking about—do they or don't they publish?

More often, I agree totally with the fourth editor, more often—well, the biggest category is the kind of weapons systems secrets which the Soviet Union has to be well aware of. It happens that this particular example is one that there would be no chance of keeping from the Soviet Union. The mere testing of it, the mere working out of it, would require the kind of signal emanation from the light that the Soviet Union would recognize. They would put two and two together, as would numerous other countries.

FIFTH BUSINESSMAN: What you want us to suppose is the fact that it is something that is secret.

PROFESSOR SCHMIDT: It is something that is secret, and as far as the CIA and everybody else knows, the Soviet Union does not now have the capacity to pick up this guidance function. Now, my question to our editor was, what would he say when Mr. Brzezinski came to him and said, "Look, don't reveal this. This is going to be very useful to us, this secret. It will mean, for one thing, we can scrap a whole bunch of cruise missiles and other things, that have been in the way of the SALT talks accommodation with the Soviet Union."

FOURTH EDITOR: I cannot make that leap. I mean, it just goes so against everything I know, that I can't do it. If you could absolutely convince me—

PROFESSOR SCHMIDT: Okay. (*Recognizes the sixth editor*)

SIXTH EDITOR: I have trouble with it, as soon as you're going to send it outside the United States, particularly if you're going to send it to the Middle East, because as soon as the first one gets there, everybody is going to know about it.

PROFESSOR SCHMIDT: We're going to send a bunch of American technicians, who are the only people who can fly this thing anyway.

SIXTH EDITOR: No way.

PROFESSOR SCHMIDT: They will operate it. For it to perform its function, for it to be of value to Olay in terms of what they think it is, they've got to keep it airborne all the time.

Look, we'll have this seminar next week on military capability and whether the military would ever rely on a foreign government for some essential. I'm not interested in that. I want you to take the value of this secret as a given. I want to ask you, would you publish it? Could you be convinced not to publish it?

FIRST EDITOR: You're making an absolute point that if this specific bit of information is revealed, it would imperil the security of the United States. You're making that specific point without respect to all of these things which have been raised. That is terribly important. In combat operations, for example, we withhold information on the movement of troops. We do things of that kind when we know that release of that information would definitely imperil the security of the United States.

A question arises really, in this case, as well as in others, and that is that you can't, in general, withhold this kind of information when you're talking about the sale of equipment, a weapons system. It's bound to leak, and the Russians become aware of it at a very early stage of the game. I think that's very important.

PROFESSOR SCHMIDT: Let me be clear. If you publish this secret, the United States is not going to blow up. The Russians are not going to attack. But we lose the effectiveness of a very promising, indeed, a technological weapons breakthrough that would give us a position that would enable us, perhaps, to make concessions in the SALT talks that could produce a disarmament treaty; that would allow us to reduce the defense budget by 10 or 15 percent and that would allow all of us to sleep a little more happily, knowing that our second-strike capability was invincible. Now, that's what they say will happen if you print this secret. Is your position like the fourth editor's, that you can't be convinced?

Whose job is it to assess that? Is it your job? Is it the president's national security advisor's job? Do you take his expert view about the defense significance of this thing or do you make up your own mind?

FIRST EDITOR: Judging by the experience of the decisions made during the Vietnam War and a number of other incidents in recent history, I would say I would have to make those judgments independently.

PROFESSOR SCHMIDT: You must make it independently because you can't be convinced. (*Addresses the sixth editor*)

SIXTH EDITOR: I'm not in trouble with the whole idea, because I can't imagine how we could find out something like this, and nobody else would, particularly since the thesis or the hypothesis is that it came in from an unknown informant. I would presume he would have more than one dime to make more than one telephone call. I just can't believe that we could come across a piece of information like this that nobody else could possibly find out.

PROFESSOR SCHMIDT: And the head of Central Intelligence comes to you and tells you, "Look, as far as we know, amazing as it seems, your reporter has stumbled onto something, and the fifth businessman knows about it, a few other people know about it, but no foreign country knows about it. No other reporters know about it, as far as we know." How about it then? Do you publish? (*Recognizes the second TV executive*)

SECOND TV EXECUTIVE: Isn't your hypothetical case really a false one? Hasn't the fifth businessman pointed it out? You're not in a war, and the times are not times when soldiers are fighting. The lead time on the introduction of any new system and its deployment is going to make it known to the other side, and isn't the danger that the media, once having acceded to the national security argument, can be led to that argument over and over again?

Now, it's the director of the CIA's job to keep everything secret that he can, and it's the Defense Department's job, too. The press has a different value to serve. It seems to me that you're posing a hypothetical case that is not a real situation.

PROFESSOR SCHMIDT: Let me pose a real one. Supposing you find out what the United States's bottom line is at the next round of SALT negotiations—what is the worst deal in terms of U.S. interests that the United States is willing to make in order to get a reciprocal deal from the Soviet Union? Now, the United States's negotiating strategy is to come into that conference and say, you know, "Our minimum deal is 3 X of this and 3 Y of that." But you know that the bottom line is that the United States will really settle for 2 X of this and 2 Y of that. Would you publish that?

SECOND TV EXECUTIVE: Let me put it this way: the gap between where we and the Soviets are on SALT is not a great one. To the extent that the American people can know something about these issues, which are really quite complicated, I would think that the best reporter in the world—who could give some idea of what the United States's position is, or the Soviet Union's position—might be performing a function because it clearly wouldn't be a case where the resulting deal would be affected by some revelation of our bottom-line position. We're that close now, and it would probably be settled—

PROFESSOR SCHMIDT: Do you know more about that than, say, the head of the U.S. Arms Control and Disarmament Agency? Supposing he came to you and said: "You know, we can make a better deal, I think, than our bottom line. If you reveal our bottom line, we'll have to start there and negotiate from there."

SECOND TV EXECUTIVE: I think the fact is that there has been enough published and read by experts to give some indication both as to numbers and as to how close we are. It isn't like a secret written on a piece of paper that the head of our disarmament agency carries around in his pocket, I don't believe. I don't think that's quite the way the process works.

PROFESSOR SCHMIDT: (*Recognizes the seventh businessman*) Yes.

SEVENTH BUSINESSMAN: You offered a chance to break in from time to time, so let me try a minute. You brought together some terribly interesting business people and government people and newspaper people. Now, let's deal with your hypothetical case and what it has done to the environment in which we live. This government-newspaper relationship is interesting fencing, but the real fact is that I think no businessman in this room could possibly entertain the kind of contract that's here, because of the environment within which we live. You couldn't do it. You could not commit the assets of your company to a deal which would put a third country in jeopardy of going to war with the Soviet Union. You just couldn't do it.

Whether that's good, from a matter of politics, or good from a matter of patriotism, is not the issue. Today, in America, this company could not enter into this arrangement simply because it is far too likely that someone would feel the need to reveal the secret. Olay would be in jeopardy of going to war with Russia because Russia would have the job of trying to get those ships out of commission, and therefore, my company could not put a significant part of its asset at risk. In this country, you can't do that anymore.

PROFESSOR SCHMIDT: Is that a business decision?

SEVENTH BUSINESSMAN: It's very simple. It's not even a hard one. You wouldn't even spend ten minutes on it.

PROFESSOR SCHMIDT: Because you would lose a lot of money.

SEVENTH BUSINESSMAN: You wouldn't put your assets at risk. You don't have to worry, you don't have to go beyond it, you don't have to—

PROFESSOR SCHMIDT: Suppose the Defense Department says, "We'll hold you harmless."

SEVENTH BUSINESSMAN: You can't hold me harmless. You can't take the stock market for the last three years, the ups and downs, you can't repay me—you can't do that. I'm a public company.

PROFESSOR SCHMIDT: We will pay you—

SEVENTH BUSINESSMAN: You can't. I'm just saying, realistically, today, you wouldn't get into the discussion.

PROFESSOR SCHMIDT: And that's because you know that the press would reveal the secret.

SEVENTH BUSINESSMAN: Not necessarily. We're in such a sophisticated world today, who knows who will reveal the secret? The Israelis? The Russians? It may not even be true that somebody will reveal it. (*Laughter*) You know, I don't want to have had the meeting. I don't want to talk to the head of the CIA on that subject.

I'm saying to you, there is a lesson for this group to learn from all the people here: if you asked the SEC, or if you asked the CIA, or if you asked the head of a major corporation, or if you asked anyone around here dealing in the sophisticated hardware, they would tell you you're talking about something that today can't happen.

PROFESSOR SCHMIDT: (*Asks the fourth businessman*) Do you agree with that?

FOURTH BUSINESSMAN: Yes.

PROFESSOR SCHMIDT: (*Asks the fifth businessman*)

FIFTH BUSINESSMAN: No respectable or well-managed technological corporation would get involved in the clear mess that they would have to get into by getting into this Broken Field project. They wouldn't touch it.

PROFESSOR SCHMIDT: Let me change the hypothetical, all right? Let's take out of the hypothetical the foreign-sale element, and let's simply suppose that you or some other advanced scientist-engineer has devised a new guidance mechanism of some sort, something that would be a useful secret for us to keep from the Soviets.

FIFTH BUSINESSMAN: On the frontiers of physics, the scientists are now breaking down the neutron into sub-particles. Half a dozen scientists, let's say at Los Alamos, are completely convinced by the theory on paper that they now have a way to create something at least as powerful as a nuclear weapon, weighing about one ounce. This could change by two orders of "bang" to the cost of a strategic deterrent system. We are now considering how to go about creating that.

One of those six scientists defects. He feels this new weapon would be bad for the world. He decides to go to one of the major newspapers and tell them about it.

PROFESSOR SCHMIDT: (*Turns to the fourth editor*)

FOURTH EDITOR: I'd call my publisher, I think. (*Laughter*) I mean, you're so far over my head with that one that I would not consider making any decision.

PROFESSOR SCHMIDT: But that doesn't bother you because you can't be convinced.

FIRST PUBLISHER: Since you called me—that is, we are playing with semantics a little bit. The fact is, we all will have secrets for the purposes of saving lives, or saving national security. There is a point at which newspapers will not print. Now, the other point is, as the example just given probably would convince you, that if you were the only one who knew it, I think that probably even then, if you thought he was going to go to somebody else, you would not print. I really do not think you would print that.

On the other hand, we've all been had so on the grounds of national security. That's why you get a lot of suspicion. We've been through some twelve years of everybody's saying, "Don't print it because it's national security." So, there is a real problem here, but I don't think that anybody wants to betray his or her country. I think that is a point that has to be made.

PROFESSOR SCHMIDT: (*Calls on the first judge*) I'd like to move to the final stage of the hypothetical, and I'd like to coalesce these two stories that we've been working with this afternoon.

One story concerns the minister of defense in Olay. It is a story that he has accepted bribes from an American aircraft-manufacturing company, and that he is a source of intelligence for the CIA.

The other side of the story is that there is some new technique—a guidance mechanism, a new way of looking at the atom, or something or other—which will give the United States a significant advantage in its second-strike deterrent weapons systems.

Now, the head of the CIA comes into district court and says, "Hey, the *Daily Bugle* is about to run a story with these two facts, and I don't want them to run either one."

It seems to me, the arguments on grounds of intelligence capability and national security, and arguments against publication, are very, very strong. Let's say it's four o'clock in the afternoon.

(*Asks the fourth editor*) When do your presses roll?

FOURTH EDITOR: They roll about eleven o'clock.

PROFESSOR SCHMIDT: At night?

FOURTH EDITOR: At night.

PROFESSOR SCHMIDT: It's four o'clock in the afternoon. The head of the CIA says, "As far as I know, he's got this story ready to go tonight." What happens then?

FIRST JUDGE: And he's asking for injunctive relief to stop the *Bugle* or what?

PROFESSOR SCHMIDT: Yes.

FIRST JUDGE: First, they have to come into court and ask for something.

PROFESSOR SCHMIDT: He seeks a temporary restraining order (TRO) to prevent publication, to enable him to make arguments to you about the sensitive nature of these two stories, why they should not be published. That's what he asks for.

FIRST JUDGE: My sense of the residue of the nine opinions in the Pentagon Papers case is that there is apart from the question of newspaper responsibility of not printing—as indeed, the *Washington Post* didn't print all of the Pentagon Papers—there is some residual power in the courts to prevent publication, in case of extreme urgency to national security, and in my view, that means there should be a day's wait. Not three days, but a day's wait, so that the judge can listen to the matter if there's a strong showing, to begin with, of something credible, and if the head of the CIA comes in or his legal representative comes in and says that there is reason to prevent publication, that gets him the first day. That gets him the TRO for the first day, so we can have discussion the next day on what it's about.

PROFESSOR SCHMIDT: Do you grant that TRO before you hear from the lawyer for the paper?

FIRST JUDGE: No, not if there's a wait between 3:00 P.M. and 11:00 P.M., you don't. If they come in at 10:00 P.M., you have to, but not if there's a wait between 3:00 and 11:00.

PROFESSOR SCHMIDT: So you would grant an injunction without—

FIRST JUDGE: A temporary restraining order.

PROFESSOR SCHMIDT: A temporary restraining order.

FIRST JUDGE: And set a hearing for the next day in chambers.

PROFESSOR SCHMIDT: (*Asks the first lawyer*) If the head of the CIA has been good enough to advise you, as the editor's lawyer, that he was going down to the judge's chambers that afternoon to seek a temporary restraining order, just a brief one, to enable the court to take evidence, and so on, would you oppose the issuance of that order?

FIRST LAWYER: Well, I would speak to the editor first. I take it, what he would want me to do for the same reason he—by hypothesis—wants to print the story, is to oppose any preliminary injunctive relief. So I would oppose it, and say, in effect, to the judge that before he grants any delay in publication at all, he should be persuaded now that the government can meet whatever the tests are in the Pentagon Papers case. That is to say that the government should have to prove that the publication of this material will so surely result in such major harm.

PROFESSOR SCHMIDT: All right, there are two pieces of material. One identifies this Olay official and the other identifies this new technological breakthrough. Do your arguments differ as between those two stories?

FIRST LAWYER: I would argue that neither of them reach the level of harm, let alone the likelihood of sureness of harm, that the Pentagon Papers case required. Now, if the government can make the kind of showing necessary to persuade the judge that this harm is sure, all but sure, and that its gravity is so severe, then we might have a different case, or it might be this very case. But what I would argue on behalf of my editor—and again, I would have consulted with him to find out the background of the story and the like. Then, presuming that he has decided to run the story, I would try to convince the judge that it isn't that certain that these harms would result. I would argue that the amount of harm is probably insufficient to meet the Pentagon Papers test. I would argue, as well, that it probably is going to leak out anyway, so an injunction wouldn't do any good. And I would urge him not to enter any preliminary injunction at all, any temporary restraining order at all.

PROFESSOR SCHMIDT: Judge, persuaded?

FIRST LAWYER: No. I think our publisher made the point that you don't print some stories, even if other people are going to have them. It isn't strictly a competitive matter, and I find that *that* argument—the argument that our lawyer makes—comes close to the absolute position which the *New York Times* counsel did not present to the Supreme Court. But it seems to me, really, the last person who should be involved in matters of this sort, is a judge—absolutely the last person who should be involved in it. But if the people who have the power and have the capability of resolving these matters cannot do so on some other basis, and the official of the U.S. government comes in and makes some kind of a showing that seems very urgent, then it seems to me that there *is* a role for the court.

As for the example about leaking information about the destination of troops, which was given in the previous case—the publisher's point about the movement of troops does not seem to me to be so much larger in its impact, the possibility of a bane upon the world, than the nixing of an important security system—

PROFESSOR SCHMIDT: How about the government official in Olay?

FIRST JUDGE: Well, that strikes me as a lesser nature, just offhand, but I realize you've got to be very objective about this.

PROFESSOR SCHMIDT: His life is in jeopardy.

FIRST JUDGE: I understand that. We know that people's lives still get to be in jeopardy without the world going—what you're worrying about there is the loss, as far as national security is concerned. It's not his life because we have no power to do anything about the fact that someone's life is in danger. It's about the possibility of compromising the intelligence function. That seems to me to be of lesser scale than losing for the United States the advantage of a possible important weapons system, or guidance system. I really don't see that that's lesser than whether the troops are on the field or on troopships.

PROFESSOR SCHMIDT: So you would enter a temporary restraining order for twenty-four hours?

FIRST JUDGE: To make sure that this isn't just a declaration, but that there's something to it.

PROFESSOR SCHMIDT: (*Turns to the fourth editor*) Would you obey that?

FOURTH EDITOR: I would argue, very seriously, to my lawyer, because I'm not a lawyer, that we should not obey that. Obviously, if the counsel recommended obeying it, I don't see how I could disobey it, but I don't think that we, as a society, want to give to a government official the right to shut a newspaper down for twenty-four hours or twenty-four days. I think the principle is so important that this "Can't you wait twenty-four hours?" argument doesn't add up. That's the argument that Mr. Mitchell made in the Pentagon Papers case. When the government was asked by Judge Gesell what its one best shot was, they came forth with a story that was in the next week's issue of *Life*, and it was in six published books, and it just didn't add up. I really don't think a responsible government official wants that right.

PROFESSOR SCHMIDT: (*Asks the third lawyer*) If you were representing our editor—for a moment, let's make you co-counsel with the first lawyer— would you advise him to obey this temporary restraining order?

THIRD LAWYER: Yes.

PROFESSOR SCHMIDT: Why?

THIRD LAWYER: I'd try to explain to the editor—and I've done this in other circumstances—that the First Amendment really ought not to interfere with the government of the country in the sense that national security is involved; in the sense in which our judge indicated; in the case that has been made out. I think that the editor has an obligation to obey, and if he fails to obey, I would, myself, feel that he should go to jail.

PROFESSOR SCHMIDT: (*Asks the first lawyer*) Do you agree with that?

FIRST LAWYER: I think I might have some comments to the editor about my co-counsel. I don't really disagree with it. I think, what I'd tell the editor is this, I'd say, "You have three choices. First, we can try to take an immediate appeal to the court of appeals, which is going to be very hard and will be very hard to win, in light of the judge's opinion as just expressed to you.

"Second, we can disobey, or *you* can disobey. (*Laughter*) And third, we can go about our business and prepare for the hearing the next day."

I would say that if this were any area but national security, I would have a lot harder time deciding what to advise the editor. That is to say, it's my view, and I think there's a pretty good argument although by no means the law, that a lot of orders banning the press from printing things are unconstitutional and so clearly unconstitutional that the press might well be able to disobey and still win legally; and still preserve the societal values at stake.

With national security, I don't think that's so. I think the Pentagon Papers case does make clear that there is some area, small though it may be, where the press should not be able to print, and and in which an injunction would be appropriate. If this is that kind of case, or if it's that close to that kind of case, I think I'd tell the editor that it would be my choice—I'm not even sure it's a legal opinion anymore—but I think it would be my sense that he would do better to obey in this area and have us go to court tomorrow and persuade the judge, as I'm sure we should and could, that he should not enter any injunctive relief.

PROFESSOR SCHMIDT: (*Asks the first editor*) You've heard the argument. Would you obey that order for twenty-four hours?

FIRST EDITOR: I think, first of all, that I would obey the order and exhaust the judicial process. Then after that, even if the court order eventually went against me, as a matter of conscience, if I felt it was in the public interest to print and to go to jail, I would do that as well. But that is a second step. I would not ignore the judicial process and a stay that would be issued by the court.

PROFESSOR SCHMIDT: Is there any journalist present who would be inclined to disobey the twenty-four-hour temporary restraining order, which the judge has issued in order to maintain the status quo so the judicial process can take evidence the next day?

SEVENTH EDITOR: I would like to review the circumstances just a little bit. We're in court on the unsupported word of the CIA director that certain information, if published, would be detrimental to the national interest? That's not the hypothetical. The hypothetical relates to some sensitive equipment that's going to be sold to a foreign country. I can't see any justification for keeping secret from the people of the United States information that's going to be exported to a foreign country.

PROFESSOR SCHMIDT: There are two parts to the story. One is, there is this person in Olay. Now, how do you feel about printing his identity as the recipient of big bribes and also someone who sells intelligence to the CIA?

SEVENTH EDITOR: I think I would give the CIA a chance to get him out of the country.

PROFESSOR SCHMIDT: Ten days.

SEVENTH EDITOR: Oh, I don't think he needs ten days.

PROFESSOR SCHMIDT: Five? Three?

SEVENTH EDITOR: I think two days would be enough.

SECOND EX-GOVERNMENT OFFICIAL: Could I add to the hypothetical that the revelation that minister of defense of Olay is a CIA agent and operates in that fashion would result in an immediate swerve of the friendly policy in Olay toward the United States, and a reimposition of the oil embargo. (*Laughter*)

SEVENTH EDITOR: I think that's one of the risks you have to take.

PROFESSOR SCHMIDT: That's a pretty big ante. That doesn't bother you.

SEVENTH EDITOR: I think that's one of the risks. There's also a risk for them, you understand, when they take that action, too. They have been friendly to the United States for some very good reasons of their own, and when they sacrificed those reasons for this purpose, I think they made a very big decision.

PROFESSOR SCHMIDT: And you're not impressed at all with the argument, the lesser argument, that to reveal this guy's identity—even if the CIA gets him out of the country so he's safe, settles him in Brazil—nevertheless, doing that plugs up a very constructive source of good intelligence. The CIA loses some intelligence capability as a result of that. Would you publish?

SEVENTH EDITOR: The CIA has had a great deal of trouble keeping its channels open, and they've had a lot of their sources plugged up. I'm not aware that it totally impaired their effectiveness. I suspect it has, to some degree, but I think that they have it within their power to re-create those channels in circumstances such as this.

A VOICE: There's always a new defense minister.

PROFESSOR SCHMIDT: Yes. We hope he's as accommodating as the old one.

FIRST BANKER: Could I inquire? While this is fascinating, what is the relevance to the topic of "Business and the Media"?

PROFESSOR SCHMIDT: The relevance is the extent to which the media is willing to cooperate with government to subordinate its own self-interest and its own sense of its own function in order to accede to the national interest, as defined by the head of CIA and as eventually resolved—we've got to get it resolved—by a judge.

FIRST BANKER: My question is whether the subject of the conference is "The Media and Business," which I take it to be. This is sort of "Media and the Law and Government," is that right? I was just inquiring as to the relevance of this case to the interaction between media and business.

PROFESSOR SCHMIDT: The relevance, as I see it, is a kind of triangular process of forces. We have the media, and then we have business, and over both, we have the government. It is not possible, in my judgment, to look at media-business conflicts without at the same time looking at the influence of government on those conflicts.

Now, the particular piece of that triangular set of forces that interests me, at this moment, in the hypothetical, is the media's sense of its institutional independence; its institutional autonomy from what the national interest is defined to be, by either government or experts. Now, I think we spent some time looking at what business's sense of its institutional autonomy is; the extent to which it will cooperate with government, whether it's to build the *Glomar* or provide information to the CIA or cover, or whatever. The thesis that I'm developing is that the media has a very distinct, different and, it seems to me, questionable sense of autonomy that is not shared by banks, lawyers, defense technologists, or whomever.

What I wanted to explore with the judge was the media's attitude toward a court order not to disclose some secret information, as sort of the final piece of this comparison. What I've been doing is drawing parallels and comparisons. (*Recognizes the seventh editor*)

SEVENTH EDITOR: Well, as far as I know, the press and not the media, but the press, and I'm willing to extend that to all the media, is the only private institution in this country that has a constitutional privilege. It's the only one.

The First Amendment says that the Congress shall not enact any law that will abridge the freedom of the press and the freedom of speech. Now, that franchise, it seems to me, puts the press in a very special category. As I read the origins of our Constitution, I'm getting into grounds here that are your province and not mine, so I recognize the danger. But at any rate, the purpose of that was to create some kind of a balancing force that would exercise some kind of restraint upon government. The founders of our government were very concerned about tyranny. They were revolutionaries. And they created the First Amendment as a balancing force that would have some restraint on government.

That creates a very special relationship between the press and the government. It's a relationship that business does not share. I think it is perfectly proper for a businessman to share information with the government. I can't see any real problem there at all. But when the press begins to share information with the government, it begins to lose its credibility. If you travel abroad, you'll be challenged on it repeatedly, particularly since it became known that some newspaper people have cooperated with the CIA.

The foreign people all say, "We don't believe you because you are CIA agents." It is a direct attack on our credibility and it's an important concern for all of us because credibility is the best thing we have.

SECOND EX-GOVERNMENT OFFICIAL: I'd like to answer that. The CIA has stayed away from the Peace Corps for at least seventeen years. The CIA has stayed away from the Fulbright. CIA has stayed away from a variety of other organizations.

There are a number of other countries that are very democratic, in which citizens, both journalists and non-journalists, have helped their intelligence service. That kind of staying away from other parts of the government, such as the Foreign Service Officer Corps, AID, the USIA, the Fulbrighters, all the rest of it, hasn't helped those organizations one slight bit against accusations that they were involved in intelligence in a variety of countries. And, they've lost people.

Now, I believe that you're never going to absolve the American press from the charge that they might be helping their intelligence services. What you're really doing is adding to the concept that some kind of mark of Cain stands on the forehead of CIA. That it must be extirpated from every form of American overseas presence, so that you end up with no way of conducting the important intelligence work of the country. This is so because you don't have any cover. That's exactly where the United States stands today with respect to cover overseas. Until the nation gets over this, the government will not be able to run an effective intelligence organization.

PROFESSOR SCHMIDT: In your view, are the editors here right in saying, "Media are different from other parts of American society"? Journalists have got to suppress even any natural instinct to cooperate with their government. It has to be "hands off."

SECOND EX-GOVERNMENT OFFICIAL: Absolutely not. As I say, I know a number of very democratic countries with very democratic press which collaborates with its country's intelligence services.

PROFESSOR SCHMIDT: (*Recognizes the eighth businessman*)

EIGHTH BUSINESSMAN: I would print the story. I would print the second part of the story, that dealing with the minister of Olay. First, because when he took the job for two million dollars, he knew his life was in jeopardy, and I see no reason to protect him from that point of view.

And second, if they want to reimpose the oil embargo, I think that this country would gain a great deal from an oil embargo now, rather than later.

Now, taking the other question, the broader question, which is a question of the defense system. Number one, I'd just have to draw upon some, at least, of the hypothetical assumptions involved in there. It is in the hands of a third country which doesn't know about it. I regard that as having an extraordinary possibility of explosion throughout the world, as far as our relationships with all countries. I disagree very much with the attitude of our government that brought that about. I'd like to do what I could to stop that sort of thing.

Second, I do know that this kind of thing will become known, regardless of whatever assumptions are made. Third, I do not accept other people's definition of national defense, no matter how much they know about the specifics of hardware. I would prefer to accept my own, and I think we would be in great trouble if various editors had not accepted their own, at various times in our history.

So given those three things, I would publish both those stories, presuming, of course, that a judge didn't get me first.

PROFESSOR SCHMIDT: Just one question. Suppose you were the head of an oil company, would you publish the story then? Would you go to an editor with the story?

EIGHTH BUSINESSMAN: If I had all this information?

PROFESSOR SCHMIDT: Right, but you're not a journalist. What I'm asking is, is your obligation as a private citizen who happens to be a business-man, but it doesn't matter, you could be an academic, whatever, is your obligation as a private citizen to disclose the existence of this story, the same as it would be as the head of a newspaper?

EIGHTH BUSINESSMAN: Well, I happen to think so, yes.

PROFESSOR SCHMIDT: (*Asks the fourth editor*) Do you think so?

FOURTH EDITOR: I hope he brings it to me. (*Laughter*)

SECOND EDITOR: Mr. Schmidt, could I say something, something to what was said a minute ago. Of course, it's quite possible to have a democracy in which the press is not as free and as privileged as it is in America. Britain certainly is a democracy; its press is not as free as ours in many areas. France is a sort of democracy; its press is not as free. The point is not democracy, which is a very flexible term, but *our* democracy. I do agree with the editors that the press here does play a constitutional role, which it does not play in other countries. I think we want to preserve that.

As far as the CIA is concerned—

PROFESSOR SCHMIDT: May I just ask a question about that role? Is that a role of autonomy that extends so far as to not let a judge tell you that you may not print some item of interest because it's a critical national defense secret?

SECOND EDITOR: It is not an absolute privilege. It is not absolute auton-omy. I think that, on the whole, I would not obey his temporary re-straining order. There might be circumstances in which I so violently felt he was wrong that I would choose to go to jail. But on the whole, I would certainly not claim absolute right to ignore it in the courts.

But on the CIA, I would defend the CIA on many grounds. I would print stories defending the CIA. We have. But I would not try to defend the CIA by cooperating with it, as a journalist. I don't think it needs that cooperation. I think it's bad for the CIA, as well as for us.

PROFESSOR SCHMIDT: What we've tried to do this afternoon was get away from direct collisions between business and the media in the coverage of particular stories. We've tried to explore instead comparisons and contrasts, the view being to try to educate one another as to the media's conception of its role in American society and how that conception of role contrasts with the conception of other institutions in American society, such as governmental agencies, other private sector institutions, businesses. We could have brought in, for comparative purposes also, academic institutions, foundations like the Aspen Institute, and so on.

My aim was to try to have you all speak to certain parallel problems in terms of your reaction to government requests for cooperation, to judicial proceedings, seeking to impose obligations on you, with the common theme being the problem of disclosure versus either confidentiality or secrecy, whatever you call it.

I've enjoyed this session very much. I've learned a lot about what I think your different perceptions are, and I hope you have found it educational as well.

Let's go to the bar. (*Applause*)

FRED FRIENDLY: Before you go, I wonder if we could stay about ten more minutes. I think there are some of you around the table that were a little frustrated this morning, a little this afternoon. That's the nature of the beast. Everyone who has something to say didn't get to say it. I think it would be good, because by the time we get to it tomorrow, we'll be busy on banking. I think it would be useful, if you'd like to spend ten or fifteen minutes saying what you would say in the cab on the way home.

PROFESSOR SCHMIDT: I'd be very happy to hear that, particularly from people who haven't had a chance to speak.

FOURTH LAWYER: You started on something which you dropped when you talked about the premature disclosure of the bottom-line position of the United States in the SALT talks. Someone said that he thought that would do no harm.

Now, I think that the premature disclosure of a bargaining position is inevitably bound to destroy the bargaining position, whether it is of the United States or of two business concerns, or in a labor negotiation.

Now, I would like to inquire about the reaction of the press as to the imperative importance of such disclosures, which are going to come out ultimately, but which if revealed prematurely have a very adverse effect on the bargaining.

PROFESSOR SCHMIDT: (*Recognizes the first TV executive*)

FIRST TV EXECUTIVE: Both this morning and this afternoon, I think that a key element of the real world of journalism has been glossed over. We are in a competitive business. It is a competition for journalistic excellence, of course. I tried to inject the fact that when a reporter here was talking about a story that the reporter had, that a competing organization with reporters every bit as skilled as the one who may have the story, is also out in the field against us. We cannot overlook, and we must not overlook, when you consider why it is that we may be assaulting the CIA or assaulting Rothwell Industries, or Boeing or anybody else, in real life, around this table. It is my job, and it is the job of the editors of these other publications to get the news and to get it first, to get it accurately, of course—accept that as a given.

When it comes to the "premature disclosure," if our reporters have found out something, then it has been disclosed. It may not be disclosed at the time that someone else wished it to have been disclosed. But we have found it out, and as soon as you start to impose certain criteria about when you publish or don't publish, based on premature disclosure or other criteria, I think you are not taking into account the fiercely competitive nature of the business we are in.

In fact, there was a government report about minority hiring practices in the broadcast industry. It broke at about four o'clock in the afternoon. The evening news goes on at six. A TV news director called his own people for a statement and got what is probably what he would get if he were calling Boeing about a report that there was a crack in a 747 wing. He got a kind of "Well, we're studying that." That's all he had to go with, and that's what he went with, because if he didn't go with that and waited for his own company or for Boeing to make up its mind about what it was going to say, his competitors would have gone with the story just as well.

Now, I'm in a real world. I don't want to dominate, but to be candid, I feel that if we were supposed to find out why businessmen at this table are concerned that the media is trying to do them in; or why we believe, in our fingertips, that all we're ever going to get from business is "Send me a letter, and I'll try and answer the fourteen interrogatories," I don't think we've succeeded here, and it bothers me, frankly.

NINTH BUSINESSMAN: This morning, the point was raised about the difficulty of access to information for businessmen. I can only speak for the industry in which I operate, but I would like to say that as far as access to information is concerned, the access to information is 100 percent. There's never any question as to whether or not the press will have the right to disclose facts about it—it's only the way in which they disclose it.

We cannot make a discovery and keep the fact secret, because we're in trouble with the SEC. We can't file any kind of a prospectus or undertake the sale of new securities without putting all the relevant facts on the line—what lawsuits are involved, what pollution regulations. I'm very sorry that in the hypotheticals we had today, and those we will have tomorrow, there has been no consideration of the environmental issues. We have touched on the medical side, but the environmental issue is a fundamental issue which is attacking the position of virtually every industrialist around this room.

Now, I'm not trying to put forward the pros and cons. It's a very serious subject, but the role that the press is playing in the discussion of the position of business in regard to environmental regulations is a major factor.

PROFESSOR SCHMIDT: Just describe that role. How do you think the press is reporting environmental issues?

NINTH BUSINESSMAN: I think the press is biased in favor of the public interest groups.

A VOICE: What?

NINTH BUSINESSMAN: Yes, I do. When our first banker made the statement that he did, I think I was the only person in the room that actually started to applaud, because we are not talking about media and business here. We're not talking, really, about the law and the media. We're not discussing the questions of access to information, from business to the press, or for that matter, from press to business.

SECOND TV EXECUTIVE: When I heard about the nature of the seminar, and before I got the hypotheticals—and this is in line with what has been said—when I just heard the title of the seminar, I thought that it would treat and get into a question that I had raised with myself a great deal.

We have a practice of inviting people from different parts of industry and people in public life to lunch. Many times, we get the complaint that the media are anti-business, that the media don't do as good a job as they should do in presenting the problems that business has. I thought that that would be a subject matter that we would be able to get into here. It's a deeply felt feeling held by a lot of corporate executives. Those of us in television—who are both in the job of presenting news, and also, we feel, often on the side of getting our own positions misrepresented—feel it both ways. I thought that that would be a central topic that would be discussed here.

PROFESSOR SCHMIDT: (*Turns to the tenth businessman*) May I ask you a question? Do you think the media, on the whole, has been fair or has shown anti-business bias in reporting the whole questionable payments problem in relation to foreign sales over the last three or four years?

TENTH BUSINESSMAN: My criticism would be less with the media, editorially, than it would be with certain writers, just one or two or three. That would be the only statement I would make. I think, in some cases at the beginning of the problem, there was a tremendous effort to disclose what might be called possibilities, claims and others, as if they were fact. I have to say honestly that I would not blame the press for that. If I blamed anyone it would be one or two writers, but I think that happens in our business, too. We have one or two or three people that do wrong things. So I wouldn't blame the press.

I think—and we're backing into the courts—I think there was a time when the courts were forcing situations that caused claims to appear as fact, and then the press picked them up, as good reporters would. So, no, I think not. I do not think they're unfair.

SECOND LAWYER: What I got out of this, and what I think disturbs me the most, is that there is a double standard between the press and business on matters of responsibility. I was, frankly, surprised to hear a TV executive say that for fear of competition he would not wait a day or two to go to press or to go on the air with the story about an agent, even though it might cost the agent his life. Whereas, I don't think the press would stand for it if a drug company rushed its product out quickly for fear of competition.

I heard it said that the press will protect confidentiality at almost all cost, whereas if a business tries to, it will be considered a cover-up.

I heard it said that the press will, one way or another, buy information, while business will be castigated for questionable or sensitive payments.

And finally, I heard today that the press reserves its right to refuse to observe orders of the courts, even when none of us would tolerate the fact that the President of the United States raised that reservation. No businessman could say, "I will reserve the right to refuse to observe an order of the court."

I think perhaps the press in looking at business could look at it from its own perspective of engaging in competitive practices, and perhaps the coverage might be a little more balanced. (*Applause*)

PROFESSOR SCHMIDT: I might say, without agreeing with your conclusions about what comes out of the comparison, that that is the kind of parallel and comparison of standards that the hypothetical was designed to present.

FIRST EDITOR: I think that our lawyer friend is making false parallels here. The question of competition, of course, might relate to the financial health of a news organization. But more important than that, competition is essential to the nature of journalism. First, in the sense that it gives the reader a diversity of approach, which is essential if he's going to have a viable press. Second, in that it provides the push and the shove which is necessary to bring important facts to the surface for the good of society.

On the question of confidentiality, I question whether or not business refused, often, to disclose information simply because it is absolutely essential to the lifeblood of that business. On the other hand, the confidentiality is absolutely necessary in order for the press to function, to operate. It's an aspect of journalism that cannot be shed.

On the third question, as far as the courts are concerned, I think that the press makes a case for being, in Burke's term, the fourth estate, or the fourth branch of government. I think that it is a position which is certainly defensible, because we have seen in the case of Watergate, for a considerable period of time, a failure of the three branches of government, including the judicial, to correct a situation that was undermining the society as a whole. It was then that the fourth branch of government became operative and brought about a resolution of the situation. That, I think, is recognized to a considerable extent in the Constitution itself and in the nature of the First Amendment. So on the whole, I feel that the parallels that have been drawn are really artificial.

PROFESSOR SCHMIDT: (*Calls on the first judge*) The parallels, the double standard of which the second lawyer spoke—does the First Amendment provide a kind of constitutional foundation for a double standard, say, with respect to the obligation to obey the orders of the court?

FIRST JUDGE: While I agree with the comments made previously about the fact that some judges have been quick on the draw to issue injunctions that don't really have standing; on the other hand, if we have a government of law, not mere anarchy in which everybody does what he wants, this is a condition that we have to put up with. So I don't think they have that kind of absolute freedom to decide for themselves whether a court order should be obeyed or not.

I think it is a constitutional privilege, of course. The First Amendment does create something like a fourth estate or a fourth branch of government. But the executive is subject to the mandates of the courts, even to some extent, to some of the legislative mandates. The courts themselves are subject to the mandates of the legislatures, in terms of appropriations. There are checks and balances throughout our system, and it seems to me that no one of them is able to be self-determining or autonomous, the word that you used before.

FIRST LAWYER: I'd just like to agree with formulation of the issue by the second lawyer, if not with his answer. His question was, is it a double standard? I think that's a proper way to phrase it, in one sense. Another way to phrase it is, is the press different? And, if so, how is it different? There's absolutely no doubt that the press takes positions for itself, which it would condemn in others, and that the courts, indeed, have gone far towards recognizing those positions for the press, as they would for no one else.

Justice Stewart gave a speech a few years ago at the Yale Law School, in which he ran through a whole list of things; confidential sources are one example. He said, in effect, "Look, if it were anyone but the press, we wouldn't even listen to them. It's a ridiculous thing for anyone else but the press to say that they should not be obliged to divulge information otherwise relevant because it was obtained in confidentiality." Justice Stewart's position was that the press was specifically set forth in the Constitution as being not the same as any other entity in American life.

Let's pass the history part. That doesn't have to be right, and I'm not going to try to persuade anyone that it's what ought to be the law. But I do think, when we think about these problems, and we try to think about them as broadly as possible, the kind of questions we have to consider are, in effect, how free a press do we want to have? We have to understand—and all the businessmen know this from personal experience—that the freer the press is, the freer it is to be offensive and reckless and to say things which are often untrue.

Now, either we get enough societal benefits out of that or we don't. In asking the question of what the framers meant and what the courts have said, each of us has to make his or her own kind of decision as to whether the price—and it is a real price that we pay for that—is a price we choose to pay. I would hope that a number of the businessmen here would think it is a price worth paying. It is a responsible position, I must say, to say it is not. Many democratic countries don't choose to pay that price. I think this is the way to view the issue.

ELEVENTH BUSINESSMAN: Let me piggyback on what our judge said. I hate to wind up this afternoon being on the side of the press. As a one-time lawyer, I grew up believing that you're supposed to respect court orders, take your appeals, get them reversed and all the rest. But I haven't heard anybody on the press side say that they want a different standard with respect to court orders than the businessman or the average citizen is asking for. We all reserve for ourselves the right, in appropriate circumstances, to defy a court order and to take the consequences if it turns out that we're wrong. The businessman does it with a subpoena. If he thinks it's improperly authorized, he takes his appeal.

The first editor particularly, I thought, went through the whole thing and said he was prepared to respect the order or take the consequences if it turned out he was wrong; that meant going to jail.

So I think on this one issue, we're all together, even though we may formulate it in a different way.

PROFESSOR SCHMIDT: (*Recognizes the eighth editor*)

EIGHTH EDITOR: I'm going to come out on the side of business. I just want to make a general observation. We, at our publication, also have many people from the business world up to lunch. It seems to me that it's clear the press is different from business and parallels have their limits. I think a lot of business people here would be more comfortable if they felt the press was doing a better job at what it's supposed to do.

It seems to me that an increased degree of conscientious editorial supervision of stories would help—I know, from our own shop, how a story about a business organization or a business controversy can evolve from the first reporting, the first discussion, the first versions on through. One of the attractive things about news magazines, I think, is that they do have a little more time. While they're intensely competitive in their world and with other press, they're not looking at the clock at five o'clock to figure out whether a competitor is going to be putting something out at five-thirty. Their journalistic process is, perhaps, a little more of a model of how things might be.

I think, as we go into the rest of this decade and the next, as the issues become more complex, the press should catch its breath, too. It's not a big crap shoot and horse race on every story. I think a little more measured reporting; a little more pressure on younger journalists to smarten up a little faster; and a little less casualness on the part of many of the stories that must disturb people here are not the full story. It's the fourteenth paragraph that throws a line in. That's where the copy editor is asleep on the job, or the assistant city editor or the reporter.

At the news magazines, every word of the magazine is read before it comes out, so that its editors are responsible. Magazine editors make a lot of questions in the margin. That works. The number of beefs are much fewer in a magazine shop than they are in others. Of course magazines run a smaller volume of type.

So I just want to make a pitch to get away from the legalisms a little bit and to remind ourselves that harder work generally produces better results.

PROFESSOR SCHMIDT: (*Recognizes the second reporter*)

SECOND REPORTER: I guess I want to respond to the businessman who said that businessmen disclose 100 percent of the information that we request. I just find that he's existing in a different world than I am.

NINTH BUSINESSMAN: I speak for my own industry, sir.

SECOND REPORTER: I can't believe that. I mean, you have trade secrets. You certainly don't disclose those to the press.

NINTH BUSINESSMAN: What type of trade secrets?

SECOND REPORTER Surely you must have secrets you want to keep from your competitors?

NINTH BUSINESSMAN: No, sir. (*Laughter*) You're quite wrong. We do have patents and we have a certain amount of know-how—but that is of no interest to the public, whatever.

SECOND REPORTER: The whole beginning of this discussion was about things that should be kept secret. Someone said there is certain information that the SEC doesn't want to go into, because it should be kept secret.

FIRST EX-GOVERNMENT OFFICIAL: No, I didn't say that.

FIRST BANKER: He said it was irrelevant. He said it was of no interest to us.

THIRD REPORTER: I just wanted to express some regret that we didn't focus a bit more on what I see as a very real problem for Mr. Josephs. When we get down to the nitty-gritty, it seems to me that most of you gentlemen who head major corporations have to be concerned, first of all, about your jobs. I think Mr. Josephs's job, in our hypothetical today, should have been very much on the line. This man was not responsive to his board of directors. And the press has to think a little bit about how we approach business. It is very important to me how we approach government. I've been in a Washington news bureau. I'm now in a different city, and big corporations are a way of life there, just as government is in Washington.

What's very interesting is, what is the approach? Today, we've been talking more about business as something big and powerful. But I think one cannot forget that publicly-held corporations go to all the citizens of the United States and ask for their money to be invested. As a result of doing that, I think, then we have a right as reporters and newsmen to go on behalf of those shareholders and ask questions. The shareholders vote for the board of directors, who in turn are to keep the top management accountable. What we're finding, as a result of the questionable payments thing—as we have discussed here today—is a much greater degree of accountability by the chief executive officers and by the chairman of the board, for example, who is really running the corporation. Boards of directors are being much more responsive. I think it's a favorable development. I would hope that we could have explored it a little more today, and tomorrow certainly might offer opportunity for that.

THIRD EDITOR: I've got some sympathy with some of the business complaints. But it seems to me we ought to make a clear distinction that the press cannot sensibly be said to be anti-business. We're anti-*bad* business, and unless we do expose and probe and pry, the public interest won't be properly represented.

Let me give you two instances. First, Bernie Kornfeld and the Fund of Funds. The investors were not protected by the SEC and the governmental regulatory agencies. They were protected, in the end, by a newspaper's exposing Bernie Kornfeld and the IOS. Millions of people's money was lost.

Second, McDonnell Douglas and DC-10 air crash. You try asking McDonnell Douglas for the drawings that were changed after the Windsor, Ontario, air crash but before the Paris air crash in which 346 people died. They're not going to cooperate. They went to the California federal courts to stop newspapers from getting information, and that information was essential to understanding the nature of the crash. The "federal bias." And we have to ask, "Why?" I think, when we look, we will see that over the last ten or fifteen years, we have tried to upgrade our newspapers and recruit from the universities rather than from our own younger staffs, that we have drawn into the press a great number of people who are very highly politically motivated. That is true.

I think, on the whole, it's true to say that the press has a healthy skepticism about business. There have been many occasions when the press has made enemies of business because of the activities of some of the new writers who, I think, in many cases, were given too much freedom by their editors. We do need to get away from the cult of the byline and the writer, and to get back to the editor.

EIGHTH EDITOR: I didn't say that. (*Laughter*)

SECOND PUBLISHER: You said we need a lot more editing. I think the press must look at itself.

PROFESSOR SCHMIDT: I think that's a good time to close. (*Applause*)

(*Whereupon this session was concluded.*)

Case Study
3: Peoples Guarantee and Security Company

Professor Miller

The Case:

Georgette Plimpton is an experienced prize-winning reporter for the *Capitol Chronicle,* the leading daily in Idyllia, which is the largest city and sole industrial center in the predominantly rural midwestern state of Nirvana. Ms. Plimpton has a flair for writing sympathetic profiles of ordinary working people at their jobs. Her method has been to obtain employment without divulging her newspaper connection. Plimpton has decided to do a piece about bank clerks and has taken a position at the main branch of the People's Guarantee and Security Company (PB&S), the dominant commercial banking organization in the state.

I

About two weeks into her new job, Plimpton finds herself in the unoccupied office of Morton Moregauge, the vice-president in charge of the bank's real estate investments. She spots a memorandum to Moregauge from Phinneas Phiduciary, the president of PG&S, and perhaps the most powerful banker in Nirvana. It is stamped "CONFIDENTIAL." The memorandum concerns a major apartment complex in a lower-middle-class section of the city on which PG&S has made a building loan. The owners of the building subsequently failed to meet the terms of the savings bank commitment; thus, there was no permanent mortgage. PG&S now holds a substantial lien on the property. PG&S also has between sixty and sixty-five million dollars invested in other building loans and single family home mortgages in that community.

According to the memo, the complex has never achieved full occupancy because of a series of highly publicized and violent incidents. To solve this problem, its management has been accepting welfare families as tenants, but, according to Phiduciary, their number has reached "alarming" dimensions. He therefore directs Moregauge to compel the existing owners of the complex, who are in default on the loan, to remove the welfare families as soon as feasible, in order to "halt any possible spread of this deterioration so that it will not endanger the neighborhood and other investments there."

II

Shortly after, at a party, Georgette Plimpton runs into J.D. Posit, a long-lost college classmate and former editor of the university's daily who has become an assistant vice-president of PG&S. In the course of reliving old times, Plimpton reveals her true identity.

Two days later Posit hands Plimpton documents revealing that the Nirvana Urban Finance Agency (NUFA), created amidst a fanfare of publicity and bold claims that it would provide much-needed planning and financing of urban redevelopment, especially in Idyllia, is on the verge of defaulting on $200 million in short-term notes. NUFA has been a pet project of Governor Aardvark, now campaigning for a third term. The election is less than two weeks away. At the time the agency was established, Aardvark and the legislature pledged that Nirvana has a "moral obligation" to support it, but NUFA's debts are not backed by the state's full faith and credit.

In addition to the notes, there are $800 million in NUFA bonds outstanding. PG&S, the Agency's financial advisor and architect, currently holds approximately $90 million in bonds and notes. It has purchased an additional $35 million in bonds and notes for various trusts it manages. Other large purchasers of NUFA paper are the Nirvana State Employees' Pension Fund and the Midwestern Construction Trades Union Retirement Plan. The *Chronicle* editorially supported the establishment of NUFA, and its civic-minded publisher, Otis "Sock" Sachertorte, is a member of its board and a major force in developing NUFA's program.

Although NUFA is promoting the construction of low-income housing and capital development in blighted urban areas, stimulating building and providing employment for thousands of Idyllians, the papers show that the occupancy rate of various projects remains unsatisfactory and that a fair number of its commercial tenants have failed. In addition, energy and operating costs have skyrocketed, and the agency's cash flow situation is precarious. Given the possible revenue insufficiency of the underlying projects, a new public issue of bonds seems out of the question.

A confidential memorandum prepared by several members of the NUFA underwriting group alleges that it is poorly administered, its operating expenses and salary structure are excessive, and there has been little or no oversight of the agency's investment program and management. Another document, prepared by the most important member of the original underwriting group when it refused to participate in the last bond issue six months ago, suggests that the only solution is to force NUFA to undertake an austerity program by not providing additional financing.

PG&S apparently has suggested two other possible solutions. The first is to secure legislation after Governor Aardvark's reelection that would provide the agency with state funding to meet its obligations. PG&S has urged secrecy until the election because rural legislators, who are generally opposed to NUFA, might use the information for political advantage. Three meetings with the governor have been held on the subject.

The second proposal is for a consortium of banks to provide NUFA with short-term financing. According to Posit, several banks have demanded (1) assurances that there will be a moratorium on new projects, (2) a veto power over completing projects they believe would not be economically viable, (3) promises that certain completed projects that have fallen short of expectation will be sold, and (4) a streamlining of NUFA's operations.

Posit feels the PG&S should not make any further commitment to NUFA. He tells Plimpton that the national bank examiners are devoting a great deal of attention to PG&S's "exposure" on loans to various less developed countries and therefore fears expanding the bank's involvement with what he considers another dubious venture.

III

Posit also tells Plimpton about another highly confidential matter at the bank. It related to Acme Appliance Manufacturing Corporation, which is headquartered in Idyllia and is the largest private employer in the metropolitan area. PG&S has extended a sizable line of credit to Acme, about fifteen million dollars of which is currently in use.

Last month, Richard Rowe, chairman of Acme, reported to Phiduciary and senior officers at PG&S that his company would probably report a net loss for the fourth quarter of this year. Rowe has concluded that the company cannot be returned to profitability without the sale of its refrigerator division, which employs about eight thousand Idyllians but requires additional investment in an amount that would overstrain Acme's financial resources. Rowe has asked PG&S for advice.

A PG&S research task force has concluded that the refrigerator division should be sold, even at a capital loss, and that it must be disposed of before the announcement of Acme's operating is announced. American Cooling Corporation is interested in acquiring Acme's refrigerator division and has assured Phiduciary that it would continue to operate the division in Idyllia.

The bank team also has found that Rowe's unwillingness to adopt modern management and control techniques has been responsible in part for Acme's poor performance and that the bank should insist upon his replacement. Two of Acme's outside directors have indicated that Rowe would be unwilling to give the appearance of resigning under pressure, particularly in view of his interest in running for the Senate in 1978. Rowe's resignation, they believe, should be postponed until Acme's annual meeting next spring, when he could intimate that political ambitions were the cause of his leaving.

IV

Under close questioning, Posit reveals that he is a member of a group within PG&S seeking the ouster of Phiduciary because of his increasing inattention to the bank's affairs and occasional serious lapses in judgment. Phiduciary's inattentiveness undoubtedly has been caused in part by concern over the tribulations of his drug-using son. Posit tells Plimpton that he is convinced Phiduciary is under treatment by Dr. Eric Enuresis, a prominent pyschiatrist, for a potentially disabling mental illness and is using amphetamines. In addition, according to Posit, Phiduciary is currently under investigation for allegedly using PG&S's facilities, such as its legal and accounting staffs, for personal matters and for exploiting his position to obtain preferential bank financing on his own investments.

SOME QUESTIONS

1. Do you approve of Plimpton's techniques for developing a story? Why?

2. Is it prudent for PG&S to seek the removal of the welfare tenants? Is it newsworthy?

3. Should Plimpton report the contents of the documents concerning NUFA? What are the competing considerations?

4. Is Acme's predicament newsworthy? Should Rowe try to avoid the publication of any story about it?

5. If Plimpton decided to do a story on Phiduciary, what aspect of his life should she report? What aspects should she omit?

The Seminar:

PROFESSOR MILLER: Good morning. I'm sorry to perform the role of a Sunday morning wake-up call for you. At least I'm not depriving you of the golf course or the tennis courts.

We have a problem in front of us; it's really five problems glued together. They are five little soap operas. They are each there to elicit some conversation about ways in which the media and business interact; how they deal with each other; what they think about each other; and how they feel about each other. This problem is a vehicle to provoke conversation on these issues, and I hope in the time that we will spend together this morning, we will get at most of these issues, one by one, in no more rational order than happens to be in the particular soap opera that we're dealing with at that particular time.

I know lots of people have lots of things to say about these issues. We talked about this last night before dinner, as Fred's remarks during dinner might suggest, about how to let everybody get it out. Fred rejected my suggestion, which was to divide you up and hand out broadswords and maces, and sort of have a do-it-yourself session. So we're going to work with the hypothetical. But let me say, there is one thing we are not going to do today. We are not going to talk about about law. (*Laughter and applause*) I talk about it all week long at school, and I find it dull then, so it would be worse today.

We're sort of going to make believe we really are in Nirvana and there is no law. Now, we may have to bump up against it from time to time, but really let's try to ignore it. The hell with the SEC and the FDA and all these other people.

Let's look at the first soap opera. It's really the unnumbered one, up there in that first preliminary paragraph, where it tells us that Georgette Plimpton is working at the bank and in the course of working at the bank to do a story, she in effect bumps into another story.

(*Says to the first banker*) Someone has just come into your office. You are the banker, you are Phiduciary, and they say, "You know, we have a media fink in our midst. I don't know how it happened, but we've got this woman working here and it turns out she's from the newspaper." What's your reaction? What do you feel? What do you think when you hear that?

FIRST BANKER: Well, I hate to break the ground rules, in not talking about the law, but— (*Laughter*)

PROFESSOR MILLER: Let it hang out.

FIRST BANKER: We have several bankers indicted, now, for breach of the company's conflict-of-interest laws. When she took the job, she signed the conflict-of-interest laws, and so I think she's committed a crime. I think the first thing to do would be to call my good friend, the publisher of the *Chronicle*, and say: "We've got a problem."

PROFESSOR MILLER: You don't like it, I take it?

FIRST BANKER: Well, I don't think it's a question of liking or disliking it, or even being concerned about it. I think it's a question of where we've got a breach of our customer confidentiality problem, and our customer confidentiality we put on the same order of magnitude as the press would put the confidentiality of its source.

PROFESSOR MILLER: Would you feel the same way if it were a fink from some bank?

FIRST BANKER: The statement that people sign when they come in—and you've got to remember that we're in one of the most regulated businesses in the country—says that they won't take money from customers, and they won't have transactions with customers, and they'll treat the information in the corporation with confidentiality, and they won't have conflicts of interest. You don't buy non-listed stocks, etc., etc. So when she took employment, she agreed to all of these stipulations, and now there's a breach, and we're under obligation to report that to the U.S. Attorney.

PROFESSOR MILLER: Well, does it make you feel one way or the other about the media, that she happens to be from the *Chronicle*? Someone else might be from another bank.

FIRST BANKER: No, I don't think so. We have pretty good relations with the media, and their job is to get stories. I think this was a little excess enthusiasm, but she probably didn't know what she was doing. No, I don't have any problems.

PROFESSOR MILLER: But you think you're going to have to report it to the authorities.

FIRST BANKER: Well, I think it would be better if we and the management of the paper could get it worked out and then report it to the papers along with the context in which it was done. It was a perfectly innocent thing, she wanted to do a story about some clerks in the bank and just unknowingly fell into this thing, and the problems resulted. We hoped that they will take it in that light.

PROFESSOR MILLER: (*Turns to the first businessman*) You're not under that statute, and in case it's not apparent, although this set of soap operas deals with banks, it's an allegory. Let's suppose Georgette Plimpton has entered one of your subsidiaries, and is looking into some of the chemicals produced by it. Again, you're sitting at your desk and somebody calls up and says: "There's a media fink in our midst."

FIRST BUSINESSMAN: She entered as an employee.

PROFESSOR MILLER: Yes, she came in—I suppose there's been a technical or maybe an overt mis-statement as to her prior vocational background.

FIRST BUSINESSMAN: I would regard it as a breach of the standards which the newspaper profession professes to hold everyone else to. (*Laughter*) I would be disappointed.

PROFESSOR MILLER: Would you be mad?

FIRST BUSINESSMAN: I would not be mad. I would fire her or him, and I would be disappointed. I would not be mad, but I would regard it as a breach of standards.

PROFESSOR MILLER: Suppose it was a competitor that put this spy into your midst; how would you feel?

FIRST BUSINESSMAN: I would feel exactly the same way, except our competitors are not as pious as the press often is. (*Laughter*) I would not feel that it was quite the same. It would be a breach of standards and a breach of professionalism, and I would resent it. But I'm not sure I would have quite the shade of indignation.

PROFESSOR MILLER: Would you take any action, other than firing her?

FIRST BUSINESSMAN: No.

PROFESSOR MILLER: Which is a rather mild sanction, because she's otherwise employed.

FIRST BUSINESSMAN: No, I would not.

In the case of the newspaper, if I knew the publisher or the editor, I would certainly call him, and say I did not think this conformed to the professional standards that I would expect. If I didn't know him, I would perform that sacred rite of writing a letter to the editor.

PROFESSOR MILLER: But you'd take no other action?

FIRST BUSINESSMAN: None.

PROFESSOR MILLER: You might even improve your screening procedures for hiring.

FIRST BUSINESSMAN: Oh, you're talking about internally? Well, our screening procedures are not designed to trap that kind of thing. I think changing rules that work ninety-nine times out of a hundred, in order to catch one out of a hundred, is a foolish procedure. We would probably not change our screening, because it would work most of the time.

PROFESSOR MILLER: (*Asks the second businessman*) Suppose this were an environmentalist, an environmental reporter, coming in to look at aerosol data.

SECOND BUSINESSMAN: I must confess that I probably, for a minute or two, might be very mad. I think, after that, I'd sort of put myself in the desk drawer and think about it for a little bit. Then I probably would come down pretty much on the side of the previous speaker. I think I'd be madder today that I would have been two days ago. (*Laughter and applause*)

PROFESSOR MILLER: Then it cannot be said that we haven't had an effect on you. (*More laughter*)

SECOND BUSINESSMAN: I've been very impressed with the very righteous atmosphere that some of the press have expressed. When I think about how they feel about taking CIA agents and other members of the government who do good work for our government, and then see this—that would rather enrage me, perhaps.

PROFESSOR MILLER: But not make you mad enough to do anything?

SECOND BUSINESSMAN: Oh, I'd do something. She would obviously go. I'd call up my good friend on the local newspaper, whose editor sent Ms. Plimpton in there. We might have a chat about it.

PROFESSOR MILLER: What would you say to him, your good friend over at the *Bugle*?

SECOND BUSINESSMAN: I'd say, I'm shocked. I can't believe it.

PROFESSOR MILLER: Don't do it again?

SECOND BUSINESSMAN: No, that's up to them. I'm not going to threaten them.

PROFESSOR MILLER: No threats.

SECOND BUSINESSMAN: No threats.

PROFESSOR MILLER: Would you think of having this person prosecuted?

SECOND BUSINESSMAN: Probably not. It might run through my mind, but I think I'd quickly realize, there probably wouldn't be any grounds for prosecution, unless she stole something. If she actually stole something, you know, I might. But basically, I think we're rational enough not to want to get into a lawsuit with her. I would think that would possibly happen.

PROFESSOR MILLER: What would you suppose—hypothesize, why do you suppose she did it?

SECOND BUSINESSMAN: Well, we're disregarding the fact that she just went in to get aerosol data. She didn't go in to write an article—

PROFESSOR MILLER: Let's take it in two steps. Before she goes in to do this human interest story, in your industry—

SECOND BUSINESSMAN: I don't think I'd be even terribly upset about that one, because I think perhaps that would be a perfectly proper way to see how people live, on their job, and all that.

If somebody came and said: "We just discovered that Ms. Plimpton is writing a human interest story about the people in the computer department; what do you think?" I'd say, "You know—" Well, I wouldn't say anything. I don't think they'd come to me with something like that.

PROFESSOR MILLER: Just let her do her thing.

SECOND BUSINESSMAN: I wouldn't be terribly bothered by that. If she came in to ferret out corporate secrets, if you will, I could understand why she's doing it. I could even understand why her managing editor sent her.

PROFESSOR MILLER: Why?

SECOND BUSINESSMAN: A story. They think they've got a story that they're trying to gather.

PROFESSOR MILLER: Just straight story-getting.

SECOND BUSINESSMAN: Well, I assume it's story-getting. I don't know what else it might be. I assume they're not trying to steal money.

PROFESSOR MILLER: Why do you think they didn't come to you?

SECOND BUSINESSMAN: Because I think they probably think that I might have declined the opportunity.

PROFESSOR MILLER: Would you have?

SECOND BUSINESSMAN: Well, it would depend what she specifically said to me that she wanted to do. Probably, if she said: "I want to get in your company and sort of ferret my way around and see what I could find and do all those things," I think I obviously would say no. (*Laughter*)

PROFESSOR MILLER: (*Calls on the first reporter*) Why would a reporter do this? First, just to do the human interest story? And second, more at the infiltration level?

FIRST REPORTER: We're doing the human interest story because sometimes it's very difficult to imagine how the people on the job would feel, unless reporters experienced it—although I've never felt the need to do that, myself.

PROFESSOR MILLER: But it is done.

FIRST REPORTER: It's done.

PROFESSOR MILLER: It's done. Why don't you, or if you haven't done it, why would you assume one of your colleagues, but not you, would go to a corporation and say: "I'd like to do a human interest story; why don't you place me inside?"

FIRST REPORTER: Fine, nothing wrong with that.

PROFESSOR MILLER: And you would assume this corporation would allow you to do it?

FIRST REPORTER: If you were going to become a clerk or something like that, sure; why not?

PROFESSOR MILLER: (*Asks the third businessman*)

THIRD BUSINESSMAN: My corporation wouldn't let you.

PROFESSOR MILLER: Wouldn't let you?

THIRD BUSINESSMAN: No, this is an intrusion upon the rights of the workers.

PROFESSOR MILLER: Which rights?

THIRD BUSINESSMAN: Their rights to privacy, and their rights to make their own determination as to whether or not they're going to talk.

PROFESSOR MILLER: And you think that your workers have a right to know that the fellow worker is a fellow worker?

THIRD BUSINESSMAN: Right.

PROFESSOR MILLER: (*Turns back to the first reporter*) How do you react to that?

FIRST REPORTER: Well, maybe I misunderstood the facts. If I'm going to go in there, and I'm not going to tell the other people that's what I'm doing, I don't know whether that really gives me a problem, as long as I'm performing the job at the same time. But, when I start asking questions of the people I'm working with, there's a slightly different order of magnitude there.

PROFESSOR MILLER: (*Now asks the first businessman*) Would you let someone come in? Human interest?

FIRST BUSINESSMAN: If they wanted to work as a disclosed employee for the purpose of getting a genuine feel of what goes on in a clerical job, I would give that careful thought. As an undisclosed employee, absolutely not, for the reasons my fellow businessman just gave.

PROFESSOR MILLER: (*Turns to the first reporter*) Now, let's look at the tougher one. You want to get on the inside to see something about a manufacturing process. It might be a pollution process. You want to get on the inside to see a banking policy that you feel will be on pieces of paper. Why don't you go to the company first?

FIRST REPORTER: I'd be forced to. By forced—excuse me, I couldn't do that. I wouldn't be permitted by the paper to do that.

I want to tell you something, though. I feel very strongly that we've given the impression, the press generally, that we never do anything which is the least bit, you know, unpleasant or off-color, and we do. We do things that are off-color.

I can think of an example, in which, one time, I was trying to get a story, and I called around, and I said, "This is Adam Smith, and I want to ask you a question," and I asked the question, and I got my answer. And I used the story. And I did not say, "This is Adam Smith from the *Financial Times*."

Now, there was some debate about that, in the shop, and I think I violated my newspaper's rule. I don't blame the people that I talked to, at all, for being angry about it, because they told Adam Smith, but there are lots of Adam Smiths not in journalism. They told Adam Smith, a presumed potential customer for the firm, something they wouldn't have told Adam Smith of the *Financial Times*.

I'm telling you that because I think we've—at my peril. I'm telling you that because I think we've given the impression that we never do anything that is the least bit off-color or unpleasant and reprehensible.

PROFESSOR MILLER: Well, we can take as a given that on occasion newspaper people do infiltrate. We can take, as a given by the way, that everything that you see in these five soap operas has happened. Not at the same time or place, but they have all happened. What I'm trying to get at, I suppose, is why, on occasion—maybe rare occasion—media people don't go directly to the corporate officers when they have questions.

SECOND REPORTER: Isn't one of the difficulties here that we have spent a lot of time talking about things that happen very rarely, and very little time talking about things that happen all the time?

In this particular instance, I suspect that you have many of the top reporters around this table, who do business investigative reporting, and my suspicion is that almost none of them have ever engaged in this technique.

Now, that's not out of piety, that's because it's not productive. We have better ways of getting information.

PROFESSOR MILLER: You wouldn't go to the second businessman, for instance?

SECOND REPORTER: No, I would not go to him.

PROFESSOR MILLER: Who would you go to?

SECOND REPORTER: First of all, I wouldn't be doing this kind of story, it's a feature-type story. If there was information inside of that company that I wanted, I would find out if there was anybody I knew who had formerly been an executive of that company. I would go to an outside director of that company that I knew. I would see if there was anybody in the paper who had any contacts with any of the executives or employees of that company. There are all kinds of things I would do. But I would not use this technique.

PROFESSOR MILLER: You wouldn't go to the operating executives?

SECOND REPORTER: At some point, I would.

PROFESSOR MILLER: At some point.

SECOND REPORTER: But I would not go to the operating executives for a piece of sensitive information. For example, if I wanted details of a loan that Bert Lance had gotten from someone's bank, I would not go to the public relations department or to the chairman of the bank. (*Laughter*)

PROFESSOR MILLER: On the theory that you wouldn't get it?

SECOND REPORTER: Of course.

PROFESSOR MILLER: (*Asks the first banker*) How do you react to that?

FIRST BANKER: Well, I think that really strikes at the heart of the problem, if the basis of your information is predominantly from disaffected employees or from hostile sources. The mind-set of the reporter doing the story is going to be influenced by that. Now, I've found that, subject to certain basic rules like customer confidentiality—and I think everybody appreciates the need for that—most managements are generally very open. But when they talk about a problem like some problems in this case, there are lots of dimensions to the problems. They do not have simplistic answers.

SECOND REPORTER: We will accept complex answers.

FIRST BANKER: Yes, but it generally does—and I think, maybe, during the course of the discussion, some of these may come up. We may see the dimensions of the complexity of the problems, but these problems can't be given sharp focus and definition, which would attract attention. At least, that's the impression that I as a businessman have. And, I have heard that expressed by other businessmen. The nature of the publication requires over-simplification of a very complicated situation with lots of dimensions, and we don't feel that it's put in fair light—whatever that means.

PROFESSOR MILLER: And how does that cause you to react when someone from the media wants to interview you on a subject you think is complex?

FIRST BANKER: Well, we try to be as open as possible and to spend a lot of time with them. We try to bring in the people who have some knowledge about the various dimensions, and here in this case, you're talking about a situation of a blighted area in the city. This is a very tough problem. You've got people living there, you've got the requirement to bring additional investment into that area. You've got the tax base of the city. You've got the institutions that serve it. We try to paint the four corners of the picture, and then permit the reporter to zero in on whatever part of it he wants, but within the context of the whole framework.

PROFESSOR MILLER: (*To the first reporter*) Let's pick up this business of inner-city blight. Let's assume you get this memorandum that Plimpton has gotten in our hypothetical. Let's ignore the question of how you got it, without throwing stones or anything like that. What are you going to do with it? Let's hear your process, your decision-making processes, as to what you're going to do with that information.

FIRST REPORTER: It's essential to know how I got this memorandum. If I've gotten it by legitimate means, I'm certainly going to—

PROFESSOR MILLER: You haven't stolen it. Maybe a disgruntled employee has brought it to you.

FIRST REPORTER: Well, there's a story there.

PROFESSOR MILLER: There is a story there; we've made that clear.

FIRST REPORTER: It's obvious.

PROFESSOR MILLER: Why is it obvious? Let everyone in the room get from A to Z, Z being it's obvious there's a story.

FIRST REPORTER: This situation is so complicated, I hesitate to review it, but—

PROFESSOR MILLER: You have one memorandum.

FIRST REPORTER: We have a memorandum here, and it tells that the whole project is in serious trouble. Okay? We have a complex that's underpopulated and our friend, the president of this bank, wants to have all the welfare families removed as soon as possible so that the investments of the bank will not be in jeopardy, and so forth.

PROFESSOR MILLER: All right, that's the story.

FIRST REPORTER: Oh, sure.

PROFESSOR MILLER: What kind of story? What do you expect to be writing about with this story?

FIRST REPORTER: Well, I'm the financial reporter and I'm going to report from the financial side, but it may turn out that this story is taken out of my hands and handled by the metropolitan desk.

PROFESSOR MILLER: It may be news, it may be real estate, it may be finance.

FIRST REPORTER: I think any one of those three. In fact, all three of those.

PROFESSOR MILLER: When you look at it, how do you frame up the story, in very general terms?

FIRST REPORTER: Again, I don't see it strictly as a financial story. I think it's, in a sense—I hesitate to say "bigger than that." But it's a story of such general interest that I feel quite confident the managing editor would want to take this story and reassign it to the metropolitan desk.

PROFESSOR MILLER: Are you going to talk to your editor about that?

FIRST REPORTER: Oh, certainly.

PROFESSOR MILLER: Talk to him. Let's hear how you two make this decision.

FIRST REPORTER: May I call you by your first name? (*Laughter*)

FIRST EDITOR: Since this is the nicest thing you call me, yes. (*Laughter*)

FIRST REPORTER: Arnold, I've got a story here that's really something. It's a confidential memo, and it touches on a variety of problems, and some of them are ours. We have a question of a potential default on a loan by one of the —you know, PG&S, you know, those guys. We've been critical of them, because of the president's inattention, but there's much more to the story than that. It smacks of sort of—there's an overtone of redlining here, at least in the mentality of the president of the bank. He wants to get rid of a lot of welfare families in this complex. I'll leave it to your decision, but it seems to me that we're going to have a piece of this story, but the city desk is going to have the biggest piece, at least in the beginning.

I leave it up to you, Arnold.

FIRST EDITOR: My reaction would be: "Adam, it's a terrific story." What I see this story shaping up as, is a conflict between two important interest groups. On one hand, we can understand the bank's concern about its investment, about maintaining the viability of that investment in the area. On the other hand, there are public policy issues concerned with welfare payments and the location of welfare families, and it seems that what we're writing about here is how two very desirable objectives have come upon a collision course. I think we'll want to explore this from the bank's aspect. We'll want to talk to them. We'll want to get their views. We want to verify that this memo is an accurate reflection of the bank's views. We'll want to go to the city. We'll want to talk to them about its policy of locating welfare clients there. Perhaps, we'll want to talk to some outsiders who can give us a broader view as to how these two points can be reconciled. I think we'll want to talk to other departments of the paper. Maybe we'll want to put together a team of several people to look into all aspects of this, because we think it's a major public policy issue.

PROFESSOR MILLER: Big story.

FIRST EDITOR: Big story.

PROFESSOR MILLER: Big story. So you're going to leave it in his ballpark?

FIRST EDITOR: No, I wouldn't leave it in his ballpark. We usually play the right of first discovery. If Adam Smith has been the person that has received this particular document, I think he's entitled to some of the action in the development of the story. But I think we'll bring in people who are expert on the city side, on the public policy issues, welfare, and put together a group and designate an editor to ride herd over the whole project, and see what we come up with.

PROFESSOR MILLER: Are you going to check this out upstairs?

FIRST EDITOR: Well, upstairs sounds pejorative. I'd check it out on our same floor. (*Laughter*) My procedure at the point when I had this information, because it would involve a jurisdictional problem between various city-states at the newspaper, would be to go to the managing editor and say: "Here's a story that seems to have a large element of business financial news in it, but there are city angles to it that we'll want to pursue through City Hall, and things of this sort, too. We're going to have to have a joint project. I, obviously, would want to run it, because I like to be involved in good stories. What do you think; is that okay? Shall we go ahead?"

PROFESSOR MILLER: Would you feel the same way if this were not a bank, but if it were a real-estate development owned by your parent company?

FIRST EDITOR: That parent company would own the property and would be seeking to evict welfare tenants?

PROFESSOR MILLER: Yes.

FIRST EDITOR: I think I'd feel the same way, but then it would go upstairs. (*Laughter*)

PROFESSOR MILLER: All right, say you go upstairs to Mr. Businessman. He is both your publisher and, at least, an influential member of the board of the conglomerate which also owns the real-estate unit.

FIRST EDITOR: I'd say, "Mr. Businessman, we've come across a terrific story here, but you might have some problem with it. Here's what we've got.

"We seem to have gotten ourselves, or the corporation, you seem to have gotten yourself, into some difficulty through your investments here. Whether that was wise or not is obviously your business. But this is now what we've come across. This seems to be a little bit bigger than I had first thought and I sort of need your thinking on this."

PROFESSOR MILLER: (*Asks the fourth businessman*)

FOURTH BUSINESSMAN: The answer is, "I don't know."

PROFESSOR MILLER: Let's assume we're going forward. I thought I heard that at least one of your lines of inquiry would be to talk to banks.

FIRST EDITOR: Yes, indeed.

PROFESSOR MILLER: (*To the first reporter*) Your editor has just bucked it down to you, and one of the things you're supposed to do is talk to the bank. The head of the bank calls you. What do you say to him?

FIRST REPORTER: I say, I have a story here. I want to discuss it with you, and I want to give you a full opportunity to hear the facts. It's something we're going to run with, and you have a right to know what we're about.

PROFESSOR MILLER: Do you tell him about the memo?

FIRST REPORTER: I tell him I have the information.

PROFESSOR MILLER: You tell him you have the information. (*To the second banker*) How do you react to this information out of the blue?

SECOND BANKER: Well, I know that this problem has been facing us for a little while. It's a big enough problem, so it's something many people in the public probably know something about; at least the people living in the complex know about it. I'd want to provide as much information as possible, so that I get the best, the fairest story possible. I'd invite the reporter to come over.

PROFESSOR MILLER: Would you ask him about the memo?

SECOND BANKER: Well, at this point—

PROFESSOR MILLER: He didn't say "memo." He said; "I've got some information."

SECOND BANKER: I don't think I'd make any assumptions about the source of the information. This is a large, complicated problem. The public interest is involved. I think I'd assume that he obtained the information in a normal course of business.

PROFESSOR MILLER: Now, are you going to go to him or is he coming to you?

FIRST REPORTER: It doesn't matter to me.

PROFESSOR MILLER: Good, we're at the PG&S.

FIRST REPORTER: Okay, I've got a story here you're not going to like. We've got a problem here with a complex that is not well-populated, and we think there's a possibility of default, and we're going to be in serious trouble with this story.

SECOND BANKER: Well, I recognize the problem, but maybe I look at it a little differently. Maybe I look at this as an opportunity to do something, perhaps to stem the blight that's starting to appear in that particular neighborhood.

FIRST REPORTER: In other words, you're going to kick out these welfare families; is that the idea?

SECOND BANKER: Well, it is possible that we should take a look at whether or not the complex can accommodate the concentrated number of welfare families, and see if perhaps this isn't a bad policy for the city to follow. Perhaps we ought to—not kick them out—but make arrangements to do something about dispersing them in other parts of the city.

FIRST REPORTER: That's very interesting. You know, my information has you on the record as saying you're going to kick them out.

SECOND BANKER: No, I think, if you have that information, it's distorted. Make arrangements to relocate them as quickly as possible.

FIRST REPORTER: Well, I'll have to read you excerpts from my material, I'm afraid, in order to get this thing straightened out. This is so because my information says that the owners of this complex—who are in default on your loan—have been ordered to remove the welfare families as soon as feasible. You've also told them: "This is to halt any possible spread in deterioration that will endanger the neighborhood and other investments." You say "other investments." I'm not saying that you say it, but it's in my information that this is the way it's stated in my information. I presume you're concerned about other investments of the bank, and this is your tactic. This is the way it's stated. You're telling me you haven't said you're going to remove the welfare families. I'm telling you, it's in writing that you have.

SECOND BANKER: No, I'm not saying that I do not plan, make plans to relocate the welfare families. I'm just saying that I have no power to order the owner of a piece of property to relocate his tenants. I can suggest that this would be in the best interest of maintaining the value of the property, but I can't order him.

FIRST REPORTER: Well, as I suggest, again, you have suggested it in the very strongest possible terms that he do that.

SECOND BANKER: That, I can do. But I cannot order him to do it, because I have no means of enforcement. I can and I have expressed my concern about the way the property is deteriorating, about the effect that an excessive—and I have to emphasize that—an excessive number of welfare tenants in a particular concentrated area would have on both the property and the neighborhoods.

FIRST REPORTER: Have you thought about the public-policy considerations here? This puts the bank in a very embarrassing position, I've got to tell you that, because if we use this information, you're going to be put in the position of being anxious to deal very harshly with welfare families. I want to be sure you understand what I'm going to do in terms of this information, so you have a full opportunity to answer in the best way possible to serve your own interests.

SECOND BANKER: Well, unfortunately, the memo, the information that you have, is only part of the picture.

FIRST REPORTER: You're assuming it's a memo. I haven't told you that. (*Laughter*)

SECOND BANKER: Your source of information is limited, because we have already started to talk to the city about this. It is a public-policy problem. It is a problem of a city department sending far too many welfare tenants to a single location without any exercise of control over the situation.

Now, I know that the financial situation with this project is pretty bad. We're a commercial bank. We do not normally plan to retain building loans for an indefinite period of time. We're concerned about getting this property up to the right financial level, so that it goes to its permanent financing. The only way this can be accomplished is if we have a first-class complex. That may include welfare tenants, but not to the degree that we currently have them.

So our plan is to work with the government in transferring some of these welfare tenants to other locations, so that we can reestablish the vitality of this complex.

PROFESSOR MILLER: Let's draw the curtain a little bit. How are you going to write the story, at this point?

FIRST REPORTER: Well, we have a fairly complete story. We're talking about what we've just developed here in our conversation. We have a fairly complete story, as far as my information and his reply are concerned.

Right away, we've got a news story. That means we've got to go with it fairly quickly. Well, we're going to go with it fairly quickly. I would go back to my editor at this point and tell him what I have. I'll tell you another thing, I don't think a reporter, in a situation like this, is necessarily qualified to consider all the ramifications. This business of going back to the editor is an important one for the purposes of finding out whether or not there may be other angles that we're overlooking. It is a complex story and there are lots of things to be brought into it.

If we sit down at the typewriter and bang something out right away, we can possibly overlook the full meaning of the story and some of the implications that should be covered.

PROFESSOR MILLER: But you're still convinced it's a story.

FIRST REPORTER: Absolutely.

PROFESSOR MILLER: And you're convinced it's a major story.

FIRST REPORTER: Definitely.

PROFESSOR MILLER: (*To the first editor*) Do you agree with that?

FIRST EDITOR: Absolutely. My concern would be to verify the authenticity of the memo to make sure that it was a legitimate document; also, to check with the owners of the building and with the welfare tenants to find out if, indeed, that was what was happening—that pressure was being put upon them to vacate it; and, to look into the city aspects of it—why the welfare tenants were there, and what purpose their presence was supposed to accomplish; once we'd satisfied ourselves that we had reported the essentials of the story, to publish it. To publish it, saying this was according to information made available to our newspaper, and then to say that the banker, when asked for a comment on the situation, replied as follows, and to say that very high up in the story.

PROFESSOR MILLER: *(To the second editor)* Do you disagree with this appraisal?

SECOND EDITOR: I do not.

PROFESSOR MILLER: Do you think it's a story?

SECOND EDITOR: Yes.

PROFESSOR MILLER: And you would run it and develop it about the same way?

SECOND EDITOR: I'd send someone down to the project and do a side bar on what life was like down there. Otherwise, I'd go just the same as he would.

PROFESSOR MILLER: *(Recognizes first banker)*

FIRST BANKER: It seems to me that this really strikes a focal point of what we would consider to be the incomplete ways that stories are reported. Let's say, a story comes out, and the whole purpose of the discussion here is really on the welfare families in this project. Now, we're taking the facts of the hypothetical here. This is abnormal. I think there are better ways of doing this than was posed in the hypothetical, but we won't change the facts.

First of all, any bank that was in this position would have gone to its board and there would have been a full exposition to the board of what the problem was. We would have gotten the benefit from the people who were sitting around the table, as to the public-policy implications and what might be done.

Second, there would have been an economic analysis of the area. The situation here talks about lower-middle-class area, where the bank has made sizable other investments, and therefore, the bank has made a judgment that additional investment can be attracted to this area, and this can be an area which can be improved. So you would be working very closely with the Economic Development Commission. We'd be working with the mayor's Manpower Development Program, to see if we couldn't find jobs for these welfare families, and perhaps take them off the rolls of the welfare so that they wouldn't be welfare families anymore.

You'd be trying to see if you could attract other industry into that particular area. You wouldn't want to have something that was in the area that might deter. In other words, if a building was going to start to deteriorate, you wouldn't want to let that create an impression so that industry would not locate in that area.

This would be a composite project of the labor community, the city community, the financial community, the industrial community, and the bank. It would seem to me that a story that was going to deal with this would not focus on the plight of the individual families, although that might be a side bar. Rather, it would be in the context of all of these other considerations that go to bear on real city redevelopment.

A VOICE: Business is being pious now.

FIRST BANKER: Well, maybe it is being pious. But, these are problems we face every day. I think we've had a fairly decent record around the country, bringing back areas that have begun to turn the corner.

PROFESSOR MILLER: If I'm hearing you correctly, you are not necessarily quarreling with the fact that there's going to be a story.

FIRST BANKER: No. On the contrary, it would seem to me that the way this would be handled, would be to call a press conference and to have representatives of all areas—to have the city, to have the Economic Development Commission, everybody else, and trace what's involved here. Then say; "We've got a problem with some of the welfare families." Now, there are lots of ways of dealing with that.

One is to say: "Okay, we won't take any more welfare families into this particular project. Let's try to get jobs for the welfare families that are there, and let's set up codes of conduct for living in there."

If they meet that goal, fine. You've got that segment rehabilitated.

PROFESSOR MILLER: (*Recognizes the first lawyer*)

FIRST LAWYER: Just two observations. One is, I'm glad there are no racial aspects to this problem. (*Laughter*) It does seem to me that there's a hell of a story. The story is about the person who is the author of the memo, and not yet about the bank.

Now, it may be that it becomes a story about the bank after the story about the person who wrote the memorandum is published. The underlying problem I'm having is the assumption that runs through every comment I've heard so far that there is a cause-and-effect relationship between the presence of welfare families and the economic plight of the project. Maybe you want to assume that as a given, but it's one hell of a given to start out with.

The facts, as we have them, have this project in trouble before you get the increase in welfare tenancy. The reasons for that are not clear. Part of what the bank's process ought to be is what's just been described and it ought to be doing that. The fact that the bank would be making those kinds of inquiries—into the economic and other influences that are affecting this loan—doesn't excuse the dumbness of the memorandum that was prepared. I regard it as a dumb memorandum, produced by a person whose vision is not very broad, and about whom, perhaps, a story would be appropriate.

But I think, as you talk it through, and as we develop all the intelligence that's around the table, to allow the assumptions to ride that there is a cause-and-effect relationship, necessarily, between the presence of welfare families—first of all, that's odd to me, frankly, because if you have the welfare family, the odds are you have the third-party payment that will insure the rent collection on the property and might make it more viable, rather than less viable.

There are a whole series of other questions that enter into this, and it's distressing to not hear any comment on those, even if we want to assume and weigh.

PROFESSOR MILLER: So if I hear you correctly, you're not quarreling with the fact that there's a story, but you're enlarging its dimensions.

FIRST LAWYER: That's correct.

PROFESSOR MILLER: We've now got the biggest story in all time.

(To the first banker) I take it from what you said, you would be willing to turn over to the reporter, to the newspaper, the economic studies you've done and whatever memoranda were generated in the course of the decision-making process about this complex, so they could analyze the facts and write a more intelligent story.

FIRST BANKER: Well, there's no question that we would turn over a good deal of economic information. Let me address this question about a particular memorandum, because we see this coming up, and this is a habitual problem, where a document may fall into the hands of the media, and they publish it, and we're not quarreling with that.

But very often a memorandum may be out of context with the total picture. Now, I don't want to be in a position of being an apologist for Phiduciary in this case. But he may have—the week before—had his staff or the economic department prepare a 350-page document on this whole problem, outlining all the various options and so forth, and this was kind of a shorthand cryptic thing, written to another officer in the organization. We just don't know the context in which that particular memorandum was written. To hang a whole story on that, without getting the total picture may not be putting it in its proper light.

Now, on a story like this that involves the city and involves an important population within the city, you bet, this is everybody's business and everybody's story, and everybody should be a contributor. As I understand the facts in this case, the publisher of the *Chronicle* is very active in this redevelopment corporation. This is a community problem. This is not just a bank problem.

Now, there may be individual bank investment involved in the totality of that problem, but the problem is bigger than that individual bank investment.

PROFESSOR MILLER: *(To the fifth businessman)* Let's suppose it's just a real-estate development company. There's no bank or anything, how do you react?

FIFTH BUSINESSMAN: I disagree with our lawyer. I think that the presence of welfare families in any project that's just starting off, would, to a large extent, be detrimental to the future of the project and may not allow it to be funded someplace in the future.

PROFESSOR MILLER: When the reporter appears, how are you going to handle it?

FIFTH BUSINESSMAN: Well, the sad part about this is that the minute this story comes into the newspaper, it's no longer an economic problem. It becomes a political problem. I would do everything in my power to keep the story from appearing, by, in effect, speaking to the reporter and explaining the problem to him. If I can't do that, the story will appear. The chances are the project will go down the drain.

PROFESSOR MILLER: You don't think there should be a story?

FIFTH BUSINESSMAN: I don't think so.

PROFESSOR MILLER: How would you try to convince the reporter not to write a story?

FIFTH BUSINESSMAN: Well, just by explaining the economics of the situation—the fact that turning this project into a complete welfare project, which is what will happen after the news gets into the newspaper, will be harmful to the city, to the neighborhood, and to the economics of the whole area. Now, that may not work, and if it doesn't work, the project is in trouble.

PROFESSOR MILLER: Do you think it will work? If you were a betting man, what would you bet?

FIFTH BUSINESSMAN: I'd bet that I couldn't do it.

PROFESSOR MILLER: But you'd try.

FIFTH BUSINESSMAN: I certainly would try, because I believe that I'm right.

PROFESSOR MILLER: Will he win that bet?

FIRST REPORTER: No, he won't win that bet, but I'll say this, that I do think that a lot of the things that the first banker has said about this story would provide a very interesting—let's say, we'll call it a think piece or a story in depth—which would have what he had to say, along with a lot of other assessments of the situation, including the one that the lawyer suggested. These are very interesting stories. This is going to be one of the, let's say, major efforts, I'd say, of the *Financial Times* for the next few—well, who knows how long the story would last. All of these implications, and they're very serious implications—if they are not touched on by the paper, then we have not really done a complete job.

FIFTH BUSINESSMAN: We had the same story in St. Louis ten or fifteen years ago, and I doubt if the newspaper now would publish what happened at that time, and show the destruction of those buildings. But I know it was a major story at the time.

PROFESSOR MILLER: It's interesting that we have rather polar views. You're feeling is that the social situation is best advantaged by no story.

FIFTH BUSINESSMAN: Yes.

PROFESSOR MILLER: And I take it, the first banker is driving towards maximum information flow, all dimensions of the story.

FIFTH BUSINESSMAN: It won't appear that way in the newspaper.

PROFESSOR MILLER: Aha, why do you say that?

FIFTH BUSINESSMAN: Because newspapers—I mean, putting a lot of information into the paper is not going to get readers. (*Laughter*)

PROFESSOR MILLER: You are making a judgment, as I hear it, about our friends in the media. You have a perception of them.

FIFTH BUSINESSMAN: Yes, I do.

PROFESSOR MILLER: Which is? Fill in the blanks.

FIFTH BUSINESSMAN: Exciting headlines sell newspapers.

PROFESSOR MILLER: So your best guess as to how this story will appear, after the banker gives the reporter at least two file drawers full of paper, the lawyer brings in a great deal of sociological data on the question of the relationship or non-relationship of welfare tenants to the economics of a project—how do you think that story is going to run?

FIFTH BUSINESSMAN: Landlord evicts welfare tenants. (*Laughter*)

PROFESSOR MILLER: (*Asks the second editor*) Is that the headline?

SECOND EDITOR: No.

PROFESSOR MILLER: You gave us this side bar on what life's like down there for those tenants.

SECOND EDITOR: And you made the assumption that it's going to be filled with rats and trash and garbage.

PROFESSOR MILLER: Me?

SECOND EDITOR: Yes.

PROFESSOR MILLER: I'm just standing here directing traffic. (*Laughter*)

SECOND EDITOR: I think the side bar could very well point out all of the social dimensions that the lawyer sees. I think there's an assumption on the part of the business community, in this, that we have absolutely no capacity to understand anything about their business, and no capacity to have a brain.

A VOICE: What would the headline be, just as a matter of interest?

SECOND EDITOR: Technically, we would avoid putting it in a one-column hole, where you have fourteen or fifteen characters per line, because it's obviously a very complicated story. What the lead is—if you tell me what the lead of the story would be, I could write you a headline. I suspect it would be, what's the area it's in—we'd have to have that— "Brooklyn project falls . . ."—no—". . . Troubled by Financial Something"—it's a long headline. "Money Troubles Plague Brooklyn Project."

PROFESSOR MILLER: "Money Troubles Plague Brooklyn Project." (*Laughter*) It sounds to me as if you'd sell a copy to everyone in this room.

    (*Asks the third banker*) Do you share our businessman's rather dim view as to such prospects for the story?

THIRD BANKER: No, I think it's a story. I agree with my banker colleague. The headline on the oldest story in the world is the banker foreclosing on the widow in a blizzard, and this is a variation of that one. (*Laughter*)

    It has to be a story.

    What I would say is that the complexity of the situation is enormous, and there are two or three things. One headline might be: "A Bank Makes Another Bum Loan." Shaky is the apparent word, "Shaky Loan in Big Project." That would be the story of the financial page, and the other regular story would be the problem of welfare tenants, what the project is like. As the editor said, a side bar on what the living is there.

    What is the city doing about it? The assignment of welfare tenants is made by a city agency, in my particular city. Why did the long-term lender refuse to take up his mortgage? That's another piece of the story. What is the occupancy rate? Is there a tenant strike? The whole Co-op City story is right here in this case. The lender was the state, but this is Co-op City, and that's the way the story was developed. I agree that you should give them as much information as you want, because it's a social problem, it's a financial problem, and it's a political problem. Whether or not the project is viable in the end, you can't foresee now. It depends on what people do between now and then. But it's certainly a story. It certainly should have a lot of information.

PROFESSOR MILLER: Are you sanguine about what's going to come out?

THIRD BANKER: Well, whether you're sanguine or not sanguine about the fact that we have a project that is in trouble, the situation doesn't make for sanguineness. I'm not sanguine about the fact that so far nobody has figured out any answer to an urban problem. This is a symptom of a disease we don't know how to cure at this point. I'm not sanguine about the fact that there will be a lot of free advice on how to cure it, but it will be with us for a good many years. As far as the story goes, it's a perfectly legitimate story.

PROFESSOR MILLER: But when I use the word "sanguine," I used it in reference to what you expect that story to contain when it hits the paper.

THIRD BANKER: I would say there might be some difference in what the headline says and that's why I asked what it would be, so that I'd be able to answer your questions a little better.

PROFESSOR MILLER: (*Recognizes the sixth businessman*)

SIXTH BUSINESSMAN: I'd like to ask the reporter a question, if I may change the facts for a second. If instead of the bank putting pressure on the landlord to evict the welfare tenants, all the people in the neighborhood, the clergymen, the community leaders went to the landlord and said: "You must get rid of the welfare tenants because they are having an adverse impact on our neighborhood," the landlord responded by saying: "I can get higher rents from the department of welfare than I can in the marketplace, and I couldn't keep up my mortgage payments and my tax payments unless I went to welfare people." But the community put extraordinary pressure on him. He owns other property in the neighborhood, and his clergyman asked him, and all the local legislators asked him, and he finally gave in and began to change the occupancy from welfare tenants to other kinds of tenants. Is that the same-size story as the one we've just been discussing?

FIRST REPORTER: That's certainly a very interesting story. I defer to my editor on that one.

FIRST EDITOR: I think it's a different story. I think it's less a financial story at that point and more a city story, and with less financial aspect involved.

I'd like to ask a banker, though, what his reaction would be to another story that we would likely run which would be, "Wall Street Expresses Concern Over Shaky Bank Real-Estate Lending—Stock Drops."

THIRD BANKER: I said, at the outset, that that would be a story.

FIRST EDITOR: "Wall Street Houses Produce Adverse Research Reports as a Result of Bank Real-Estate Difficulties." That would be a story?

THIRD BANKER: Certainly, no question about it. Whether the story would compare the size of this loan, which is about fifty million dollars against the forty billion dollars outstanding—that would be a question of whether that would be in the first paragraph; one-tenth of one percent of loans are shaky. Then we might discuss whether it really is a story. Is that a fair comment?

FIRST EDITOR: Right. We would relate the extent of the problem loans to the bank equity capital.

THIRD BANKER: And the total loans?

FIRST EDITOR: I think equity capital would be a more operative comparison.

A VOICE: I wonder if I could comment on those points, also. If the stories are written in quite that bald form, "Wall Street Reacts to Shaky Real-Estate Loans, Stock Drops Two Points"—

A VOICE: Five points.

A VOICE: Five points. I wonder if there isn't an implicit assumption in that, that work-out situations always end up in total losses? It seems to me that you may have lots of patients in the sick bay, but for heaven's sake, only a small proportion of them die. Depending upon the skill of the doctors, a greater proportion of them recover, at least partially. I wonder if you couldn't look at this same situation and say: "Hopeful Sign, Project Facing Money Problems, Under Remedial Process, Has Hope for Entire Community." (*Laughter*)

A VOICE: I think you can influence how that comes out, in the way that you react to it. If you react to it in the way one businessman was suggesting, that is, try to focus on the damage that a story might do, you're very likely to end up with that kind of conversation with the story. There's no way you are going to kill a story like this. You would end up with a story that focuses on—

PROFESSOR MILLER: Look, could I just hold you and say, there's no way you're going to kill the story.

A VOICE: No, it's too good a story.

PROFESSOR MILLER: Too good a story.

A VOICE: Right.

PROFESSOR MILLER: What do you mean by "good"?

A VOICE: It has too much public interest.

PROFESSOR MILLER: Public interest, public interest, and that's something you decide when you decide it's newsworthy, that this story has public interest, and nothing a businessman can say to you about the deleterious side effects of the story—

A VOICE: Given the facts as we have them.

PROFESSOR MILLER: Okay.

A VOICE: Yes.

PROFESSOR MILLER: (*To the first banker*) You've gone back to a theme I think you sounded earlier, which was the slant that you perceive the media give stories. Before, you remarked about one editor's focus on the welfare tenant aspect.

FIRST BANKER: I don't think I used the word "slant." I said, we'd like to see the story in context and in fair light.

PROFESSOR MILLER: And you would not charge the media with slant in the headlines that we've been discussing or in the focus on the welfare?

FIRST BANKER: Slant can be used a lot in headlines, because they are abbreviated or obviously incomplete. But I do think that if we can develop complete understanding on the dimension of a story, we, at least, have found that ninety-nine times out of a hundred, let's face it, everything that comes out in a story we're not going to like. There's not going to be a love-fest, but at least it's going to be balanced. We find it much better to lay it all out on the table, and if you're dealing with competent reporters of good will, you get that balance in both the headlines and the story.

THIRD REPORTER: This was the point that I was starting to make, that if you adopt the approach that the bankers take, you're much more likely to get a story that would be more acceptable to you. No, I don't think any story that could come out of this set of facts would be enjoyed by the bank. The facts are painful. But I would see the story in this case, if all the facts were laid out, focusing on the problem of the welfare people and how the bank is trying to make the project work. There's a conflict here, as an editor explained it. The alternative, if the facts are limited, is to go with what's hard, which is the memo saying welfare tenants are going to be evicted. That's going to be a much more damaging story.

PROFESSOR MILLER: (*Calls on the fourth reporter*)

FOURTH REPORTER: I think there's a bit of piety creeping in, because we're ignoring the fact that the reporter has this memo, and suddenly I understand the idea of calling a press conference and broadening the story, bringing in the whole picture. If I were the reporter, I'd be very angry that my exclusive had been blown. That's an honest gut feeling. I'm a reporter, and I do like to be first, and I think we reporters have to admit that. It's a weakness of ours. I'd hate to see the press conference called. It happens to us quite frequently. We get an exclusive piece of information and suddenly we're blanketed. Why should the bank take a story one day, in the reporter's paper, and then call a press conference the next day and have all the rest of us catch up? But it is a gut instinct, I think, of the reporter. I speak for myself, at least.

PROFESSOR MILLER: Well, your point is interesting because I heard the reporter refer to this as a news story. When we first started talking, and in line with your comment that a news story has a certain urgency to it, a certain feeling that you've got, maybe not a deadline today, but a short fuse on publication. Then I heard a conversation between an editor and this reporter that involved at least an eight-year Ph.D. course in economics, sociology, anthropology, etc., etc. Now, what's the real world?

THIRD EDITOR: In the real world, the banker was saying, you can't talk about this because he wants to respect the confidentiality of the owner of the property.

FIRST BANKER: No, I think a story that would be like this, would already have been discussed, as I said, with the mayor's department. It would have been discussed with the labor community. It would have been discussed with citizens' groups within the community. This is different from going into the files and asking, what is your loan to such and such, and what is the financial conditon of such and such. We would protect those files with all of the ability that we would have.

This is a question of what's going to happen in a community, in a sector of the city, and what's going to happen to various populations there. It seems to me that there's a substantial distinction between the situations.

Now, if somebody asked: "What is the status of the borrowers of that building?" we would draw the line there and say, "We'll discuss anything about the community, but if you want us to talk about the financial condition of these particular borrowers, we're not going to do that."

Perhaps I can make one other point, too, and it was made earlier. People have the impression that the banks are able to order actions to be taken. Until you foreclose on the property—and that's a long, complicated procedure—you don't have any authority. Banks are very reluctant even to try to influence that, other than to say it would be better if such and such happened. But as often as not, the borrower says, "I'm not going to do it," and then you get into a confrontational situation where you do have to go through foreclosure and the borrower tries to deter the progress of that, which is a complicated procedure. So this isn't a case where the bank is in control at this particular time.

PROFESSOR MILLER: (*Turns to the first businessman*) How would you react? Would you react the way he reacted, assuming you had a subsidiary in real-estate development, this was your problem? Would you react the way our bankers are reacting?

FIRST BUSINESSMAN: I share the feeling that the story is out. I would not only try to prevent it but I would try to get our point of view included, because if we wait until the story is out, and then we formulate a point of view, it will never catch up with the story. So it is in our best interest to deal fully and openly immediately, so that the first story includes our point of view as to the importance of the problem and why it's difficult and complex.

PROFESSOR MILLER: (*Turns to the third editor*) When you call him, what do you expect to get?

THIRD EDITOR: He would ask me over. I would sit down and he'd try to lay it out.

PROFESSOR MILLER: He would try to lay it out. I take it, the comment you made a couple of minutes ago was not a generalization about how business reacts . . . (*Laughter*)

THIRD EDITOR: The standard problem we have is with bankers who use a smokescreen to hold off giving out information, and then they sit back and say: "Well, we should give out all the information. We want to see all this in print." but, it doesn't happen on the first confrontation.

PROFESSOR MILLER: (*Asks the fourth banker*) He says your group masters a smokescreen. How do you react to that?

FOURTH BANKER: Well, I react by saying that things are different in my state. (*Laughter*)

PROFESSOR MILLER: No smoke in your state.

FOURTH BANKER: I think that anybody on the newspapers in my city would call me up, and I'd talk to him on the phone, and he'd come see me. It's too important for me to talk to anyone else, because if my bank's involved in a big deal like that, I've got to talk to them.

PROFESSOR MILLER: And you would say our third editor's experience—

THIRD EDITOR: I don't think he would try to call me, because they don't have much to do with us. If you asked the fourth editor, I'd bet you he wouldn't say that that's not true.

PROFESSOR MILLER: I'm not going to put him on the spot.

FOURTH EDITOR: Well, I would say that you cannot generalize because in some situations we find companies that will respond, and in other cases, we find companies that say: "Give us your questions in writing and maybe we'll get back to you."

PROFESSOR MILLER: Does that bother you?

FOURTH EDITOR: Yes, it bothers me a great deal. I would tell them where to go, with their questions in writing.

PROFESSOR MILLER: Why does it bother you?

FOURTH EDITOR: Because when I have a story, I'm going to get it done and I'm not going to wait for somebody to take questions in writing and then put it through a law firm and then come back with a nothing response, which is what we almost always get from a written sort of correspondence.

I would also say that, with all due respect, that I agree that most often the first call to a businessman or banker, on a really sensitive subject, brings more of a stonewall response. Now, later on, it may warm up. But, we don't get a rapid response very often from the business community.

PROFESSOR MILLER: What do you think about the comments that we heard from our reporters about the deadline issue, saying they're going to do deep background research.

FOURTH EDITOR: Well, it depends on the story. If I know that some other newspaper has the same story, I'm going to be in a hurry. Now, that doesn't mean I'm going to put it out as an incomplete story, but I'm going to work very fast and very hard and the story is going to come out sooner than it would if I think I had the story to myself. Or, if the story is indeed very, very complex, in that case, well, I might have the reporter work a month and a half on it.

That certainly happens.

PROFESSOR MILLER: If you think you've got the story, you work on it.

FOURTH EDITOR: Right, and sometimes I would even work on it for that length of time, even knowing a competitor might have it, but I certainly would admit that we try to be first.

PROFESSOR MILLER: So you are responding to competitive instincts, just the way any business would.

FOURTH EDITOR: Absolutely. It's part of the drive.

PROFESSOR MILLER: And how do you factor in the social considerations? Let's assume you feel that the *Wall Street Journal* or the *New York Times* is onto a story like this. I realize I've got this housing project spread over thousands of miles, now. But ignore the metaphysics. You know that the competition is onto the story, but you had a conversation, as they did, and you understand or are beginning to understand the social implications of this. What would you do?

FOURTH EDITOR: I think the more complex the story is, perhaps the more people you put on it, if you're in a hurry, or you do what you can to get the materials as fast as you can. But I must concede that, although you might go with the story the first time around, it would not be totally complete. That doesn't mean there isn't another day.

PROFESSOR MILLER: Do you have some scale on which you weigh social significance versus competitive drive?

FOURTH EDITOR: No. (*Laughter*) There is no scale. I suppose it's a gut feeling. You would see how many people are impacted. Is it a few people or a lot of people?

PROFESSOR MILLER: Just a few welfare people. They're really not impacted. They are on the way out anyway, right?

FOURTH EDITOR: No, it's a few welfare people, but perhaps we have here, if we go back to case itself, discriminatory practice, which might in itself be a story. Now, we've heard explanations here that soften that a good deal, and we would certainly want to see whether those softer explanations are correct. I think it would be possible to find out, because I think we could go to that community and find out.

PROFESSOR MILLER: Twenty-four hours.

FOURTH EDITOR: We could also go to the city and find out, and we could do that in twenty-four hours, we could.

PROFESSOR MILLER: Because the *Journal* is going to run a story about something happening in your home town tomorrow morning. Boy, won't you look silly when the *Wall Street Journal* has something about your city?

FOURTH EDITOR: Well, we're in a tight spot. (*Laughter*)

PROFESSOR MILLER: All right. We'll pick up some of these things in the context of the third soap opera. The third soap is this NUFA, this urban finance organization. It's been operating for about six years, let's say. I think the first banker came very close to bringing us into this soap opera when he referred to the bail-out situation. Because here, you're just given documents showing that this organization is in trouble on these notes. How do you react?

FOURTH EDITOR: I react by thinking that we've got a good story and we'd better get on it pretty fast.

PROFESSOR MILLER: Why fast?

FOURTH EDITOR: Well, I think we ought to get on it fast, because it's important. I mean, I don't think my first consideration here would be competition, although that would cross my mind at some point during the day. My first reaction would be that there are lots of bondholders, there are lots of people involved in the community, it's both financial and general in its impact. I'd want the information out as soon as possible.

PROFESSOR MILLER: Why as soon as possible?

FOURTH EDITOR: The public should have it, as soon as I can get it to them.

PROFESSOR MILLER: Where have you been for six years?

FOURTH EDITOR: Well, I didn't know about it for six years. I'm sorry, I just don't know, that's all. I wish I were omniscient, but I'm not.

PROFESSOR MILLER: This is a tough one to get at. I'd be the first to admit it. I really would like to know why six years have gone by, with this massive urban-financing organization periodically issuing bonds—they have had three or four bond issues during that six years, and they're putting up massive projects. Suddenly, you have a sense of urgency because one day, someone hands you some confidential documents. Suddenly, you're worried about the bondholders and the public.

I'm asking you a very difficult question that's really very abstract. The business reporters, do you think that it is their job just to keep abreast of things like this, to come in one day to the office, three years ago, and say: "Gee, I wonder how NUFA is doing." Or do you just react when people hand you documents?

FOURTH EDITOR: Well, I would say we try to do both, but I would concede that we're often remiss in not sort of just keeping track. But we should. We try to, but I must say there's more urgency when we are presented with a document such as we're talking about here; that lays out a real problem. Then we feel, obviously, there's a story and we're going to get going on it.

Now, when I say there's an urgency, that doesn't necessarily mean we're doing a story tonight. We might not even be doing the story for a month, depending on how complex this thing is. But there certainly would be pressure on, with the document in hand.

PROFESSOR MILLER: Please do not misapprehend. I'm not throwing stones. I am really just asking. You're worried about those bondholders now. You feel you have a duty to inform them. I'm asking, where was the duty for five years, so many days? Do you read the official statements that accompany bond issues from municipal corporations?

FOURTH EDITOR: Well, I would say, probably, most of the time, no, because there are too many of them. We have to be directed, in some way, to a story, probably because otherwise just a routine reading of lots and lots of material is probably not going to get our paper out.

PROFESSOR MILLER: To be sure, there are lots of official statements, compounded by S-1s, compounded by 8-Ks, and 10-Ks, right?

FOURTH EDITOR: Correct.

PROFESSOR MILLER: And you can't read them all.

FOURTH EDITOR: Cannot.

PROFESSOR MILLER: Do you think it should be a job of the media to monitor those things, and is it a resource question?

FOURTH EDITOR: In a way, it's a resource question, but I think it would take an impossible number of people to do it. I'm not saying we shouldn't have more people doing it, and there certainly are situations we should be monitoring better than we are. I certainly agree with that.

PROFESSOR MILLER: Okay. So here we are, you've got the documents and there's a sense of urgency. How do you go about this story?

FOURTH EDITOR: Well, probably with more than one reporter because it's complex and there are so many places to go. Often, with a project approach, you get more minds on it, you get more ideas, you get more complete coverage of it, so that's probably the way you begin internally. You plan a project.

In terms of going out to get the story, you simply go to all the people that are involved in it.

PROFESSOR MILLER: You go to the bank.

FOURTH EDITOR: You go to the bank. I'm not sure you go to them first. I think you make a judgment, right off the bat, where you're most likely to get help first.

PROFESSOR MILLER: That presupposes, I take it, that you have some sort of a sketch as to what the story or stories might be.

FOURTH EDITOR: Well, you probably do if you have a document like this.

PROFESSOR MILLER: Okay. What do you see, at this point, as potential stories here? Which are these newsworthy elements?

FOURTH EDITOR: Well, I think, to begin with, you have a story just simply on the whole project's being in financial difficulty and probably going to need some infusion of capital in some manner, to keep it alive. Perhaps there's mismanagement. I mean, I can go on—most of it is newsworthy. Finally, you might get down to the fact that you have a bank official trying to keep this thing quiet until this governor can get reelected, because he's more likely to pass legislation. That would be a story, if you really discovered that. But certainly, it would be no reason that I could see to allow anybody to hold this story up, so this governor could get elected. I mean, you would wind up with quite a political story. You have quite a series of stories here, as I see it, probably more than you could handle at one time.

PROFESSOR MILLER: You've got lots of stories. It's too bad that we've only got two weeks to election, right?

FOURTH EDITOR: That presents a problem.

PROFESSOR MILLER: So is that going to be your first line of attack?

FOURTH EDITOR: It might be, yes. If we discover that aspect of it, early on, we certainly want to try to get a story out, of some kind, on that, before the election.

PROFESSOR MILLER: Now, you know or you're informed that if that story is published, that governor may not be reelected or if reelected—the idea is going to be, defeated or reelected by a slim enough margin, so that it is politically impossible for him to get legislative approval for infusing more money into NUFA. Right?

FOURTH EDITOR: I don't think I follow what you said. You mean, if we do a story, we're going to make it such a close election—in other words, if we do the story, this financing bill will not ever get through.

PROFESSOR MILLER: Will not get through. Does that cut any ice with you?

FOURTH EDITOR: Not at all.

PROFESSOR MILLER: None?

FOURTH EDITOR: None.

PROFESSOR MILLER: And you make that decision in what constellation of values?

FOURTH EDITOR: I guess I make it simply as a newspaper reporter seeing a good story and seeing the public impacted.

PROFESSOR MILLER: Which public impacted?

FOURTH EDITOR: I think all the public. What do you mean, which public? The general public. I can't judge that. I've got to put the information out and let the public react the way they'll react.

PROFESSOR MILLER: I mean, the public, in one sense, is better informed to exercise its franchise, right?

FOURTH EDITOR: I guess so.

PROFESSOR MILLER: On the other hand, major capital investment, in which the state is committed, on which the city depends, on which jobs depend, may go down the tubes.

FOURTH EDITOR: My publisher may be involved in it, also, if I read this case.

PROFESSOR MILLER: Yes, he's on the board.

FOURTH EDITOR: I still say we have to go with the story. I mean, in this case, at least, we have to go with the story, and let the chips fall where they may.

PROFESSOR MILLER: (*Asks the first reporter*) Do you agree with that?

FIRST REPORTER: Definitely.

PROFESSOR MILLER: (*Asks the second editor*) Definitely?

SECOND EDITOR: Yes.

PROFESSOR MILLER: (*Asks the fifth businessman*) Is that surprising?

FIFTH BUSINESSMAN: No, I expect them to do that. (*Laughter*)

PROFESSOR MILLER: Does it disappoint you?

FIFTH BUSINESSMAN: Well, I think there are a lot of questions to be raised, if you were looking out for the public good.

PROFESSOR MILLER: He doesn't think you're looking at the public good.

FOURTH EDITOR: I disagree. I don't think that we can make a judgment ahead of a story about what the public good is. I think we have to give the information to the public and let them decide. I don't think you want to put us into a situation, too often at least, where we're trying to decide whether it's in the public interest, in having an important story or not.

I'm not saying we don't, sometimes, find ourselves compelled to hold up on a story because of some of these factors. But in the case you're presenting to me here, I certainly would not see any reason to do that.

PROFESSOR MILLER: You view yourself as sort of a sieve, information comes in one ear and out the other?

FOURTH EDITOR: No, not as a sieve.

PROFESSOR MILLER: No judgment made?

FOURTH EDITOR: No, no, of course not. We have to make a judgment of what's newsworthy, and that's a gut judgment at times. We may be right. We may be wrong. We make that judgment often, so hopefully we learn how to do it, but that still doesn't say we don't make mistakes.

PROFESSOR MILLER: (*Asks the fifth editor*) Could you see holding up this story?

FIFTH EDITOR: No. We've got an opponent to Governor Aardvark and I think we'd like to know how he feels about NUFA, for example. They're running. The election is two weeks off. I think you would owe it to the people of the state to know how the two main candidates feel about this issue. There is absolutely no way you can wait or hold up or take the publisher's ties into consideration. There's no question in my mind.

PROFESSOR MILLER: (*Turns to the sixth businessman*) I'll put you in the entirely hypothetical position of being the head of NUFA. Would you expect any media organization to hold off in this situation?

SIXTH BUSINESSMAN: No.

PROFESSOR MILLER: Would you like it if they did?

SIXTH BUSINESSMAN: I don't even think I'd reach that question. I think I'd be preoccupied with how to make the story responsible and accurate and one that would least injure the public purposes of the corporation and the corporation's creditors.

PROFESSOR MILLER: I think everybody around the table or almost everybody around the table knows this story is going, with an election within two weeks away. (*Says to the fourth editor*) Let's take that election out of the picture. No election. You've got the same story, no election. Do you still have the sense of urgency, even though it's not a two-week election situation?

The memoranda tell you that they're trying to work out an arrangement—an arrangement that might prevent the default on those notes.

Putting that arrangement together involves getting some bankers together. Will you go to Phiduciary? He tells you: "For God's sake, let us put the arrangement together. Then you have your story. Yes, we're in trouble, we're in deep trouble, for a lot of reasons. Let us put the arrangement together. We've got some skittish people who will run if the story is given full media coverage this afternoon, tomorrow, next week. Give us time." How do you react?

FOURTH EDITOR: In this case, I do not feel that I could wait—in this case, no election, but bondholders involved, public involved, the scope of the story. I do not feel that I could wait for the arrangement. I also do not believe that the printing of a story would, in some way, make it impossible to make that arrangement. I've heard that argument many times, premature disclosure of a merger, premature disclosure of this or that, I just simply don't believe it. I don't think it has that much impact. So the argument wouldn't affect me much.

On the other hand, I have encountered situations, not quite like this one, where there is less reason to go with the story more rapidly, where it is conceivable that that kind of argument would convince me. It's possible.

PROFESSOR MILLER: You seem to making two points. There is reason to go quickly with this story. And you don't believe the representations that are made to you about the need for breathing time.

FOURTH EDITOR: Correct.

PROFESSOR MILLER: (*Recognizes the first businessman*)

FIRST BUSINESSMAN: I personally think that none of this would happen. I don't think it would happen because I do not think, if I read this correctly, that a chief executive would let it happen. I don't think the chief executive would let it happen because, if I read this correctly, there is a surprise pending. A profitable company is going to have a loss—

PROFESSOR MILLER: No, we're not talking about Acme. We're talking about NUFA.

FIRST BUSINESSMAN: Then it's a story and I would go right away in the public interest, as soon as I was sure it was accurate and responsible. I, personally, can't see the debatable issue on NUFA.

PROFESSOR MILLER: What is the sense of urgency? Can you define it?

FOURTH EDITOR: Well, I guess you'd have to define it as a sense that a newspaperman has when he goes into the business, that you're sort of seeking the truth, which is kind of a pious way to put it, but you're seeking something. You're seeking information and you try to get it, and get it out. I mean, you have daily deadlines which tend to tell you, well, the paper is there and sooner or later, I'd like to have that story in it.

You want to get it done. And you feel, also, that the public is served better by having information sooner rather than later, and then you're also faced with competition.

PROFESSOR MILLER: All right, we've got this motor inside you, you've got to generate so much truth per day. And this happens to be on the front end of the assembly line. (*Laughter*) It's your own narcotic. We all have our own narcotics.

The second thing is, people may be hurt. And the third is competition. Right?

FOURTH EDITOR: Yes, I suppose, in that order, maybe. In some cases, the competition might be at the top. I don't know, but they're all there together.

PROFESSOR MILLER: Okay, let's drop one and three. I just want to focus a minute or two on this sense that people may be hurt if you don't get it to them today versus tomorrow. In this situation, how does that work?

FOURTH EDITOR: In this situation, it wouldn't be today versus tomorrow. Taking it in a more general sense, if you want a specific reason, the sooner the bondholders know about this, the sooner they can take action.

PROFESSOR MILLER: Assuming the values are going to go down.

FOURTH EDITOR: The bonds may be traded.

PROFESSOR MILLER: You're really benefiting them, telling them today, a week before Christmas, that they can't buy Tinkertoys.

FOURTH EDITOR: No, there's an answer to that. The answer is that if we put it out, at least everybody has a crack at it at the same time, which is the way the game is supposed to be played. If we don't put it out, it may leak out. For example, somebody inside that bank, knowing we're working on the story, may make an illegal trade and get away with it, or something like that.

PROFESSOR MILLER: I know we left SEC outside the door this morning, but do you view yourself in the capacity of public avenger?

FOURTH EDITOR: Not public avenger.

PROFESSOR MILLER: Is that your role?

FOURTH EDITOR: No, just providing public information. We are certainly a vehicle for disclosure.

PROFESSOR MILLER: We don't doubt that. We agree on principle. We're only talking about timing. The bonds are going to go down, right? People are going to sell. People are going to think, gee, there's a value, and buy. That's going to happen whether the story breaks tomorrow, breaks next week, breaks a month from now. If they work out an accommodation, the bonds may never go down, or they may go down modestly. They may avert a panic. Do these things go through your mind?

FOURTH EDITOR: Well, they go through my mind, but I certainly would report in the story that an arrangement is in the process of being worked out. That's what I've been told.

PROFESSOR MILLER: Would you also put in, because I'm writing this story, however, there's reason to believe it will fall apart?

FOURTH EDITOR: No, I wouldn't put that in, because I don't necessarily know that that's true. It could be that a good, complete story will not hurt, but help. It's quite possible.

PROFESSOR MILLER: What about the purchase of bonds?

THIRD REPORTER: The bond-buyer in the open market the week before Christmas doesn't have the benefit of this information.

PROFESSOR MILLER: We are worried about him. Given my history, it's going to be me. (*Laughter*)

FOURTH EDITOR: We're doing you a service this time. (*Laughter*)

PROFESSOR MILLER: Oh, I appreciate the service. (*Laughter*) I'm not disputing that there are people who are going to get caught in the Mix-master. What I'm really trying to get at is, how much of this publication decision is narcotic or is fear of the *Wall Street Journal,* or is real sense of social anguish for those bondholders who are going to get nailed next week? What are the other values in this case? (*Now addresses the first union official*)

They are going to stop building in Idyllia. (*Laughter*) They're going to put up a big sign saying, "Closed for the Season." Construction is going to stop. Your workers—your people—are going to have some difficulties. How do you feel?

FIRST UNION OFFICIAL: I think they have to go with the story. I don't see any alternative. I think the fact that money will be available, through the consortium of different banks, is a way out. I don't think the drop will be as great as it would have been, had that not been in the picture. If they don't go with this, someone else will.

PROFESSOR MILLER: What about your pensions?

FIRST UNION OFFICIAL: Well, I think, in terms of the laws that exist today, under ERISA, they would be guaranteed. (*Laughter*)

PROFESSOR MILLER: Now, remember, we're only talking about *when* they go with the story. We are talking about a possibility—the fourth editor doubts it, he doesn't believe it, that's his privilege—that the ability to achieve that consortium may come apart if the story is published this week, as opposed to next week.

FIRST UNION OFFICIAL: I think he has some obligation to give it very careful thought.

PROFESSOR MILLER: Would you try to help him in thinking about it? I mean, would you make a telephone call?

FIRST UNION OFFICIAL: I think I would go to see him, yes, talk to him.

PROFESSOR MILLER: If you were on the board of the *L.A. Times,* might you bring it up with your peer group?

FIRST UNION OFFICIAL: I'm not likely to be on the board of the *L.A. Times.* (*Laughter*)

PROFESSOR MILLER: (*Asks the first stockbroker*) How do you feel? Let's assume you're part of the underwriting group.

FIRST STOCKBROKER: About what?

PROFESSOR MILLER: About the notion that the newspaper must go today rather than next week after you can work out an accommodation.

FIRST STOCKBROKER: I'd be inclined to let him publish his story as he would. I'd explain the facts to him. If he wanted to break the story, let him break it. I have no power over that.

PROFESSOR MILLER: I know you've got no power. The question really is twofold. You've got no power over him, but we always assume that everybody in life is subject to sweet reason. So one aspect is, would you talk to them? The other aspect is, really, the visceral one. How do you feel about media involving themselves in a decision-making domain— yours—about what to do about NUFA, in a way that sort of rocks the boat a little bit.

FIRST STOCKBROKER: I would (a) talk to him; I'd explain what was going on. (b) Tell him about the consortium that we were trying to put together. State that at such time as we came to a conclusion in that consortium, we'd give him the story, or give the story to the press. I don't see any harm in letting it be known that there is a rescue group being formed for NUFA.

THIRD BANKER: The case says that they are moral-obligation bonds, which means that the state legislature in this mythical state, with its mythical group, has passed a resolution saying that in the event that the debt service is not met on the bonds, they will appropriate the money. That means that at the end of the day, the bonds get paid if the political process operates the way they committed themselves to do it.

Now, would that be in the beginning of the story, or would it be in the story, or is that a relevant fact, or what?

PROFESSOR MILLER: Ask the fourth editor. He's writing the story.

FOURTH EDITOR: It is certainly a relevant fact. I can't tell you where it would appear in the story. We would certainly try to avoid, in writing a story, something that would knock the bonds down in the first ten paragraphs, and build them back up in the next ten paragraphs. I can't guarantee we'd write the story well enough to do that, but we'd certainly try.

THIRD BANKER: I'm not concerned about the value of the bonds. I'm just concerned that the fact situation is that if the state legislature is responsible—they have passed a resolution, that's a fact. And the fact is that they will make the bonds good. Now, it seems to me that's a very important element of the story. I would think it would be somewhere near the top of the list. I'd just inquire whether that's just a bum judgment on my part.

FOURTH EDITOR: I think I agree with you on that, but on the other hand, I think we would probably be inclined to point out what had happened in the case of previous moral-obligation bonds. But I agree with you. I think it would be fairly high in the story. There's a lot of material here, but we certainly would want to point out what kind of bonds these were, and explain what the situation governing them is.

SECOND LAWYER: There's one additional piece of the decision of the legislature that would have to go in. In addition to saying they would appropriate, the legislature also says, "But we're under no legal obligation to appropriate, and if we don't appropriate, you can't do anything about it. If you put that in the story, the bonds go down, because they are only a moral obligation."

THIRD BANKER: I understand. The question is whether it's a relevant piece.

SECOND LAWYER: It certainly is.

PROFESSOR MILLER: (*Asks the first editor*) Can you see any set of circumstances in which you'd hold up for a few days?

FIRST EDITOR: No, I don't see any point in holding it up.

PROFESSOR MILLER: Is it that you agree with the fourth editor that you just don't believe that they can effect a consortium?

FIRST EDITOR: Well, it's a combination of things that the fourth editor was talking about, too. It's material information, not necessarily in that legal SEC sense, but it's information that the public has a right to know. It affects buying and selling decisions. All the juices are running, I can tell you, instinctively. I tell you that this is a story in which you're representing the public. You're acting as an agent here.

PROFESSOR MILLER: The public. What about his eight thousand workers? What about the fact that your typesetter's union holds $2,000,000 worth of the bonds in their retirement fund?

FIRST EDITOR: Well, I'm very sorry, I can't account for their own investment decisions.

PROFESSOR MILLER: What about the credit of the state of Nirvana, which will be hurt more this way, let's say, than if they work out the consortium?

FIRST EDITOR: We'd consider all those things, and we'd publish the story tonight. (*Laughter*)

PROFESSOR MILLER: So you'd consider them quickly.

FIRST EDITOR: We're adept at doing that.

PROFESSOR MILLER: Now, if I take competition out? Let's take competition out. We have a hypothetical situation where the fourth editor has gotten this stuff from a friend, and has gotten a blood oath from the friend, that Xeroxes will not be given to a competitor.

FIRST EDITOR: Sometimes we ask for that. (*Laughter*)

PROFESSOR MILLER: The competition isn't going to do it. I'm now working with an equation that says a few bondholders are going to transact in the interim, versus his eight thousand workers, the credit-worthiness of the state, the impact on the banking community, and I guess we have to souse it all with your juices.

FIRST EDITOR: I'm sorry, it's part of my make-up. There's an inner compulsion to publish that story. I'm very sorry for the construction workers, but I don't see any reason not to publish that story.

PROFESSOR MILLER: (*Asks the sixth editor*)

SIXTH EDITOR: In a daily newspaper or in a magazine?

PROFESSOR MILLER: We'll make you answer that one. If you were working on a daily newspaper?

SIXTH EDITOR: I think I would take the time to interview as many people as I thought it was necessary to interview. I would withhold any judgment as to whether to go with that story until I'd gotten all sides of the picture. I'm talking about a period of two or three days.

I think, in most cases, I would end up deciding that we should go with the story.

PROFESSOR MILLER: But you might give it two or three days to fill out or flesh out the ramifications.

SIXTH EDITOR: Yes.

PROFESSOR MILLER: (*Recognizes the seventh businessman*)

SEVENTH BUSINESSMAN: I'd like to ask a question. Would it make any difference if we could just take all of your facts, everything that we've talked about here, and put them into a one-newspaper town, in a city of two hundred thousand, where the publisher's involved, as he is here. Would that be a different type of decision-making process?

SIXTH EDITOR: Well, certainly, it would remove the possibility that the competition was going to come in with the story. So it would give me a little bit more time without fear that I was going to get hit by the competition's coming out with my story ahead of time.

PROFESSOR MILLER: (*Addresses seventh businessman*) I take it you're also magnifying the impact and making it much more direct and human.

SEVENTH BUSINESSMAN: Well, the paper is very much a part of the community and all those issues, I think, then might arise. How would the publisher react then?

PROFESSOR MILLER: (*Asks the first editor*) Would that affect you? If you were not the *New York Times*, but you were the one paper in a community of two hundred thousand?

FIRST EDITOR: Yes, I think that would make a difference. There's a way that you do banking in Georgia and there's a way that you—(*Laughter*) act on the national scene. I think there's a way that you operate a newspaper in a smaller community.

PROFESSOR MILLER: The First Amendment reads a little more slowly in some parts of the country. (*Calls on the first publisher*)

FIRST PUBLISHER: No, I don't think it makes any difference. You'd write the story. There's public money involved. I think it's outrageous to suggest that you'd ever suppress this.

PROFESSOR MILLER: You use the word "suppress."

FIRST PUBLISHER: Well, withhold it. Hang back.

PROFESSOR MILLER: Would you be more judicious?

FIRST PUBLISHER: You can be judicious in a story like this. You've got a document here which is genuine, which is telling you that an important public agency is going bust. There's a lot of public money involved. You've got a stockbroker going out to start selling some more bonds. The people he sells them to should know about this.

PROFESSOR MILLER: We're not selling more bonds.

FIRST PUBLISHER: Well, you're putting together a consortium of underwriters, or whatever.

PROFESSOR MILLER: To bail out the community. If this were your town and you were on the board of the bank, and if you were also on the board of the newspaper—

FIRST PUBLISHER: I wouldn't be, I wouldn't approve of that for a minute. I would never do that. I don't think people ought to be in that position.

PROFESSOR MILLER: You should just be a newspaperman?

FIRST PUBLISHER: Right.

PROFESSOR MILLER: That allows you to have that single focus.

FIRST PUBLISHER: Right.

PROFESSOR MILLER: (*Calls on the second publisher*) If this were your town?

SECOND PUBLISHER: I think the story would go.

PROFESSOR MILLER: And you wouldn't seek to stop it or slow it down?

Again, I keep saying I'm not out to stop the story. I'm simply suggesting a week, five days, three days.

SECOND PUBLISHER: Not for that purpose, but for the purpose of talking to the people. It seems interesting to me, if it's a moral-obligation bond particularly, that you might want to talk to the leaders of both parties. The moral obligation was probably incurred by a previous legislature, and you might want to get their position on how they feel about the state's standing behind moral obligation bonds.

PROFESSOR MILLER: That's interesting, because in that is a fact that we really have not focused on, namely, that it's a quasi-public corporation, isn't it?

SECOND PUBLISHER: Right.

PROFESSOR MILLER: Suppose it was a purely private corporation. Now, it's pulled in the Acme Appliance Company. It's just a straight private corporation. It happens to be the largest employer in your town. It looks as if it's going to have to spin off a subsidiary in order to provide internal financing. Everybody wants that subsidiary spun off in town, so those eight thousand jobs can stay in the community.

If the story as to their financial difficulties is broken, they may be forced to accept a buyer not willing to keep the subsidiary in town. I know, maybe the real business world doesn't operate that way. This is a philosophical issue. Does that make any difference, if it's a private corporation?

SECOND PUBLISHER: No.

PROFESSOR MILLER: None. (*Asks the second editor*) Does it make any difference?

SECOND EDITOR: No. But realistically, are we in the one-newspaper town now?

PROFESSOR MILLER: Yes, for the next couple of minutes.

SECOND EDITOR: Realistically, in a one-newspaper town, the publisher is going to be on the board of the bank, and if the story *is* going to be withheld because the courageous editor is not going to be working there, the business editor probably has an AP wire, and yes, it will be held.

SECOND PUBLISHER: I want to point out that when you get up to eight thousand jobs, the *Wall Street Journal* may very well be on a story like that. That's a big employer.

PROFESSOR MILLER: Is that why you would decide—

SECOND PUBLISHER: No, I was just weighing, I was quarreling a little bit with the second editor.

PROFESSOR MILLER: The second editor seems to be quarreling both with you and our first publisher. He said, in your town, dammit, you're going to hold that story.

SECOND PUBLISHER: Oh, I think there are some publishers in the United States who would attempt to sit on a story. I don't think there's any question about that. But I think the story should go.

PROFESSOR MILLER: (*To the second editor*) You wouldn't?

SECOND EDITOR: I wouldn't what?

PROFESSOR MILLER: Sit on it.

SECOND EDITOR: No, I would not.

PROFESSOR MILLER: You would not. (*Calls on the fifth businessman*) Should they sit on it?

FIFTH BUSINESSMAN: I'd like to borrow a word from the first publisher. I think it would be outrageous to print the story.

PROFESSOR MILLER: What's the harm?

FIFTH BUSINESSMAN: Well, I don't see what good is accomplished by printing the story. The argument that a few bonds may trade, compared to the possible harm of the whole syndicate falling apart, as in NUFA, or the eight thousand jobs being lost, as in Acme, really is a minor consideration in the overall picture. I don't buy this argument of competition at all, because a newspaper should do what's right, and not worry about whether another newspaper does something that's wrong.

PROFESSOR MILLER: The first editor says he is doing that which is right, as dictated by his juices. The fourth editor has a motor. (*Laughter*) The second editor is his usual cynical self. (*Laughter*)

FIFTH BUSINESSMAN: Well, we're in a very sorry state, then, when his motor and the other guy's juices control the destiny of eight thousand jobs.

SECOND LAWYER: The first thing—if I am about to be involved in a story that's adverse from my point of view—the first thing I'd do is to say to myself, "Don't be outraged, because if you allow yourself the luxury of paranoia, you're bound to get into difficulties." I proceed on the assumption that the newspaper is going to act like it always acts. That is, it's going to run the story, regardless of the consequences. And there is nothing that I can do to persuade the newspaper not to run the story—by persuasion—or even to slow it up. In fact, I will assume that if I try, that that will definitely insure that the story will be run. Whereas there is a possibility—remote as it is—that they might, on reflection decide not to do it, as long as I do not try to interfere with the story's getting published.

What I would think about is how the story could get projected in a way that would be less unpalatable to me. I would again assume that there is no way I can do it by calling up and saying: "I'm a nice fellow, will you treat me kindly, and write in a way that will not be damaging."

What I'd try to do is to think, if I can, the way a newspaper thinks, in terms of what motivations it has. For example, I know one of its motivations is that it doesn't want to be scooped, and that it is absolutely psychotic on that subject. I will, therefore, focus on that aspect of it—namely, that the competitor might get the story, and I would even negotiate in terms of exclusivity. It's amazing the amount of attention you can get for an exclusive story with a newspaper. Or I might break the story to another newspaper, immediately, in order to offset the consequences of an exclusive story.

In other words, what I'd try to do is not fight the system, but work within it, in exactly the way the newspaper does.

PROFESSOR MILLER: I have a set of hands that have been building up. (*Points to the seventh businessman*) Let's start with you.

SEVENTH BUSINESSMAN: It seems to me that you're dealing with a situation that has no alternatives, because a newspaper that sits on that piece of information is building up its own liability in very large amounts of money, simply because it is market information. For better or for worse, you can get sued for that. It's serious. So we're dealing with something that's a very real—I understand the juices and the motors, but the fact of the matter is that you can't sit on that, and nobody does. I mean, no newspaper of any reliability at all could possibly sit on it. It's too volatile.

Now, the problem, as you look at urban-development corporations, in New York and the small towns, is that newspapers uniformly have not decided what role they want to play with business information. They come in at an exciting moment and provide a snapshot and not a story. And when you deal with market information, when you deal with things that the rest of the world deals with in a different way, and come in just for the excitement of the moment, with whatever lack of expertise you may have with that particular problem—expertise that is absolutely necessary, because it's hard to deal with some of this information—what it means, for example, to say that you have a projection report fourth-quarter loss. Any manager, for example, has to decide for himself, is it real? What can I do to avoid it? In any given week, you may have a memo on your desk saying you're going to go bankrupt next week if you don't do something. And then you want to do something.

You may have a situation where somebody is going to sue you for treble damage action, and the whole roof will fall in on your head. Therefore, you have to do something, and so if you take these snapshots of anything that's of a financial nature, and if you don't have people that are willing to stay with it, then that's when the newspaper strikes me as being irresponsible.

If you look at recent history, you see the failure of the newspapers to have the same kind of interest in some of the city's problems, over a long period of time, that they now have in these kinds of problems, largely because they have brought to their staffs the investigative techniques they did not used to have. Some of our problems are caused by those facts. I think the newspapers should realize that they didn't used to do the things they're doing now. Even the *New York Times* didn't used to do the things it's capable of doing today.

That strikes me as illustrating the kinds of problems we've been building up and the tensions we've been building up among us.

If I could make just one comment. In this country, there are only three or four newspapers that even have a competent financial person on them. There are only a very few, and maybe there are ten or twelve, but in several of those cases, there's not enough staff to do anything. You may have a very good person on a major newspaper—let's try Seattle, because I don't think there's anybody here from there. There's one, just one, and that person can't do a damn thing with a financial story.

Throughout the rest of the country, you have no interest in it. You can wander around the country, you can send your people from the SEC and talk to people, and it doesn't do any good at all. They will only cover the story when it pops, and then they leave it. They'll send the stock down, but they'll never bring it back up. (*Laughter*)

PROFESSOR MILLER: That's a very juicy statement and given the hands, I've got a surplus now, I'm sure Dean Fouraker's going to pick that one up. (*Recognizes the third businessman*)

THIRD BUSINESSMAN: First, I've got to point out that there have got to be at least six newspapers with competent financial staffs, because this conference has been put together by six newspapers. (*Laughter*)

I'd like to comment, as a businessman, which is unusual, and with no journalistic juices flowing, in opposition to a previous point of view.

Number one, NUFA is, in every sense of the word, a public corporation. It impacts all aspects of the society in which it lives; almost all aspects of the society have some form of interest in what happens to NUFA.

Number two, NUFA has been operating for apparently about six years, under the mantle of secrecy. It has done an absolutely wretched job, and the newspaper is far too late in coming out and putting some light on this situation. I can't imagine that NUFA could do a worse job, certainly, if it's given the help of those people who are interested in seeing it succeed.

This kind of a corporation has to succeed in one fashion or another. Behind the closed doors, it has made it almost impossible for itself to succeed, through its inept management, and through the fact that it has not taken into account the people that have a direct interest in it, and so forth. So therefore, I think the newspaper, if anything, is late in breaking the story.

PROFESSOR MILLER: How do you react to Acme?

THIRD BUSINESSMAN: Well, I have to follow there, a general principle, and that is, I know that the newspapers are going to break that story, and in my experience—I hate to say this, but I'm just generalizing— but in my experience, they are right more often than they are wrong in throwing the light on a corporate situation. There are a few times when the situation is so delicate that publicity, premature publicity, if you will, does detract from the resolution of a particular situation, but I would have to say, in my experience, more often than not, it does not detract from the resolution of a situation.

PROFESSOR MILLER: (*Recognizes the first businessman*)

FIRST BUSINESSMAN: Well, I'm disturbed at part of the tenor of this, because we're debating something on this—I'm not Acme, or whatever its name is—because I really don't think the newspapers have a choice. I think they have an absolute duty to break the story. I do not want them speculating about what the consequences are, because while in this particular case I might like them to speculate my way if I'm here, ninety-nine percent of the time I don't want them to speculate, because then they're exercising a role that I would prefer they not exercise. I want them to come with the news.

My only concern, generally, is that it be fair and balanced—put the thing in perspective. If they do that, they have a duty to publish. They didn't make the consequences. They didn't make the events that precipitated this. They are strictly the messenger boys. We don't cut off the heads of the messengers with the bad news. So what they should do is publish, making sure that they have the facts, that it's balanced and fair; and I think that it would be a crime to withhold, not because they might be sued, not for any reason, because then, I think, they are forfeiting their franchise.

PROFESSOR MILLER: (*Recognizes third publisher*)

THIRD PUBLISHER: I'd like to leave the hypothetical and deal with some realities. In connection with NUFA—it so happens that about three years ago, a friend of mine who was chairman of UDC asked me to take over his part-time chairmanship of UDC, because I was interested in urban affairs, and I was quite tempted and finally asked to see the balance sheet, and I'm no financial genius. I looked at the balance sheet, and my reaction was: "Gee whiz, if those guys get in trouble, it's going to be pretty bad." But like the fourth editor, I wasn't about to raise the flag and say: "Wow," because the situation had not occurred. That's the reality of why you don't catch a NUFA early enough.

The other non-hypothetical is that New York City, which seem to be somewhat involved in this paper, has gone through several years of great trouble, and it strikes me that it's in large part due to the Byzantine form of accounting that the banks never seem to have caught up with what was going on. If they did, they're in trouble; if they didn't, they're in trouble. Surely, the press didn't catch up with what was going on. But it is also probable that due to those two facts, the city did not go into bankruptcy, which is an interesting question in itself. I suspect that we are better off for not going into bankruptcy. I would also say, if we had known the facts, we should have printed them instantly.

PROFESSOR MILLER: Let me turn both of your points around a little bit. I would have a personal disagreement with you about the UDC, since there were a series of official statements that accompanied the bond issues, which apparently the media did not explore. But do you believe that the media have a role that they could, should, or oughtn't to perform in looking at the variety of corporate documents that are available, through a variety of sources; and if you think they have a role, can the media provide the resources for doing that?

THIRD PUBLISHER: Sure, they should look at the documents. Providing the resources is more difficult. I think the press has been late in obtaining financial reporters. I agree with whoever said there are only maybe twelve around at this moment. I sense that the press is trying to catch up very rapidly on this score, and that it will learn not only to get the documents but learn how to read them, which is not that easy.

PROFESSOR MILLER: (*Recognizes the first union official*)

FIRST UNION OFFICIAL: I wanted to comment a bit on the case of Acme. Here we have a case of an individual, Posit, who is trying to get rid of the president, perhaps to make himself the president. He makes certain moves and gives this information to the reporter. Here we have eight thousand people who are involved, who have jobs. Here we have a case where there is available a buyer who agrees to keep the eight thousand people working if he can purchase the refrigeration complex.

There's a deal about to be made. There's nothing to stop the deal's being made, except the publicity that relates to the fact of the general conditions. I don't believe that any attention should be paid to Rowe. I think Rowe has to take his chances in terms of running for the Senate. I think that's something not to be considered. But I think the fact that this relatively small city has its largest industry about to go down, causing a great deal of hardship to the people, perhaps a great loss in taxes to the city. I think the common good of the community has to be considered by a newspaper, in the same way as anyone else in the community has to look at the common good of society. So I think the common good should be considered by the newspaper in the same way as it would be considered by a worker who might be employed by the company.

PROFESSOR MILLER: How do you answer our first businessman, who said that he really doesn't want the press second-guessing or trying to decide what's the greater good for the greater number. They've got a duty to perform. That's their function under our scheme.

FIRST UNION OFFICIAL: Well, I think they have a duty to tell the public the truth about what they see. I think they have a duty to tell the public the facts about the matters that take place in daily life, so the proper decisions can be made in a democratic society. But I think in this kind of situation, where there is the obligation to try to preserve the economy of this small town, where this company is the biggest employer, I think they have a great obligation not to use this information which they have obtained in a very surreptitious way. I think they have an obligation not to use it, because of the impact it will have on the community.

PROFESSOR MILLER: You're not going to focus on the surreptitious way, or are you?

FIRST UNION OFFICIAL: Well, I think you've got to consider all the facts that you've given us. It was obtained surreptitiously.

THIRD PUBLISHER: How is the press ever going to be believed—and the truth always comes out finally—if it turns out that the press is hiding, keeping back the facts, depending upon how they feel about a particular situation? It never will be. You'll say: "Well, they're hiding the facts about something else, too."

FIRST UNION OFFICIAL: Well, had these facts come out publicly, had they come out in what I would consider an ethical way, or had they come out in the normal course of events—that might be a difference. But here, the newspaper has an opportunity to make a judgment. They have to make a judgment as to what this impact is going to be on the community. They are the only ones who have the information. There's no chance of anyone else's getting it, presumably. So, when they give it out, it's going to have a very adverse effect on the economy and on the lives of the people. It's going to have a very adverse effect on the tax structure of the city, etc. In fact, it might cause a real decline in the city.

THIRD PUBLISHER: My case on New York City and bankruptcy is a clear-cut case. It would have had a very adverse effect on New York and the U.S., and yet the truth is going to come out sooner or later, and if you don't print it when you've got it, you're never going to get believed.

FIRST UNION OFFICIAL: We have a small town, maybe one newspaper, two hundred thousand people; we have a special case. We can't compare it with New York City.

FIRST PUBLISHER: But should the truth of the company's financial troubles be kept away from your members, the employees? Don't they have a right to know that their jobs really are at risk?

FIRST UNION OFFICIAL: I think when you have a deal pending, almost accomplished—selling the refrigeration unit to another company that has given assurance that it will keep these people working, keep the economy moving in the community—I think there is an obligation to consider that.

FIRST PUBLISHER: I think it's almost impossible to imagine that a company would pull away from a chance to make money because of some publicity. If there's an opportunity there, someone else would come in.

SECOND LAWYER: I don't think the issue is bottling up the story at all. It's not going to be bottled up. The question is, what does the story contain and how is it written? That's the important question.

PROFESSOR MILLER: (*Calls on the third editor*)

THIRD EDITOR: I was going to agree that the economics of the deal are going to keep the employees in the town or put them on welfare. They're the same as the economics of the steel industry, which closed the Johnstown plant and put people out of work.

PROFESSOR MILLER: I'm trying to see whether you're focusing on the doubting Thomas defense, "Ah, it will work out." Or, on the more pristine flag of, "We've got information, we have a duty to disclose, that's our job. If we make curves and bends and twists in this context, they're not going to believe that we're telling them the truth in the next context."

THIRD EDITOR: That's my job.

PROFESSOR MILLER: That's your job. What do you say to the union official who says you're a member of this community, and it's also your job to be a citizen and protect these eight thousand people?

THIRD EDITOR: We want a free press.

PROFESSOR MILLER: The free press is more important than your concern for his eight thousand workers.

THIRD EDITOR: I'm concerned, but I have a job to do, and there's some information, the distribution of which is of value to people.

PROFESSOR MILLER: (*Recognizes the third businessman*)

THIRD BUSINESSMAN: I would like to try to answer my good friend the union official. To come back to my generalization that we're not in a position, or no one is generally in a position to determine whether or not something is going to work out in a business situation. But more times than not, if there is public knowledge of a situation, in my experience at least, more times than not it has worked out well. Think of what might have happened, for instance, if the newspapers had gotten hold of the Pennsylvania Railroad story, at least in time to tell the directors. (*Laughter*)

FOURTH REPORTER: My newspaper sent me to run a bureau four years ago, and one of the prime things that I ponder every night is, "Do I have a Penn Central going belly-up in my jurisdiction?"

THIRD BANKER: Wait, tell us. (*Laughter*)

FOURTH REPORTER: I don't mean that I'm cynical and always looking for the negative, but the Penn Central—it would be my feeling that we did a very poor job there. I'm talking about all of the press. It really came up, and there it was. We had not been reading the documents that had been filed, to the extent we should have. We had not been watching the commercial paper.

So just as it would be to a person responsible for looking on behalf of the public investors, it seems to me that the possibility of a recurrence of that kind of situation is a real fear to the press. One point I'd like to make here. We have now seen about three examples of PG&S. They're popping up here, they're popping up there. It would be my impression that we had written the initial story, it's amazing how much this process would have been accelerated—I hope in a thoughtful, reasonable fashion.

But the most interesting thing happens. When my competition beats me to a story, I'm coming back, I'm going further, I'm looking, and I might not have gotten the documents. He might have kept getting them. But I'd be in there pushing and so would everybody else. The networks would be there. Other reporters would be there. These people would all be looking. This whole process would have been accelerated. PG&S is the dominant banking and financial institution in the state of Nirvana. That seems to me to perhaps be a bigger bottom line that we've been talking about. The whole process of getting to the root of their dominance, of getting Phiduciary, if he's really not a very good manager, of getting him out of the way and improving that whole situation—all the investors and businesses involved there would have been working at an accelerated pace, and the free press would have been working, all of us. Our competitive pressures—I'm not being pious—

would have paid off because the information would have flowed faster and created more diverse views; the truth would have been somewhere in there.

THIRD REPORTER: We recognize that too often we lunge into a story, either because we've stumbled onto it, or because a competitor has broken something on that story, and that we don't have time, because of competitive reasons, to put the first day's story into perspective. But there is a second day's story, and a third day's story, and those are the stories where we try to get at all of the ramifications of what we're doing.

PROFESSOR MILLER: I know it's Sunday morning, but this is a delightful *mea culpa.*

SECOND PUBLISHER: I'm really going along with that same remark, it's probably only fair to say that in the great majority of newspaper sales— in which one business is being sold to another—the owners, including the publishers, make great efforts to make sure that no one finds out about it until it is a *fait accompli.* (*Laughter*) So they actually consider the fact that if that were public information, that would be somewhat detrimental.

PROFESSOR MILLER: Two more comments and we'll go to the fifth soap opera. (*Recognizes the third banker*)

THIRD BANKER: May I ask a question? Our third publisher says that Byzantine accounting in New York, which is a charitable description—we have a situation, today, in which the Social Security system of the United States is in terrible jeopardy. It's busted. It's a technical term. (*Laughter*) It's a hell of a story. Nobody writes about it. Wait a minute.

THIRD PUBLISHER: Oh, come on. How the hell do I know it if I haven't read it somewhere? How do you know it?

THIRD BANKER: What I'm saying is that, despite the Penn Central, the day it *does* go bankrupt, it will be a front-page story. But what is being done right now, about explaining the situation? The accounting in New York made me think of it—every year, the Citizens Budget Commission put out a report, which was on page twenty-six of the *New York Times,* saying that the public group said the numbers were phony. That went on for five years. It was not a story.

I'm just asking, as this train goes down the track, at what point do you accelerate what is going to be a national problem?

PROFESSOR MILLER: (*Recognizes the first lawyer*)

FIRST LAWYER: I just wanted to ask a question. In the one-newspaper town, would the union official's concerns weigh more heavily in delaying that story if Acme, in addition to being the largest employer, was also the largest advertiser?

PROFESSOR MILLER: (*Recognizes the sixth editor*)

SIXTH EDITOR: I'm sorry, I don't want to respond to that point. I'd like to respond to the third banker. I think today there's another story, other than Social Security, which is in the kind of building stage and which the press has been making attempts to get at, not doing a very good job, because it's such a complicated problem. That's the problem of big loans to the LDCs (Less Developed Countries).

Now there's a case in which every time the press has raised the question of danger, the banks have vigorously attempted to tell the press that it's off base. They may be right, but I think that's a similar question, and I'd be interested in what our banker has to say on that.

THIRD BANKER: I would be delighted to address it. A bank recently published a book written by an expert on this subject. Two weeks ago, a major newspaper ran on the front pages of the financial section, a "Church Committee Report," which was written by a young lady of twenty-three years, and they published—

FIRST EDITOR: Was that an error, per se, that she was twenty-three years and a young lady?

THIRD BANKER: No.

FIRST EDITOR: Why did you mention it?

THIRD BANKER: It's an indication of experience. If you had a reporter who had been on the job one day, you probably wouldn't assign him to a very important story.

SECOND REPORTER: We operate under a system of collective view. We take responsibility for that.

THIRD BANKER: May I finish my answer? The newspaper published a box containing the amounts that were due to "less developed countries." The newspaper didn't break it down between foreign currency and across-border-risk and local currency, so that the numbers were totally useless. The newspaper did not break them down by maturity. There's a difference between financing sixty-day coffee bills out of Santos and a fifteen-year loan to Recife. The newspaper didn't break that down.

The newspaper didn't break down, at all, the difference between these loans and loans to, say, Volkswagen in Brazil, guaranteed by the Export-Import Bank, which has an entirely different risk from anything else. The newspaper did not break down the numbers by World Bank classifications, so it didn't say there are no loans to Uganda. There aren't any loans out to the poorest LDCs. So what I'm saying is, all that information is available, but it was not in that chart, which was simplistic. I think that that is a failure of the journalistic function, which is to tell the complete story. This is quite apart from the question of whether you're going to get the money back; that's another problem. But why would the newspaper run that chart when all of the information was available, broken down the way I described? Is that a fair comment?

SECOND REPORTER: Very fair, if I can respond to that. It's a very fair comment. I think you said the Church Committee Report. I'm not aware of how much material was actually contained in that report or what the constraints were or how much space was devoted to it.

THIRD BANKER: It was front page, and the newspaper ran about, I'd say, fifteen columns.

FIRST EDITOR: That doesn't sound quite true.

THIRD BANKER: It was very large. It went over onto the next page.

FIRST EDITOR: I don't think it was fifteen columns.

The newspaper could well have broken that down into more detail than it did. I can only think that, on this particular story, too, there is some limit as to how much the newspaper can go into. I would think that, perhaps, this was the conclusion of the subcommittee or the staff—

THIRD BANKER: The committee never saw it. It was a staff report.

SECOND REPORTER: Well, I presume it was presented as a staff report, which is sometimes dubious and sometimes not dubious. I think the report was carried on the basis of what the staff said. Perhaps there was some press obligation to question the work of the staff of the Senate subcommittee and to go beyond it and to seek comment from banking institutions. I will say that shortly after that, bank opinion was surveyed at the IMF meeting, and the consensus of all the bankers was that the LDC loans presented no problem. That story wasn't believable either.

THIRD BANKER: That is because we're facing the worst depression that we've had.

SECOND REPORTER: But that article was prominently displayed—stating that the bankers at IMF see no problem in LDC loans.

THIRD BANKER: I have no quarrel with that. I'm just saying that about the story, about the box; it was false and misleading. If we had filed such a statement with the SEC, we would have been in jail, because one cannot lump cruzeiros and dollars and cross-border and private and government obligations. It just was not a good news story. I have no quarrel with the judgment that we're dumb or smart—that's your judgment. But what I'm saying is that the facts in that story were misleading.

SECOND REPORTER: I think we can do a better job on the LDC problem, which many people think is a real problem.

FIFTH REPORTER: I'm not aware that that information is available.

THIRD BANKER: It's in a bank's annual report.

FIFTH REPORTER: But it's not in the aggregate. You're talking about an aggregate story. I was at the Fed last week, and they don't have that data yet themselves.

THIRD BANKER: Well, the aggregates, by World Bank classification, are available.

FIFTH REPORTER: I don't think they're available in local currency, maturities, what is trade finance for the major twenty-five banks, let's say.

THIRD BANKER: They're available in local currencies and in foreign currencies, correct? And by World Bank classification and countries.

FIFTH REPORTER: Well, it's a technical thing, but that's a misunderstanding. I was told that is just a beginning—to send out questionnaires on that kind of thing.

THIRD BANKER: We filled one out, about a year ago.

FIRST EDITOR: Do you make that information available in terms of your own banking institution, your exposure in various currencies, by maturity, by country?

THIRD BANKER: Yes, it's prominently displayed in our annual report, which I'm sure you've read.

FIRST EDITOR: I'm sorry, I don't have occasion to read all the details in your annual report.

THIRD BANKER: Well, if you criticitize on LDC loans on lack of information, and we publish it, I think we have a right to raise the question as to why you publish information from the detailed report that we gave out—classified by maturities, by currencies, guaranteed, unguaranteed, and by World Bank classifications. That's about all the ways you can slice the bread.

PROFESSOR MILLER: That's great. I've never had ringside seats at a heavyweight match before. (*Laughter*)

Let's spend the last ten or fifteen minutes on a subject no one around here gets emotionally involved—

SEVENTH BUSINESSMAN: Let me quickly say again, that in this area of financial reporting, we too often rely on a memo, although the person who has the memo doesn't necessarily understand all the facts and sources. I'm not speaking of a few major dailies because they have good financial staffs; they do those things for whatever reason, based upon the exigencies of the moment. But in fact, and throughout the country and even in Washington, and even in New York, you see somebody with a memo. They take a memo out of the SEC, they take a memo out of the Federal Reserve. It's a staff memo. They don't know what staff they're talking about. They don't know what significance it has. And because of this lack of basic training over many years, that memo is published.

Now, I happen to agree a hundred percent that the memo should be put out, that the information should flow. But when you have a combination of little experience in this area and a precise piece of information, that precise piece of information gets far more coverage that it really ought to get. I would hope that most newspapers kind of appreciate that fact and this penchant for using something they have because they've got it. A memo may or may not be confidential—the issue isn't whether it should be confidential or not. In fact, many memos, I might say to you, are confidential because the people involved are afraid it will be pulled out of context. So there is a very real problem. I would hope that most newspapers would appreciate that, particularly in the financial area.

PROFESSOR MILLER: Let's close out this portion of the program by taking a few minutes for the last of the little soap operas, and that consists of broadly conceived questions of personal privacy concerning individual members of the business community.

(*Turns to the sixth reporter*) Your editor has assigned you to do a profile on Phiduciary, and you've got information in there. What is it that you think should be included in a profile of Phiduciary?

SIXTH REPORTER: In regard to this information, I think I'd certainly look into his misuse of company personnel, his mismanagement of funds.

PROFESSOR MILLER: Misuse, mismanagement. We'll start with that.

SIXTH REPORTER: Yes, according to what people have told me, yes. I think that's important.

PROFESSOR MILLER: Yes, except he's under investigation, and you're interested in that. What else?

SIXTH REPORTER: I would not go into his psychiatric problems or his son with drug problems.

PROFESSOR MILLER: Why not?

SIXTH REPORTER: I feel that would be a violation of his privacy, his son's privacy. I don't think it would belong—

PROFESSOR MILLER: If he were the President of the United States, would you go into his difficulties?

SIXTH REPORTER: Yes.

PROFESSOR MILLER: How do you draw the distinction?

SIXTH REPORTER: In that case, he more or less affects all of us. I mean, Jimmy Carter on amphetamines—he could push the button. (*Laughter*)

PROFESSOR MILLER: And you don't say that about the man who can push the cash-register button in the community, affects everyone?

SIXTH REPORTER: I don't think that part of his problem would come into this story. Certainly, it's in the background, it's in my mind, but I would concentrate on what I could document and what people told me. I couldn't prove that he was on amphetamines, really.

PROFESSOR MILLER: Suppose you could.

SIXTH REPORTER: Even if I could, I wouldn't.

PROFESSOR MILLER: You wouldn't?

SIXTH REPORTER: I wouldn't.

PROFESSOR MILLER: You wouldn't prove or want to, that the number-one banker, or a number-one corporate executive, or the head of the largest union in the community is someone who is unstable.

A VOICE: I think that's a given. (*Laughter*)

PROFESSOR MILLER: (*Asks the fourth reporter*) How do you react?

FOURTH REPORTER: I think I would want to stay away from—well, I'd want to proceed the same way. I'd want to pursue the handling of the bank's assets and personnel. The amphetamines, certainly the son's drug problem—I would not at all go into that. The amphetamines—I just can't see it in this case, and it's a very slippery slope between President Jimmy Carter and Mr. Phiduciary.

PROFESSOR MILLER: Well, how do you make this decision? What's your standard?

FOURTH REPORTER: Well, in this case, it seems to me that his ineptness has been so nicely laid out—by now we're all the way through into the last soap opera—and it's all so clear that I think it's really unnecessary at this point. He's probably in enough trouble with the SEC. He's probably in enough trouble with his board of directors. The amphetamines really—

PROFESSOR MILLER: Overkill.

FOURTH REPORTER: Yes. But privacy—

PROFESSOR MILLER: Why? Let's say you are just sent out to do a story on Phiduciary. Let's take out what you know about messing up. You're just doing a profile on the most powerful banker, the most powerful labor union chief, the most powerful corporate employer in your community, and you discover, in the course of your investigations—

A VOICE: Should we include the most powerful editor?

PROFESSOR MILLER: We will get there. (*Laughter*) And you discover, in the course of your inquiring around, that he hasn't been minding the store, however you want to define "store," because his son is on drugs. Some of his judgments have been a little askew, and it may be because of an emotional difficulty. Let's leave out the stuff that you can nail him with; this would be overkill. Put it in a narrower perspective.

FOURTH REPORTER: It seems to me that if this was the only thing that happened, I would immediately begin checking with associates in the company who might be willing to speak with me, people I might know. I'd be checking social friends. I'd be checking his board of directors. I would be trying to ask doctors in the community. It seems to me they talk a lot more than they should, sometimes, at least to each other. If it's the only game going, and he is this important executive, yes, I'd be checking it out. If this were happening, I'm just convinced his board of directors would know it. I'm convinced his personal secretary would know it. There would be evidence in his personal life and in the way he operated in the executive suite. I think you could get to the bottom of it, and I think you could find out if the board was about ready to fire him for philosophical reasons.

PROFESSOR MILLER: I'm hearing that now you are onto the story. If you couldn't nail him the other way, you'd nail him this way.

FOURTH REPORTER: No, I'm going to let the board of directors make the decision as to whether he is a fit executive. I'll report what they're getting ready to do, and I'll take the reasons they give.

PROFESSOR MILLER: But you have no evidence that the board of directors is doing anything. Maybe they're going to do something; maybe they're not going to do something. All you know is, you're going out into the community, you're doing a profile and you're coming up with this instability, partially caused by the drug-using son, and perhaps very serious judgment errors as a result of the instability.

FOURTH REPORTER: I'm afraid I'd stay away from any story that would suggest he's using amphetamines. I'd try to document every mistake he was making in public. I would take his misstatements in speeches. I would be sure I covered him everywhere he went. I would try to go to unusual lengths to cover his public appearances, everywhere I could have public access. I would try to document mistakes—silly, stupid, unreasonable things he might be doing.

We have this problem with alcoholic executives, and it raises a real question. I don't think, very often, we do it. We don't do it in Washington, certainly, with the legislators we have there, and the personal problems they have. (*Laughter*)

PROFESSOR MILLER: The theory is, the public has a right to know.

FOURTH REPORTER: I think the public has a right to know everything I can document about this executive's behavior. But I would be very loath to suggest—let's say, I got the prescriptions. I've got Xerox copies, and he's taking five hundred something-or-other pills a month. That would be awfully good, but I believe I'd hold back and simply try to describe his actions.

PROFESSOR MILLER: I take it that what I'm hearing is that whatever private facts you learn about him, you would want to connect to something in his operating capacity.

FOURTH REPORTER: That's correct.

PROFESSOR MILLER: That's your standard. (*Turns to the third editor*) How would you go at this?

THIRD EDITOR: I would try to see the implication of his drug-taking with his functioning as the chairman of the bank. Not as somebody who goes home at night, runs around the block, a flasher, something like that. (*Laughter*)

PROFESSOR MILLER: You wouldn't report that the CEO of the company story was a flasher? (*Laughter*)

PROFESSOR MILLER: (*Turns to the fifth reporter*) What would you do?

FIFTH REPORTER: I tend to agree. I would not carry it into this guy's private life, I think. In this case, it's a very simple decision, because he's already under investigation. You focus on the investigation.

PROFESSOR MILLER: No, I want to take that out.

FIFTH REPORTER: I don't know. I don't think I'd be quite as diligent as the fourth reporter.

PROFESSOR MILLER: What about the past?

FIFTH REPORTER: What do you mean?

PROFESSOR MILLER: His past. Let's say, twenty years ago, three thousand miles away, he was involved somehow in organized crime. And has been relocated by the FBI. He was a very talented man, and he came up through the ranks of the bank, or through the ranks of Northwest Industries, or through the ranks of the union, and now he is where he is.

FIFTH REPORTER: I'd protect it. Some of our great state leaders were people like Sam Houston, who were flinging out prison sentences and legal problems—I sort of like the idea of fresh starts.

PROFESSOR MILLER: Fresh start, give him a fresh start.

FIFTH REPORTER: This is easy. You're asking me to be Pontius Pilate. He'd be bumped off in a minute if I printed this.

PROFESSOR MILLER: Oh, you're worried about his life.

FIFTH REPORTER: I would worry about his life, sure.

PROFESSOR MILLER: (*Now asks the fourth reporter*) How do you react? He's been relocated.

FOURTH REPORTER: I'd document it and print it in a minute.

PROFESSOR MILLER: Really? How do you come to disagree with your learned colleague across the table?

FOURTH REPORTER: Well, I think fresh starts are for preachers, and the born-again Christians. It seems to me that I really think the past has to be something we live with. I'm sorry, I've got a problem, though, with the relocation. Is that part of the question to me also?

PROFESSOR MILLER: Yes.

FIFTH REPORTER: Those guys get killed all the time.

FOURTH REPORTER: I'm sorry, I forgot about that part. I'd check it out with the government.

PROFESSOR MILLER: If he should be killed, you'd leave him alone?

FOURTH REPORTER: Yes, I would.

PROFESSOR MILLER: If he shouldn't be killed, you'd do it. (*Laughter*)

FOURTH REPORTER: No, it's two different things. If he was an informant who had been relocated—I mean, it's so tough to relocate these people that the Justice Department doesn't do it casually; it's very expensive—and I believed his life was in danger. I believe I would not identify that part of his past. If it were simply the fact that he would lose his job as a corporate executive I would definitely print it.

PROFESSOR MILLER: Go with it in a minute, right?

FOURTH REPORTER: In a minute.

PROFESSOR MILLER: A couple of minutes ago, you said, the private life you would write about only when there was a connection with his performance. This has nothing to do with his performance. He is a damn good corporate president. The only thing is, he's a real keg of dynamite.

FOURTH REPORTER: What did he do for the Mafia?

PROFESSOR MILLER: Is that relevant to his performance? Fifteen years, he's been running that corporation A-okay.

FOURTH REPORTER: That doesn't matter. If he'd been convicted—

PROFESSOR MILLER: Not convicted, given immunity, relocated.

FOURTH REPORTER: As I said a moment ago, if the documents were there to prove it, I would print it in a minute.

PROFESSOR MILLER: (*Turns back to the fifth reporter*) And you wouldn't?

FIFTH REPORTER: No, if he was convicted, he started over again, and he's running this operation very successfully, I don't think so. I think if I had some weird information about a guy, let's say, on amphetamines, and there was also, on the other hand, some information that he was really making a mess of his job, I would certainly use the amphetamine information to really look into the managerial situation. I would use it as kind of input, to work on how well is he performing. But if there's no connection; if there's no indication that the one has led to the other, or had influenced the other, I don't think it's our business, really.

FOURTH REPORTER: He is making a mess of his job, is he not?

PROFESSOR MILLER: I'm taking that out.

FIFTH REPORTER: He took that out.

PROFESSOR MILLER: The hypothetical changes constantly. Performance is a prime discussion. We have a helluva bad ancient record, but a helluva good corporate president right now.

FOURTH REPORTER: If he's a banker, I'd still do it in a minute.

PROFESSOR MILLER: And if he's a union leader? (*Laughter*)

FOURTH REPORTER: I'm an ex-labor reporter for four years, and I could say that in the case of a labor union leader, I'd take longer to decide.

A VOICE: How about an editor of the *Wall Street Journal* or the *New York Times* or the *Washington Post*?

FOURTH REPORTER: The editor of the *Wall Street Journal* or the *New York Times* or the *Washington Post* with a past criminal record? (*Laughter*) The point is, I simply couldn't control the story. I believe I would consult my editor and then write.

I can remember coming across an allegation that a former managing editor of my own newspaper had been involved in a pension fraud. This was a con man trying to sell me an exclusive story to get me off of his payola out in California. I think we were prepared to go on that, if it had proved true. It certainly wasn't; it was a complete sham. No, I would insist, and I hope I would resign if they didn't print it.

PROFESSOR MILLER: (*Recognizes the third reporter*)

THIRD REPORTER: Isn't the question here, really, whether the standards should be the relevance to the present activities of the president of the bank. If you have documentation that he was, in some way, associated with organized crime fifteen years ago, and you discover that he may have picked up some of those old ties, then I think that's highly relevant to the story and should be used.

If, on the other hand, he had these ties fifteen years ago, and they bear no relevance to his present activity, I think there are better stories to work on.

PROFESSOR MILLER: So you line up with the fifth reporter?

THIRD REPORTER: In this case.

PROFESSOR MILLER: Just work with this one ten seconds more. Suppose he is doing a good job, but he's getting to be a very powerful man in the community. When he goes to a party meeting and says Jones should run for mayor, Jones runs for mayor. Does that make any difference?

THIRD REPORTER: No.

PROFESSOR MILLER: None. Leave him alone.

THIRD REPORTER: Right. What if I have no evidence that these ties are being resumed?

PROFESSOR MILLER: (*Recognizes the third businessman*)

THIRD BUSINESSMAN: I think it might have been nice if the newspapers had been able to blow the whistle on Philip Musica, before he took the shareholders of McKesson and Robbins for a ride in 1938, because he had a twenty-year history of criminal involvement before that.

THIRD REPORTER: But it was a continuing history, was it not?

THIRD BUSINESSMAN: But never reported.

THIRD REPORTER: Okay, but if you find it's a continuing history—

PROFESSOR MILLER: I think you are saying that if you found any evidence of continued ties to organized crime, you'd go with it.

THIRD REPORTER: Absolutely.

PROFESSOR MILLER: Absent that, you leave him alone.

THIRD REPORTER: Right.

PROFESSOR MILLER: Let me try one more and then the dean has to take over.

Let's up the ante a little bit more. Not a relocated witness—let's suppose you get word from Simon Wiesenthal that he's an ex-Nazi camp guard.

THIRD REPORTER: That's a tough call.

PROFESSOR MILLER: We were talking about headlines before—"From Buchenwald to Banking." (*Laughter*)

THIRD REPORTER: That's a nice headline, there's no question about that.

FIFTH BUSINESSMAN: I think I'm a little upset about what I'm hearing now. For the last two days, the newspaper told me that as a member of the public I have a right to hear everything, and it just doesn't seem to be working out that way. I think every newspaperman and editor makes his own decisions about what I'm entitled to hear. I mean, they don't mind lopping off eight thousand jobs, but suddenly whether they know somebody or don't know somebody becomes a major factor in what the guy's career is, and how it's going to affect him personally becomes very important to them.

I think newspapers are trying to decide what I should hear and what I shouldn't hear, but they're not admitting it. I don't think they're any different from the rest of us. They all have their prejudices. They all have their friendships. They all keep certain confidences. I think a lot of what we've heard for the last two days is a lot of bunk. (*Laughter*).

PROFESSOR MILLER: I think that that is a terrific point for me to get the hell out of here. (*Applause and laughter*)

(*Whereupon this session was concluded.*)

Review and Discussion

Dean Fouraker

The Seminar:

DEAN FOURAKER: There are a lot of ways that one might summarize the range of issues between the press and business. One of the questions we might raise is how business is liked by the press. I think the answer to that is straightforward, that they would like to be covered in the same way the press covers stories about themselves. (*Laughter*) They would like to have birth notices, marriage notices, obituaries that are well-written and edited, and for other things that are personal—a dignified filing. I have a lot of sympathy with the press.

The basic problem, as we have had described in these papers that my colleagues from the law school have done so brilliantly, is very much the same as the kind of problem that any scholar undertakes—very complicated phenomena, increasingly complex. Abstract those crucial areas; put them together in a fashion; and you have a theory (as we would call it in the scientific community) which gives you a fundamental understanding of the process and is a useful guide as to future events. Your ability to do that in a very competitive situation, I think, on balance, commands the respect and admiration of all of us.

I'd like to ask a few of the people on both sides to sort of assist in the summarization. I'll bring in a few general concerns.

One is the aspect of competition. We used to have a case that Paul Cherington taught at the business school in a business-government relations course, the students of which came from everywhere, all cultures and countries. In the case, you had to act as a representative of a company dealing with a key legislator who had some pending legislation that would affect the company. The question was, what would you be prepared to offer this legislator, who was known to be interested in such transactions? Would you buy him lunch? Would you buy him a drink? Would you buy him a week at a New York hotel? Would you buy him a woman? The point that would quickly emerge is that, depending on the background, the culture and the training of the people in the class, that legislator was going to end up completely surfeited. (*Laughter*) He could get everything.

The process of discussing in this group the question of whether you would publish a story or not has shown us that, if a story is available, it's going to be printed. As has been indicated, broadcast journalists are not represented, except by their executives, and the situation for the broadcast journalists is not exactly the same as for the print reporters. Once a story is released, everyone else is going to pick it up very quickly because of the competitive pressure. So there's a mechanism at work that is going to insure that almost everything gets into print very quickly, for good or bad.

On that, I'll start with a businessman who is responsible for a modest organization and has had some experience with the press. Would you give some views on this issue?

FIRST BUSINESSMAN: Okay, Larry. First of all, I'd like to express appreciation for an opportunity to be here this weekend. I must admit, the weekend didn't turn out quite as I expected it, so far at least. I will tell you, I don't think I've ever spent a more stimulating and fascinating weekend that this one has been.

Yesterday, we heard editors and reporters here talk about the place of the press or the media in our society today. The guaranteed freedom of speech and expression, the obligation to the American public to see that they get information that is timely. Their place as the representatives of the fourth estate, and their own dedication to principles—I, for one, accept this description of the press. I believe in their honest efforts to meet every single one of these obligations.

We businessmen might not agree with you in every instance on the methods that you use to obtain those objectives. We might not even agree that the methods you are proposing will allow you to obtain the objectives that you want. But for the moment at least, let's say that we agree that the press had made a significant contribution to the success of this country, and for that, we applaud you.

However (*Laughter*), I hope that you in the media will concede that the business community, businessmen and women, at least, have also played a part in the success of this country. Rather than the robber barons whom we've all read about, who go back in the history of business in this country, business people today are almost entirely hired hands. We are hired professional managers, and like you, we have obligations, of course, to our investors, and for that we usually get criticized for being only bottom-line-oriented. But, I can assure you that we are the first to say that we can meet our obligation to our investors only *if* we have satisfied customers. Because, without satisfied customers, you've got no business.

We accept our responsibilities to our communities, where we live, and we do everything we can to uphold them. We don't fight government edicts on environmental controls, for example. We think that they should come. We know that they must come. But at the same time, we do feel that we have an obligation to utilize the expertise that has been developed in the business community over the years to point out the most efficient and most effective way to accomplish those social goals at the least cost to everybody, and to be sure that the public is aware of the trade-offs involved in these programs.

We are, if you will, just as dedicated to the well-being of this country as you in the media are. Sure, I'll admit we've had some bad actors in business. But, I ask you, haven't there been some bad actors in the media, too? I will admit that there is information that we think is privileged, and we are not going to give it out. But isn't that also true in the media? Don't you have those trade secrets, if you will?

The thing I'm trying to say is, it's about time for you and us to recognize that we both have a job to do and that we're going to accomplish that job better if we do it together. It's about time we forget about antagonisms that have been spoken about here—mistrust, skepticism. It's time, if you will, for trust and fair play. Maybe you feel that you haven't received such treatment from the business community. Well, I want to tell you that I know damn well that my industry, at least, has not received that kind of treatment, in all instances, from the media. We've been treated pretty shabbily on occasion, and let me give you some "for instances."

There was a recent story about a Supreme Court decision that affected our business. But tied into it was a decision of the United States Court of Appeals that had come out six weeks prior to that. The entire story was written about that Court of Appeals decision, with a great number of completely erroneous suppositions covered in the story. There was nothing about the United States Court of Appeals decision when it came out. The result—our investors lost hundreds of millions of dollars in the value of their stock in two days.

Another one. There has been a great deal of difficulty for our company in a particular state. There's been a lot of publicity there. That case has been going on for three years. Within the last few months, there was an article that went back and picked up all of the old allegations made by someone who had been fired for misfeasance—dipping into the money in the till and other things. Only what that person said. That reporter refused to talk to the company's people, refused to accept a written rebuttal offered to him. Only the allegations of the guy that was fired.

Another one. The first time a billion-dollar profit was reported, the news shows interviewed two people, a consumer advocate and a member of the FCC staff. No security analyst, no company people, nobody to explain that the rate of return of eight and nine-tenths percent was less than the commissions allow, and far less than that earned in average industry—only a consumer advocate and a staff man from the FCC.

Another instance. I had lunch with the publisher and editors and the reporters of a national magazine one day. I answered questions afterwards, and one of the reporters asked me about financing in the company. I told him his statement was wrong and told him what the facts were. The next issue of that magazine came out and quoted me as saying that our financial needs were going to be exactly what *he* had said, not what *I* had said. That one, I will say, was so bad that the publisher of the magazine called me up and apologized.

Another one. You all know of stories that have come out about mishandling the books, from the standpoint of how property is depreciated. These charges were made by a former IRS agent, who was stationed in New York and audited our records. The man was fired by the IRS. He asked us for a job. We turned him down. He said, if you don't give me a job, I'm going to wreck you. He took his story to the Congress; they refused to listen. He took his story to the IRS; they refused to listen. But the media did. They printed it.

So I'll say this to you: we're not asking for much—fairness, a willingness on your part to accept the fact that maybe, just maybe, sometimes we are right; factual statements, rather than rumor or speculation, or at least a willingness on the part of the press to print our part of it in the same story; an opportunity to obtain facts that are not readily available—and sometimes a call from the reporter catches us when we don't have the information, but we're perfectly willing to put it together; knowledgeable people to report on our activities, instead of a guy who comes to my press conference at a security-analyst meeting and asks me the difference between stocks and bonds; and lastly, serious consideration of the source of your information, of the qualifications of the people providing it, and of their incentives. That's not very much, I think.

You, the media, say you have your rights. We accept that. But we have our rights, too. And we hope that you'll accept that. That's where

I come out of this whole thing. (*Applause*)

DEAN FOURAKER: It sounds like the start of a Harvard Business School field case. Do we have someone on the press who would like to respond? (*To the first publisher*) Yes.

FIRST PUBLISHER: I'll take him up on what he said about one of those stories. It is true those stories ran. It is true that they came from disaffected employees or people who had been fired. The newspaper believed the stories were true. His subsidiary company was given every chance to deny them, to make its statements. This story ran for a long time, and it was a big story and seemed very important.

If his people were still unhappy about it, or felt that there was something wrong, they certainly—no one contacted us or pointed this out. The editor believed in the story, and I still believe he was right. Very serious allegations were made, certainly by people with doubtful motives, but the newspaper believed the allegations were true. I'd like to ask you—were not a lot of them true?

FIRST BUSINESSMAN: No, sir, none of them was true. Not one single one of those allegations has been proven.

FIRST PUBLISHER: Why didn't you come to us—

FIRST BUSINESSMAN: We did. I beg your pardon. Our people have been in constant touch with the newspaper over this. We have given them every bit of information we could possibly provide. It is true that that judge put a gag on us, and the other people, but the other people didn't pay any attention to it. We did. So a lot of it came about because of that.

FIRST PUBLISHER: And the judge prevented you from talking further to us.

FIRST BUSINESSMAN: The judge prevented us from talking to anyone.

FIRST PUBLISHER: He didn't prevent us from continuing to run the story.

FIRST BUSINESSMAN: That's correct.

DEAN FOURAKER: (*Asks the first editor*)

FIRST EDITOR: I'd like to make a couple of points, because some of these examples mentioned involve my newspaper. But first, I'd like to say that one of the misapprehensions here, I think, on the part of the businessman is that there is this great monolith—the press. There is my newspaper, and there is another in my city, and its publisher is perfectly able to defend his. I'll be damned if I will. (*Laughter*)

We all do things our own ways, and at my newspaper we do it one way, and that means that I don't want to be lumped with the press as a whole. I think that's essentially true of most of the editors and reporters here. My colleague here will be happy to speak for his magazine, but he's not going to speak for someone else's magazine, and I think, in fact, that's the way it should be.

Listening to the businessmen here, it sounds as if when I want to check a story, I call the president of a bank and he answers the phone. Well, to see a bank president takes more arranging than an audience with the Pope does. We don't have easy access. On most stories, we don't anticipate going to the top dog in the corporation. We work through the public relations departments to start out, but in an enormous number of the major corporations in America, we do not have easy access to the people in charge. We are either blocked by the public relations department or blocked by the lawyers.

We have a marvelous example of the use of the gag order. There is, in a Southern court, a lawsuit against the president of General Motors. That suit has caused enormous consternation within the corporation. They don't want to talk about it. So they went to the court and got a gag order because it wasn't opposed by the other side, who didn't care. They got a gag order, and they will now look you right in the eye and tell you that because of the gag order, they can't even tell us who went and got the gag order. (*Laughter*)

This is an embarrassing situation for a major corporation, but it's a very serious internal problem at that corporation. Those problems, I think, are of very great public interest, to GM's employees and to GM's stockholders, who together outnumber the total population of America, nearly, and they don't want to talk about it. Yet they anticipate that *that* corporation should have high credibility with the newspaper people. It's very hard to maintain credibility under those kinds of circumstances.

We in the press make some terrible mistakes, partly through stupidity, partly through haste, and partly through, sometimes I suppose, just plain meanness. It ain't an easy job, but it's not made much easier by the corporations, especially on sticky stuff. Nine out of ten times, there's no problem at all. We do take the corporation's word most of the time. But when United States Steel is involved in an environmental matter, you can bet your boots they're going to fight it like hell. They're going to make a big fuss over these unfortunate and unfair costs. It's a controversial issue, and their first instinct is to say not a damn thing until they can get their ducks in a very long row. It goes on for days and days before you can actually start talking seriously to them. I think business has got a long way to go in dealing with the press, despite enormous efforts to develop public relations systems.

FIRST BUSINESSMAN: May I just take ten seconds? As you say, *Newsweek* or *Time* can't speak for you and neither can the *New York Times* or the

Washington Post. Neither can I speak for General Motors or United States Steel. They can't speak for me.

We all make mistakes, on both sides. We all have a lot to learn about getting along together. I have never immediately turned down but one request for an interview. I have even asked for interviews with your people. Your people have been given the number of a private line that comes directly to my desk and is answered by no one but me or my secretary, and only by her if I'm talking on another line, so that they can call me anytime they have a question about anything in our business.

SECOND EDITOR: What is the number? (*Laughter*)

FIRST BUSINESSMAN: The point is, they have never called it—not once.

FIRST EDITOR: Are you going to be in on Monday?

DEAN FOURAKER: (*Asks the first editor*) Do you think the forces of competition are the best regulator of the quality of the service that the press renders to all of us? We're all consumers.

FIRST EDITOR: The officially sanctioned answer from the journalism business, the newspaper business, is yes. I have grave doubts about whether that's true. I do not think that you can demonstrate, for instance, that newspapers in monopoly towns are better or worse than newspapers in competitive towns. Competitive-town newspapers are quicker, but the real issue is, are they better? I do not believe it can be proven one way or the other.

I do believe that competition does stimulate those juices; that to keep your newspaper from going dead on its ass, you've got to keep your staff interested and excited. If you tell them: "Turn the story in next week or next month," that's the kind of newspaper you're going to put out, a very lifeless sort of newspaper.

DEAN FOURAKER: (*Acknowledges the first reporter*) Yes?

FIRST REPORTER: I think, to some degree, there's a misimpression here about our deadline pressures. Sometimes, and I can give a recent example, you may spend two or three weeks developing an important story. You constantly have an ear cocked to the competition. As you talk to your sources on a major story, you are always waiting for someone to say: "Well, I've already talked to the *Wall Street Journal*," and that may throw into a cocked hat your carefully constructed symphony of news sources that you plan to put together over time.

But there is frequently, on an important story, time to develop and get a story together without rushing into print just to beat the competition. This may sometimes be because the story is an interpretive piece on something that has happened over a period of time. But there is very frequently that kind of story in which the two or three competitors are working toward that same end.

DEAN FOURAKER: Do you think reporters are much more professional, now, in terms of the preparation for their jobs than they were back in the thirties?

FIRST REPORTER: That's an interesting question. I remember looking back in the files of my newspaper at a stock market column that was prepared at least thirty years ago, and I was astonished at the implication of this piece of work. It would have made any of us proud. So I'm not sure that's generally true. I do think it is quite true that most financial writers are not trained in economics, necessarily. I don't necessarily think, either, that that's required. Any learning situation is worthwhile to the person who's receptive. You don't have to go to the Harvard School of Business, necessarily, to be qualified to write about finance. But there are a great number of people writing about finance who have never bothered to make themselves expert on the subject.

The wonderful thing about finance, if I may take just one more second, is that if I want to find out something about an accounting matter, I can assemble a group of men who are the most expert people in the country and use them as my sounding board and get my story, just by a private learning experience that would never be duplicated in a classroom.

THIRD EDITOR: May I just make a point on the competition before we leave it?

DEAN FOURAKER: Of course.

THIRD EDITOR: It's fascinating. Many of the business people have been horrified by some of the vices that arise from competitive reporting. But I do think you mustn't lose sight of the fact that the other side of competition is plurality of choice. You get very different judgments made by different newspapers. I hate the thought of all my information's coming from one gatekeeper. So bear in mind there are some vices in competition. There are some virtues, too—keeping reporters on their toes. It also has the virtue of plurality of choice, which is absolutely vital.

SECOND BUSINESSMAN: Is the free press prepared to extend that argument to other forms of human activity like business?

THIRD EDITOR: Yes, of course.

SECOND BUSINESSMAN: Would you argue that free and open competition is the best means to provide services to consumers?

THIRD EDITOR: Certainly. I wouldn't like to live in the Soviet Union and have a choice of just a Joe Stalin limo.

DEAN FOURAKER: How about the labor government that controls higher education, the production of steel, automobiles and a number of other items?

THIRD EDITOR: Let's stick to journalism. (*Laughter*)

DEAN FOURAKER: I think it's one of those odd lacks of symmetry that the press universally argues that there must be free competition, the First Amendment, the fourth estate; yet often, on the editorial page, it is not prepared to extend that. I agree with all of you.

　　We make the same argument in our field. Academic freedom— absolutely required to have a reasonable assurance of a reliable product in universities, and I would defend it to the death. The press have often been the architects of the most deadening regulations on everyone else's business, demonstrating some failure, it seems to me, to extend to others those rights that they so perceptively understand are necessary for the performance of their own duties.

THIRD EDITOR: Just getting back to the point about business. If there's bad press, say, for General Motors, or whatever it is in one paper, it is just as likely, because of competition, that another newspaper will be taking a slightly different view of it. I think business should realize that some of the disadvantages of competition have tremendous virtues of offering choices, and we mustn't lose sight of that (*Inaudible*).

DEAN FOURAKER: Again, I think the point is, there is probably not a businessman here who would propose any restrictions under the First Amendment of the press in the United States. We would probably, on balance, say that given all the pros and cons, we'd rather have libel laws as they are interpreted here, rather than as they are interpreted in England. We'll live with the consequences of open competition in the press.

　　We also feel, probably, on the business side, that the same forces would produce the same sort of results in guaranteeing the quality of the products that we produce. (*Turns to the second businessman*) I don't know if you would agree with me on that?

SECOND BUSINESSMAN: I would say yes. I have a minor point to make first, and then I'd like to come back to that. The minor point is this, that when a chief executive officer is called by a reporter, the reporter may have been working on the story for twenty-four hours, forty-eight hours, maybe several weeks, and oftentimes, you've heard it repeated around here, the reporter "never goes to the CEO first." He's last. The reporter suddenly wants to get that CEO's opinion or statement for a story. He expects the CEO to drop everything, be completely knowledgeable about the story, and reply within a half hour or something. When the CEO comes up with a "No comment" or "I couldn't comment on that," or "You have to give me time," the reporter says: "Well, look at the idiot; he doesn't want to comment on this big story."

We are not sitting there, waiting for a reporter to call, and we don't know what else is in the story. We have to go gather facts. We're under the mandate of the SEC and if we come out and make some outrageous statement that affects our stock one way or the other, we're liable for what we have to say. So we can't just pop off an answer to a reporter from the top of the head. I would suggest that they come to the CEO a little earlier. That's the minor point.

The major point that I notice is that, curiously enough, I'm from one of the few firms here that reverses this coin. We send people in to question publishers about their organizations. When our analysts go in to talk to the publisher, they get many of the same replies as the reporters get when they come in to us. (*Laughter*) As a result, we do not usually go to the publisher. We go to the chief financial officer or we go to other sources, trying to track down something other than the handout they're giving us about their quarterly earnings or something of that nature. We want to go behind those facts, but we're held to a much higher standard because what we publish, we are liable for. We can be fined, we can be suspended, or anything else in relation to the Truth in Securities Act.

I find it very curious, listening to members of the press report what they say in their paper and how they go about their work, that they are not held to the same rules as we are. Now, I don't suggest that a reporter be fined for a misstatement or even for an omission, as we could be, but I suggest that they should have a little patience with what business is saying to them, because they are not playing by the same rules that we have to play by. You play English football by American football rules and you're going to get killed. It's just not the way the thing is played. So I suggest that there is kind of a double standard here.

Take the question of payments. They all say that when we make questionable payments, we not only have to rush down and tell the SEC or what have you about it, but also we have to put out a news release about it. But when they make a questionable payment for a story, which I heard them say yesterday they will do—I won't say it shocked me. I'm over being shocked by what's going on in this world, but nonetheless, it is kind of eyebrow-raising that they don't have to report that. Now, it's a questionable payment that they paid for a story. Why shouldn't they be required—

DEAN FOURAKER: They don't have to tell you anything about the motives of their sources.

SECOND BUSINESSMAN: Why shouldn't they be required to say that they paid for a story just as we pay the commission to get a piece of business overseas? Why shouldn't they say that they paid a commission to get that story? Or is that a double standard?

DEAN FOURAKER: Is there a question? Yes?

SECOND REPORTER: No, this is a comment. A couple of months ago, a public relations firm called me—

DEAN FOURAKER: A little louder, please.

SECOND REPORTER: A couple of months ago, a public relations firm called me on behalf of a drug firm that has a representative at this meeting and said they would like a writer with a technical-scientific reputation to write a story about some of their products and place it in a women's magazine. I said, knowing perfectly well what the answer would be, that of course if I did so, I would be able to say that the research for this article was paid for by such and such a company. The response was, we can see you wouldn't be very comfortable with this assignment. (*Laughter*) I was then asked if I knew another science writer who might be willing to do such a thing. I said, "No, I didn't, and that was not my way of doing business." I then said: "Is this a common way of doing business?" The caller said: "Yes, it happens all the time." Now, I would suggest to you that what is going on here is evasion of the Food and Drug Administration regulations about labeling on products.

All I am saying is that I think this disclosure business goes both ways. When the business community says to us, we think we should be working together, quote-unquote, and you hear this—I also hear this from the scientific community—you know, why doesn't the press work with us, quote-unquote—as the medical profession does, and so on. Yes, we don't always do our job properly, but I'm not sure it would be in the public interest for journalists to be "working with" these various communities. (*Applause*)

DEAN FOURAKER: Have you seen any publications about that firm? That is, was the work done somewhere? Are the forces of competition so strong that someone will take the money to do that? I'm certain no newspaper here would but—

DEAN FOURAKER: On the question of sources—there's a question here, yes.

FIRST LAWYER: I have a question I'd like to direct to the press. As I listened to one of the bankers, particularly, what I heard was something that, it seems to me, did speak to the conflict and wasn't easily disposed of. I heard him saying, "These are complicated matters, and what we want is fairness. We want the story reported with all of its different ramifications—the labor connection, the economic connection . . ." and so forth and so on.

Now, I'm a reader, and as I heard you talking I found myself thinking, "That story is getting duller and duller. It's getting very fair." (*Laughter*) "But it's also getting duller and duller."

The question I'd like to put to the press is, who do you consider your audience to be? Is your audience somebody like me who gets up in the morning, looks at the morning paper, can't swallow a four- or five-column story with all its complications? I would love to read about some banker who is kicking out welfare tenants, and see what the mayor has to say about it, and then go to work. Or is your audience the banker and the business community, who are going to read your stories, and be a relatively select audience for them and consider them fair? Now, I expect the answers to be different. One editor has one answer and another would have another answer, but if that's true, then I don't see this conflict going away very quickly.

DEAN FOURAKER: (*Calls on the second publisher*)

SECOND PUBLISHER: This relates to a word that has been used fairly often this morning, "simplistic." The answer to "simplistic" and the answer to your question is, yes indeed, the press, generally speaking, is simplistic or somewhat simplistic for three reasons: one, there may be lack of competence; two, there is the pressure of time; and three, we are writing not just about business, which we've been discussing today, but we're also writing about science and medicine and what's happening in Israel, and biology and laws, and so on and so on. We are not trying to bore our entire public. We are trying to make it as clear as possible, in as few words as possible because, indeed, we think that the general public wants to read about a whole variety of things and not just about business. I'll exclude the *Wall Street Journal.*

So yes, we are simplistic, because we cannot run on and on. We cannot satisfy the banker on his story, and at the same time satisfy an atomic scientist on his story.

We try to come as close as possible to getting a good middle ground and, hopefully, a bit above the middle ground, in terms of explaining what's going on in all these different fields. But some of you would be awfully bored if we took the same attitude towards an atomic energy question, as the banker wanted us to take towards the hypothetical questions this morning.

THIRD BUSINESSMAN: I would like to make a comment that I think needs to be made. That has to do with the reporting of the industries in which there is public regulation of the charges, namely, utilities. The reporting is always slanted this way: Phone company asks toll increase which will increase cost to consumers by three hundred million dollars.

The telephone company, at the end of the war, was charging a nickel for a telephone call. The *New York Times* was selling for three cents. The telephone company is now charging a dime for a telephone call and trying to get twenty cents.

A VOICE: The *New York Times* has been at twenty cents for about two years. When the *New York Times* increases its price overnight, there's no statement about the cost of this to the public. It's a simple statement that due to the increased costs, which are legitimate and which we understand have to be covered—but there is a simple statement that due to increased costs, they're raising their price.

THIRD BUSINESSMAN: And the *Washington Post*, which has done somewhat similar work, and other journals, and it is understandable that prices are rising, because costs are rising. They're rising for everybody. In the case of the utilities, the reporting is slanted so that it seems as if they're trying to milk the consumer; actually, their costs have gone up, but the background discussion of the cost increases that have forced them to ask for rate increases is often either completely lacking or relegated to the end of the story.

Now, this is one of the problems, I think, that the business community has with reporting. It is an example of a case where the publishing industry has very different rules for itself. I don't know that the *Times,* for example, ever publishes the fact—I may be wrong on this—that they've just raised their advertising rates.

FIRST GOVERNMENTAL OFFICIAL: The difference is that I have to make telephone calls, but I don't have to read the *New York Times.*

THIRD BUSINESSMAN: Well, perhaps so—

DEAN FOURAKER: We didn't have an alternative, really.

FIRST GOVERNMENTAL OFFICIAL: I think the point is, wouldn't you grant that somewhat selective public attention to the rate structure of a monopoly is justified.

THIRD BUSINESSMAN: I grant that. I'm just asking the question about the double standard because usually there is an editorial denunciation of the utility for even asking for the increase.

FIRST GOVERNMENTAL OFFICIAL: Why shouldn't there be a double standard? There are two situations. One is a monopoly, one isn't.

THIRD PUBLISHER: There are 1,730 newspapers in the United States, and close to 1,700 are monopolies.

DEAN FOURAKER: (*Calls on the third reporter*)

THIRD REPORTER: Just think for a moment about access, because I think that goes to the heart of much of what we have been discussing during this session. There has been criticism of the press for rushing into stories, for writing incomplete stories. We have heard an executive tell us that he has a telephone on his desk, which he will use to answer our questions directly any time we want to call him. We have heard another company official tell us his company has no secrets. I don't doubt any of that. I think all of that is true. But I think we have an unusual group of people in this room; and that in the real world in which we report, attempts are made every week to block us, to intimidate us, to bribe us, to prevent us from getting stories; and that that really goes to the heart of one of our basic difficulties in getting the kind of complete stories, authoritative stories, timely stories that the businessmen in this room would like to see.

Now, I don't know what the answer to that is. I know that the businessmen here, for the most part, are accustomed to dealing with the press. But, that is not generally true of businessmen across the country, including the heads of many very large companies. Increasingly, they are being subjected to the kind of scrutiny that politicians have been subjected to for many years.

That trend is not going to go away. That's a very comfortable experience for many businessmen. Many of them have gotten to the top of their companies, not without a tough fight, but without having that kind of outside scrutiny which they get from a vigorous press. And somehow, I think, we're going to have to come to grips with that situation, if we're going to eliminate some of the hostility which I think, very happily, has begun to come out in today's session.

DEAN FOURAKER: What counsel would you have for a chief executive officer of a corporation that is, for better or worse, regarded almost as a public trust? What would you suggest that he do in terms of his continuing relationship with the press? If he gets in trouble, he's not going to give a quote that will hang him at the SEC or expose him to risks that are avoidable, and you wouldn't, I think, assume that he would. But in terms of the general concept of his office, how would you like him to behave?

THIRD REPORTER: I think, essentially, I have no quarrel with his tending to his own affairs and working in his own interest. I don't think he has any obligation to help a newspaper have a story that serves this interest in truth that we all have been trumpeting. I do think that if he recognizes, and increasingly, chief executive officers are recognizing the importance of this kind of story in the paper—say, a crucial story that comes up about his company—that maybe he has to do what we have been told is difficult to do. That is, drop everything else that he's doing at that moment. If he is under the impression that tomorrow morning there will be a page-one story in the *Washington Post* or the *New York Times* or the *Wall Street Journal*, then maybe his first priority had damn well better be that he drops everything else he's doing and gets his team together.

DEAN FOURAKER: If he drops anything that he's doing for any length of time, his job is redundant, and he wouldn't have it.

THIRD REPORTER: But it's not every day that that kind of situation comes along. I'm not saying, for every press inquiry that he gets, he should drop everything he's doing. Obviously, he's going to delegate much of what comes along. But in instances where it is a difficult situation and a potentially explosive situation, I think—if you're asking me what my suggestion would be for the chief executives, that would be my suggestion.

FOURTH BUSINESSMAN: I'd like to issue a mild criticism of the business community, rather than the press. I think it's come out in the last two days, and I've long felt it, that the business community is too reliant on the press and too willing really to cede to the press the role of being the only channel of communication and the only forum for communication with the public.

I think that if the business community does, as I perceive here and elsewhere that it does, have problems in getting its story to the public— that is really the issue involved, not whether we're going to convince reporters one way or another—I think the business community has really been very remiss in experienting and exploring in other channels of communication, in getting its story over to the press.

We sit here and complain about the press's not doing what we would like them to do. Well, if we do have a better story and we think that we do, we ought to be experimenting with other channels of communication, rather than just complaining to the press about the job that they're doing.

DEAN FOURAKER: (*Recognizes the fifth businessman*)

FIFTH BUSINESSMAN: Well, first of all I think we've all gotten a great deal out of these last two days. I think, one thing that is apparent to me, though, is that across the range of possible attitudes that we brought to the main ring here, business and the press, which might range from antagonism on one side to skepticism or maybe even something more constructive on the other extreme, that probably "distrust" still expresses the consensus position.

I think, after these two days, I draw that conclusion with some justification. I guess I'd like to throw out a question that pertains to that, though, because I think the business community does have a responsibility to attempt to work to see that that distrust is overcome. But how should the business community trust the press, when it's readily apparent, and I think it came out a number of times in the last two days, that the media doesn't trust business?

I think it was interesting, in yesterday's case, that the press was asked how they would develop that story, and the company was not identified as the source of information that they would utilize without a lot of help from Mr. Nesson, and even then, they didn't respond. Eventually, we got to it. I think there were a number of situations that developed in the last couple of days where that, in fact, was the case.

So I hear, on the one extreme, that companies attempt to bribe the press, that we lie to the press, that bankers hide behind the veil of confidentiality, that the press gets stonewalled by business. I think that is probably, to some extent, true. On the other hand, I don't think that that attitude exists generally within business if there is some understanding on the part of the press. We have to take time to respond to questions that are thrown at us in a very complex environment, where those who are asking the questions are far more knowledgeable, with justification, than those of us being asked to respond.

So I think it will help if the press will have a little more understanding of the fact that we do need that time, that we have the legitimate objective of communicating to the press, in a fair, honest way. It will also help if the press will listen to the appeals that I think you've heard in the last couple of days from the business leaders here that all we're looking for is honest, balanced reporting.

DEAN FOURAKER: If a company is in trouble, the reporters are not likely to go to the chief executive or any other officer of the company as a reliable source of information. It's probably too late. Isn't it?

THIRD REPORTER: Not in the beginning. Ultimately, they will come to the chief executive.

DEAN FOURAKER: Shouldn't his company try to keep you informed about the problems all the time, before they get in trouble, so that you have reason to assume that he's not trying to be self-serving?

THIRD REPORTER: If we're doing our job, we're reading the AK's and the 10-Ks. I'm not saying we always do our job, but we are reading the AK's.

DEAN FOURAKER: One banker said that his annual report, even though he had put it in the form of a newspaper, had not been read.

FOURTH EDITOR: It seems to me that one of the things we touched on in the first seminar was the ethics of obtaining information; how we, as newspapers, get information; the techniques we use; whether we should buy information at any time; whether we should insinuate ourselves into situations to get information. All of us in the press are concerned with these things, of course.

I would just make one observation. The art of investigative reporting is essentially the business of getting information that somebody else does not want us to have. In a perfect world, we could go to people who we have reason to suspect have information and ask them whether they have committed a crime or a misfeasance or made serious bad judgments, and have them say: "Yes, indeed." That would be one thing. But we do not live in a perfect world. The press has a terrific handicap in getting this kind of information. We are not like district attorneys, able to subpoena records. We're not like the FBI, able to wiretap conversations. We're not like the police, able to arrest and interrogate people under great psychological pressure. All we have, really, available to us, is a certain degree of creativity, some tenacity, perseverance, originality; and some of those qualities are going to take us a little close to the line, sometimes perhaps across the line.

But I would just suggest that if we did not pursue those avenues to the best of our ability, we would not get any of the information. Without them, I doubt very much that the *Washington Post* would have come up with the political story of the century about the top of the government in this country. The day when hostility between business and the press vanishes will be the saddest day in our history. (*Laughter and applause*)

DEAN FOURAKER: (*Recognizes the first banker*)

FIRST BANKER: I hate to be the first speaker after that statement. (*Laughter*) I'd like to address this question of ethics and the necessity for investigative reporting because I think the rules of the road are very much at the heart of some of the discussion we've had today.

I'll give you an incident. A columnist called up my secretary. We had had a meeting in the export area. We had invited the bankers in the community and the leading exporters in the community. A high official of one of the agencies that deals with exports came up to an off-the-record meeting for a question and answer period. We talked about foreign trade and exporting and what have you. Nothing much—I mean, it was just an information session.

The columnist called up my secretary and said, "I want the names of the guest list, of all the people who attended that meeting, and if I don't get it, I'm going to go after you with hammer and tongs." The secretary rightfully turned it over to our vice-president of public relations and he called back the columnist and told him about everything that was done at the meeting and about the type of people who were there. There were the bankers, the exporters, and the questions. He said we would be happy to provide him with the names of one or two other people who were there who would be happy to answer his questions to verify what we were saying; but we thought that in the interests of privacy we were not going to give out the guest list.

So a week later in his column, I got the love treatment. Then he called up that agency of government, and said that he would like to have the information of all the business that my bank had done with the agency six months before the Carter Administration took office and six months after the Carter Administration took office. I haven't the faintest idea what business we've done with the agency. I hope it's a lot. I hope it increases. But the point is that here was a question of a kind of intimidation and extortion. The real question is, are those the rules of the road by which we're going to develop communication back and forth, with each other?

I might just carry that forward to another point that was brought up earlier in today's discussion. We believe, in the business community, that we have a certain accountability and responsibility in the communities where we're located. Now, maybe this is misguided. Maybe the nature of a corporation is such that we ought not to be thinking about anything other than making a profit for our stockholders. But rightly or wrongly, the climate in which we have grown up has taught us to believe that we should do everything in our power to try to make the community work—to try to make it work for the labor community, to try to make it work for the citizens, to try to keep calm. The community cannot work if it's in a constant state of turmoil. And if an emergency comes up or a crisis comes up, as has been indicated, by training we're inclined to seek the alternative solutions and to try to avert the crisis by putting together those solutions and then moving toward them. That's the way we're schooled.

If we have that accountability; if we try to marshal all the facts, to get the full picture; if we're trying to tell different constituents within the community that, somehow, we have to balance their respective interests, to try to get something done; if the media has to abbreviate that and put it out in entertaining fashion so that rather than being descriptive, it becomes so much entertainment so that our friend can go to work learning about this rascal banker who kicked out these welfare tenants, (probably rode down in his limousine and handed out the notices) (*Laughter*) then we have a built-in conflict between what we perceive to be an accountability of trying to make that community work and what the media feels to be its responsibility to (a) inform and (b) entertain, but yet not to be part of the accountability that's necessary to make that community work. I just don't understand how we're ever going to resolve that conflict because a larger burden is being placed on our shoulders than the media appears willing to accept.

DEAN FOURAKER: (*Recognizes the sixth businessman*)

SIXTH BUSINESSMAN: I've enjoyed this theater in the round for two days, and I would just like to make a comment or two here before leaving.

First of all, I think the emphasis in our discussions has been largely on what the press thinks and how the press behaves and what they consider their guiding principles to be. I have felt a bit frustrated, as a businessman, in not having an opportunity to voice some of my own thoughts along this line.

Let me just point out to you that I don't believe that anywhere in our discussions for the last two days has the point really been made that the media are profit-making organizations, also. We've heard about their pious declarations of responsibility—that's carried on the shoulders of the press to keep everybody honest in our society. Yet, they're working for a competitive profit-making enterprise, and this deadline business is all related to this. I don't say this is wrong. I think it's a point that ought to be made and ought to be recognized.

I would hope that this conference might be followed up by another or others, where we might have, as businessmen, more of an opportunity to have our say than has occurred up to this point.

DEAN FOURAKER: (*Recognizes the fourth publisher*)

FOURTH PUBLISHER: Well, I'd like to make about a thousand points, but I will just address myself to the last one, that we are a business. We are a business, and I think the other publishers in the room would agree that we are a profit-making business. We don't seek circulation through headlines. You get newsstand circulation through headlines, and that is not the majority of our circulation, nor does it make money for us—I mean, except in the long run.

We have a responsibility, under the First Amendment, to inform, and we are also a business. They are very separate things. I have long held they are not contradictory. If you are responsible, and in fact, if you preserve your credibility and do a good job, sometimes you get clocked as a business, temporarily, but you have to do it because that is what, in the long run, leads to your profitability, which is your excellence.

And that leads me to a second point, that most often, when we're perceived as being unfair, it is because we've been unprofessional and not because somebody is biased or somebody is out to get somebody else. It really is sloppiness or bad reporting or lack of checking, or somebody who isn't qualified reporting on business when they shouldn't be reporting on business.

Now, we are trying to make that an area of improvement. All of us have been aware that we came too late to business reporting. I think the editors here are aware of it and they're trying to improve their staffs and their competence, their professionalism and their experience, which is half of doing it well.

I wish to make a last point, which is, if you all think you have a problem, just try being a business which is reported on by yourself. I know the charge has been made that we don't report on ourselves. In fact, we didn't used to. We didn't used to report on ourselves and we didn't used to report on each other. That was one of the complaints made about the press, that we reported on everybody else, but we omitted ourselves.

This is a very tricky area, but we are, in fact, trying to do this, We do report on each other, all too much, and rather boringly at times. Then we're accused of making media stars, or the opposite. It is very hard to report on yourself as a business, and you are quite right, we don't do it enough. We try to report our own labor disputes because they impact on the town, and it's very tricky, but we are trying.

I think you're quite right. We do not report on when we raise our advertising rates. We don't explain it enough. I do think that next to the telephone company, we have raised our rates the least of anybody. The fact is that when you can buy a newspaper on the newsstand for 10 cents or 15 or 20, or 25 in some cases, you are getting a hell of a bargain. But last, fairness is very tough, and none of us achieves it, nor will we ever, but we keep trying. Thank you. (*Applause*)

DEAN FOURAKER: (*Recognizes the seventh businessman*)

SEVENTH BUSINESSMAN: Well, yesterday I certainly enjoyed this meeting. It was delightful, and I thought, as a lawyer, it was a great show. Today, I am listening to it as a financier, and one or two things occur to me, and I would like to jump through them very quickly.

I am concerned with what I seem to feel is an attitude by some members of the press that they have been given a divine right, that someone has laid hands on them, to determine what my future should be, what the United States should be, what the world should be like, despite the fact that we have a government, we have people in the Department of Defense. I doubt if there are very many von Neumanns in the room, or Gene Vickers or Ed Tellers, and when you come down to the question, what is good for the national press, I want someone in whom I have great confidence, to make that decision. I don't want a fellow who is harried in a very complicated world, and who has to make decisions on a number of other things, suddenly to say: "Sure, we'll go with the story." It's as though we've got, for example, a one-ounce atom bomb that anybody can slip into his pocket and set off, and I'm going to make the decision to explode it and not the Department of Defense or the President of the United States.

I think that is very, very dangerous, particularly to a group which is accountable to nobody, under the First Amendment. And at the time of the First Amendment, you will recall, there was no time pressure. It took two to three weeks to get a packet from London to Boston and three days' high-speed riding by Paul Revere to get it down to Philadelphia, and then you doubled the time to get it back to London, and by that time, the crisis had disappeared. But today we say, we're pushed in this, we're pushed in that, we've got to make a decision, go with it in twelve hours. And, the problems are much more complicated than they were when we founded this republic.

So I would offer some suggestions. First of all, I think you ought to become a profession. I don't think you are. You wouldn't let me fill your teeth, most of you, if you had any sense. You wouldn't let me take out your appendix, if you had any brains. But you are perfectly willing to let somebody tell you what's going on in the Near East, what's going to happen in China, whether he's ever been there, whether he has any competence or not. And you are not subject to any criticism if you're wrong—I mean by a government or by anybody else.

Now, a congressman, a private businessman, or anybody else is checked, but the press is not. I would suggest that the best thing you could do before the situation gets out of hand, is to set up your own set of disciplinary actions, as the medical societies have done, the legal societies and, God bless them, even the architects. (*Laughter*)

You do insist on certain education, that you do have certain examinations, that you do have certain boards, before you can start selling advice about stocks, for example, or military problems. Finally, I would like to start the discipline by going to the English law of libel, because I think that that might slow everything down a little bit. Thank you.

SECOND EDITOR: I think you've surfaced the problem that's gone unarticulated. You are saying, in a very general way: "Who the hell appointed you?"

SEVENTH BUSINESSMAN: Precisely. How did you get anointed?

SECOND EDITOR: Well, I was appointed by a publisher, a business person, and you don't want us to make a decision about any matters of national defense, but you're perfectly comfortable with Neil McElroy's making it. I'd like to tell you, sir, that his is rather more limited than some journalists' experience. The basic conflict of interest between business and the press has finally surfaced. We don't have anywhere near a similar commitment to the truth, whatever it is. You're like the President of the United States. You don't want the truth out. You want the news out that shows your company in the best possible way.

The President of the United States holds a press conference, not to let the news out, but to let the news out that shows him to be the most lean, hungry, triple-spaced fabulous leader. And we can't even agree on words. The English language is a marvelously flexible tool, but you and and I can't agree on what's honest, on what's fair, on what's reasonable, on what's accurate. I can sit with a document in my hand and disagree with a banker about what it contains or on whether it's news. I think that conflict of interest doesn't do you any harm, and I don't think it does the American public any harm.

SEVENTH BUSINESSMAN: I would add only that Mr. McElroy or whoever happens to be the secretary of defense, has many thousand, in fact, millions of people , including some extraordinarily competent scientists. He may not be himself—but others working with him have been extraordinarily competent scientists, and their judgment, in my opinion, is much better, in all due deference, than yours.

SECOND EDITOR: You belittle them—I'm not talking about you personally now, but you belittle the competence of the journalists covering scientific matters. They have access to almost as many scientists.

SEVENTH BUSINESSMAN: But how competent are they to interpret?

SECOND EDITOR: How competent is a manufacturer to interpret? A man who did not make any scientific equipment, that I know about?

Let me ask one thing about your suggestion that we become a profession and take board exams, and have special education. Is that okay for business, too?

SEVENTH BUSINESSMAN: Yes.

SECOND EDITOR: You would have special boards to decide whether you could be a president?

SEVENTH BUSINESSMAN: We can't get anywhere in big business without an M.B.A. or a Doctorate. It's zero.

(*Many voices from the audience*)

DEAN FOURAKER: Let me get my fellow dean. Bill?

MR. DONALDSON: One of the things I thought I learned at the Harvard Business School is that if you sit in the back of the room, you don't get called on.

I've been sitting here with a different hat on than I would normally have on at a meeting such as this, and I've been listening to what's been said over the last two days. I think that obviously the business-press relationship is an adversary one. I suspect that our reporter Georgette's juices were running when she got down to the company. I suspect that she's incompetent to write the story that finally evolved. I suspect she'll try to write it under a deadline that's impossible. She'll try to write it, and somebody will put a disembodied headline on top of that, which will maybe sell more newspapers. I suspect that this will be satisfactory to nobody in Metropolis.

The thing that I've been interested in is whether any real education has gone on in this room over the last two days. I suspect that it has begun. I suspect that the way it begins is that this stereotyped feeling that we have about businessmen and the press begins to break down. We find out that there are all sorts of good guys and bad guys in the press and in the business world. They're going to act the way they act, not necessarily because they're a member of the press or a member of a particular company. Rather, they're going to act because of a set of values that they have inside of them. I suspect that the education that's beginning to happen here is that we see some of those stereotypes break down. We see businessmen beginning to say some things, some of them, that we didn't expect them to, and some of the press saying some things we didn't expect them to. I think that's the first step in the educational process.

At Yale I've gotten a lot of advice as to what we should be teaching. One of the biggest pieces of advice I get from everyone is "You'd better have an ethics course. You'd better teach ethics, because that's the greatest thing that's lacking in the business world, the press world, and so forth." I said, in answer to that, "We can't teach ethics. We're not going to have an ethics course for people of an average of twenty-six years who are coming back to a professional school." They're mature human beings. All we can do is expose them to the peeling off of the shades of innuendo that happens when you look at a subject from all different sides. All we can do is make sure that our students, when they get out in the big, wide world and start to make decisions, will never be able to say: "Gee, I didn't think about that. I didn't realize that there was that implication to a decision that I made."

I think that's what's beginning to happen here, although I must say that I'm sorry this is coming to an end right now, because I think we're just beginning to get down to some of the things that we should have been talking about two days ago. But, that's the educational process, too. Thanks. (*Applause*)

DEAN FOURAKER: I think Bill's exactly right, that there's not only antagonism, but there's a lot of ignorance on both sides, of what the other does. I think it's probably increasingly a responsibility of chief executives to understand the values and the priorities that the press have, and to spend some time on that before the big story breaks.

I think, equally, it's probably the responsibility of a reporter to understand a little better how a chief executive spends his or her day. Their schedule is like a dentist's. They have a new patient about every fifteen minutes. They come on your agenda because no one else can resolve the problem they have. They can't make the decision of who's going to be promoted or given that responsibility. They have to come to you, and you just can't put it aside. In that regard, I'd like to ask still another businessman to give a few thoughts before we close, as an overview of what we've been doing.

EIGHTH BUSINESSMAN: Let me say just a couple of things about this session and try to avoid repeating points that others have made. I thought the object of this was to deal with the process—what happens on the press side, what happens on the business side, how does the system work, why do these things take place. One can't help but comment on the process of this meeting. It seems to me very strange that when businessmen and the press are going to do business with each other, the midwives are lawyers and law professors. Why? Can't we have a meeting and discuss these issues without going through the whole business of the Constitution and what the law requires and what the SEC requires? I leave that for consideration for the next time we meet. I think that we might have a meeting in which we throw a businessman and a newspaperman in the pit, and let them jointly run a discussion on the nitty-gritty, which really involves the way we do business together.

Now let me shift gears for a moment and talk about the First Amendment. I agree with the comment that was made by one of my friends in the back room. I'd go so far as to say that it's absolutely critical that the press have all the rights that the First Amendment grants it, and that businessmen make sure that that happens. I'll come back to that in a moment. But the other side of that coin, in my judgment, is that if you're going to wrap yourself in the Constitution, you also have an obligation to the Constitution. One publisher touched on that briefly, but the fact is, you've got your best people in this room, now. The weakest performers are still back home. The people that we normally see from most of the newspapers we deal with don't measure up in quality. If you're exercising a Constitutional prerogative, it seems to me, you have an obligation to get quality people, to train them, and to manage them.

When we submit to a twenty-minute tape for television and ten seconds of it appears on the screen, with the CO picking his nose, you have to ask yourself: "Where is the management of the network?" Is that, by anybody's definition of fairness, an appropriate presentation of two points of view?

My final point—and this, I think, I make with some emotion. I can't think of anything in this country that is more important to a businessman than to have the press as free as it can be. Because, unless we can get our story across—not just the good news, but all the news, good and bad—unless we can get it across through you, we're dead. We have no chance at all. That says that opposite the government, opposite our employees, opposite our stockholders, opposite the public at large, you are our mouthpiece, whether we like it or not. What does that say to the businessman? I think, the obvious thing. Whatever some of us may do in running our own businesses, I think it is a fact that most business-men, or at least a lot of businessmen, are afraid of the press. They hide behind their walls. They don't want to talk. They say to me, it's time for the business community to mature, to grow up, and no one ever died from a poor newspaper story. It's time for the businessman to open his door, let the press come in, and ask all the damn fool questions they want to ask.

You may have good answers. You may have damn fool answers to damn fool questions, but so what? The important thing is to turn on the lights, let the question get asked, let the facts go out. If you've got facts that can't go out for a legitimate reason, there's nothing wrong with saying: "These are facts I can't disclose at this time, for this reason, period." The world won't come to an end, from the First Amendment standpoint, even if that happens.

The important point is that the businessman has to change his way of doing things and hope that the press will become true to the First Amendment in doing its work. I suggest, with a few exceptions, up until now it has not been. (*Applause*)

DEAN FOURAKER: That usual summary—that I think the press may regard business as a disaster and business, the press as a disaster, until you consider the alternatives. Then, I think we have a pretty good system.

Mac, thank you very much for bringing these groups together.

MR. BUNDY: We were going to have lunch, and then I was going to thank you all, but there are many who need to get on their way. Let me first thank Dean Fouraker for conducting this last, and extremely illuminating, session. Those of you who have been there know that the widest river in the world is the one which separates the faculty he runs from the faculty I used to run. If I can go back, just for a moment, I will say that the one group that has not been picked on, that you could have picked on, except in a glancing way, is the academy. I will tell you, for your mutual comfort, that among scholars, to call somebody businesslike is no compliment, and to call him a journalist is an insult. (*Laughter*)

I will draw from another part of my past, and say that I think it is a counsel of imperfection to ask chief executives to drop everything to tend to the press. When I was in Washington, I worked for two such executives, and it was not always conducive to orderly business. I do not think that four television sets are the perfect furniture for a chief executive's office. (*Laughter*)

What we've been participating in the last two days is, as Bill Donaldson said, a learning process. The reason we think we have learned more today is that we were learning yesterday, even though it wasn't always pleasant, and not always on the point that any one of us might have wished to put it on.

We are grateful, therefore, to those who framed and executed the hypotheticals. With all respect to our last speaker, I think the interlocutor does help, although I would love to see businesslike and journalistic people in the pit, where the rest of us could work them over, and I think perhaps we'll try that.

We are grateful to those who framed the hypotheticals, to those who executed them, and to those who corrected them. I think the hypothetical introduced in mid-session was vastly better than the one that we had when we went in. I know that if I had been asked, as a hypothetical national security advisor, what I would do about that strategic system, my answer would have been that I wanted to know how long I'd been in office, because if I had had anything to do with designing it, I should have been fired. (*Laughter*)

What we are exploring here is, of course, states of mind, as well as modes of behavior. We don't get to each other's states of mind, even with the best of efforts at candor, in two days. We begin. The process either goes on or it slows down.

One of the things that somewhat separates the press, I think, from all the rest of us, is that nearly all the rest of us—and I don't mean business people, as distinct from government people or university people or foundation people—nearly all the rest of us want to be loved. The press, on the whole, prefers to be hated, and succeeds. (*Laughter*)

There is an obvious and inescapable built-in conflict of interest between what some of us know in some of our capacities and what we do not yet want the press to know that has been referred to repeatedly. It's there. We all know it's there. There isn't one of us who really believes that he can tell everything about his institution, let alone himself—and those are two different things. We do seek to speak so that people will understand. What we want them to understand is how good we are, and how constructive we are, how helpful we are. And I am constantly reminded of the time when I was making this speech to my own trustees and one of the older and wiser trustees said: "You know, it's not entirely clear to me that we want the Ford Foundation to be understood." (*Laughter*)

So one needs a certain modesty about the perfection of one's own institution, and a certain modesty of aspiration as to how widely and universally one can be loved. But what we can, I think, say, is that business and journalism in this country—the free press, at least as an opportunity, free enterprise as the preferred option of commercial action—are like democracy as Winston Churchill described it—the worst form of process except for any other.

I should now thank those who did the hard work behind the work that you all have been doing, and especially Dick Clurman, Margaret Drain and Stuart Sucherman, and finally our invisible and inaudible producer, Fred Friendly. (*Applause*)

We stand adjourned.

About the Editors

JOSEPH A. CALIFANO, JR., is the Secretary of Health, Education, and Welfare. After graduating from the Harvard Law School, where he was an editor of the *Harvard Law Review,* Mr. Califano practiced law in New York City from late 1958 until he joined the Kennedy Administration in April 1961. Beginning as one of Secretary McNamara's whiz kids in the Defense Department, he served as special assistant to the Secretary of the Army, general counsel of the Army, and Secretary McNamara's special assistant and top troubleshooter. In 1965 he was appointed special assistant for domestic affairs to President Lyndon B. Johnson.

After leaving the government in early 1969, Mr. Califano practiced law in Washington, D.C. For several years, a large part of that practice involved First Amendment issues on behalf of the *Washington Post* and other publications. He returned to government at the request of President Carter.

Mr. Califano is the author of *The Student Revolution: A Global Confrontation, A Presidential Nation,* and coedited with Howard Simons *The Media and the Law.* He has written numerous articles that have appeared in the *Washington Post,* the *New Republic* and the Op-Ed page of the *New York Times.* He was general counsel to the Democratic party from 1970 to 1972.

HOWARD SIMONS is managing editor of the *Washington Post.* Before taking on his pressure-cooker job in 1971, Simons had spent ten years at the *Post* as science reporter, assistant managing editor, and deputy managing editor. In 1962 and again in 1964 he won the Westinghouse Award for the best science writing in the United States, from the American Association for the Advancement of Science. In 1966 he won the Raymond Clapper Award for the best Washington reporting.

A graduate of Union College, Mr. Simons was awarded his M.S. from the Columbia University School of Journalism in 1952. From 1954 to 1956 he studied Russian studies at Georgetown University.

Mr. Simons joined Science Service in Washington in 1954 as a reporter and later became an editor. He was a Nieman Fellow at Harvard University during the 1958-1959 academic year. Union College gave him an honorary D.Litt. in 1973, and in 1974 he received an alumni award from Columbia University Graduate School of Journalism.

He is the coeditor, with Joseph A. Califano, Jr., of *The Media and the Law* and the author of *Simon's List Book.*